Dear Reade

The book y the St. Martin's True Crime Library, the imprint the *New York Times* calls "the leader in true crime!" Each month, we offer you a fascinating account of the latest, most sensational crime that has captured the national attention. St. Martin's is the publisher of bestselling true crime author and crime journalist Kieran Crowley, who explores the dark, deadly links between a prominent Manhattan surgeon and the disappearance of his wife fifteen years earlier in THE SURGEON'S WIFE. Suzy Spencer's BREAKING POINT guides readers through the tortuous twists and turns in the case of Andrea Yates, the Houston mother who drowned her five young children in the family's bathtub. In Edgar Award-nominated DARK DREAMS, legendary FBI profiler Roy Hazelwood and bestselling crime author Stephen G. Michaud shine light on the inner workings of America's most violent and depraved murderers. In the book you now hold, THE STRANGER IN MY BED, Michael Fleeman discusses what happens when a happily married woman discovers her husband's sordid past . . .

St. Martin's True Crime Library gives you the stories behind the headlines. Our authors take you right to the scene of the crime and into the minds of the most notorious murderers to show you what really makes them tick. St. Martin's True Crime Library paperbacks are better than the most terrifying thriller, because it's all true! The next time you want a crackling good read, make sure it's got the St. Martin's True Crime Library logo on the spine—you'll be up all night!

Charles E. Spicer, Jr.
Executive Editor, St. Martin's True Crime Library

"Where's My Mom?"

"John, this is Deanna. Where's my mom?"

"I thought she was with you," John replied.

"How could she be with me? Why would she be with me?" asked Deanna.

"Well, I came home to a note Tuesday night that said, 'Feed the fish, I'll be back in a couple days,' and she had talked about coming to visit you or your brother in Florida, so I thought she had come to see you."

"She's not with me," said Deanna, incredulous. She asked him just how her mother was supposed to get to Florida or Texas with a broken hip. Scooting on her butt across terminals?

"I don't know," John said. "I guess maybe she had a friend come pick her up." He noted that the airport bus did stop right in front of their condo complex.

"What do you mean, 'right in front'?" asked Deanna, becoming increasingly frantic.

"There's just a main thoroughfare that runs right in front of our apartment that the bus comes by from the airport, and you can just get on it there," he said.

Through her panic, Deanna was trying to sort this out. John didn't seem concerned. Far from it. He seemed more miffed than anything, like Fran had brought a big inconvenience upon him by taking off and leaving just a cryptic note.

And what about this note, Deanna asked John, where was it?

He said he had crumpled it up and put it in the trash.

Deanna would later recall: "I knew that something was very wrong here."

ST. MARTIN'S TRUE CRIME LIBRARY TITLES
BY MICHAEL FLEEMAN

"If I Die . . . "

The Stranger in My Bed

THE STRANGER
IN MY BED

MICHAEL
FLEEMAN

St. Martin's Paperbacks

THE STRANGER IN MY BED

Copyright © 2003 by Michael Fleeman.

Cover photograph of couple courtesy AP/Wide World Photos.
Photo of bed courtesy Photonica.

ISBN: 0-312-98417-0

Printed in the United States of America

St. Martin's Paperbacks edition / March 2003

10 9 8 7 6 5 4 3 2 1

ACKNOWLEDGMENTS

My thanks to *People* Los Angeles Bureau Chief Jack Kelley, my editors Charles Spicer and Joe Cleemann at St. Martin's Press, my agent Jane Dystel, and all the dedicated professionals who were so generous with their time: Detective Brian Potts of the Wayne County Sheriff's Office; Detective Dave Mansue of the West Windsor Police Department; retired Detective Michael Dansbury of the West Windsor Police Department; retired Detective Frank Barre of the Milford Police Department; Agent Robert Hilland of the Federal Bureau of Investigation; Jocelyn Stefancin of the Wayne County Prosecutor's Office; attorney Kirk Migdal of Akron, Ohio; Detective Gerald Burman of the Newton County Sheriff's Department; Newton County Coroner Larry Bartley; Dr. Frank P. Saul and Julie Mather Saul; and Sandra Anderson of Canine Solutions International. I would also like to thank Richard C. Armstrong of Armstrong Funeral Home, Seville, Ohio, and Eileen Mintier. A very special thanks goes to Betty Lippincott, and to the entire Hartman family. And my deepest thanks, gratitude and love to my biggest supporter, my wife Barbara.

"I thought she was with you."
—John David Smith, in a phone call to Deanna Wehling

CHAPTER 1

As the afternoon shadows grew long in a lonely corner of Indiana, Sam Kennedy brought his truck to a stop, looked in the rearview mirror, and saw that the rest of the road crew from the Newton County Highway Department had fallen behind. If the afternoon had been any colder, Sam and his partner Russell Trail would have stayed in the truck, heater blasting, waiting for them to catch up. But spring had finally come to northwestern Indiana, with temperatures in the 50s and the skies clear. Sam got out of the truck and surveyed the landscape: miles of farmland dotted with silos and barns. Dead trees lined the side of the road. The warmer weather was thawing out the cornfields from the winter freeze.

It was Tuesday, April 22, 1980. Sam and the rest of the crew were repairing winter damage to a section of County Road 400 North, known locally as Hopkins Park Road. One of the few paved east–west roads in the area, Hopkins Park Road connected busy Route 41 on the western edge of Indiana with the little town of Hopkins Park in far-eastern Illinois, 40 miles south of Chicago. Sam and Russell squirted oil in the cracks and the second crew came along behind sprinkling little rocks in the oil, creating what is called a "chip-along" road surface. But Sam and Russell had gotten too far ahead. The oil would harden before the second crew got there with the rocks.

As Sam stood on the roadway, he let his eyes wander to the surrounding farmland. That's when he saw it, lying in the weeds on the far upslope of a drainage ditch that ran parallel to the road. A wooden box. It was about five feet long and a couple feet wide—the size and shape of the toolboxes in the beds of pickups. Sam pointed it out to his partner. They trudged into the three-foot-deep ditch and walked up the other side to get a closer look. From its darkened, weathered surface, the box appeared to have been outside for some time. It looked to have been constructed by hand with plywood and finishing nails.

They picked it up and carried it back up to the roadway, where they set it down next to the truck. With a crowbar from the truck, Sam pried open the lid and peered inside. A faintly musty smell hit him. Stuffed inside were a soiled blanket or quilt, green and old, and a tangle of clothes made of denim and plaid cloth. Sam poked at the quilt with the crowbar, pushing it aside to see what was underneath.

As an object appeared, he gasped. Sam shouted to the other workers to stay right where they were until he called for help. He jumped into the pickup cab and radioed his boss, Highway Superintendent Ernie Collins, telling him to come out to Hopkins Park Road, just a couple miles west of 41, immediately.

The old quilt in the box was covering a human skull.

Larry Bartley had been driving home in his work car, a white Malibu station wagon, when over the radio he heard the dispatcher say, "Signal 8—10-79 at 400 north, west of US 41 in Newton." A crime scene technician for Newton County, Bartley knew the lingo: a body had been found on Hopkins Park Road. Turning around, he drove five miles to a spot on the road just west of Route 41 where he saw the highway workers standing near an old, weathered wooden box. They looked shaken, their faces ghostly white. At about the same time he arrived, his friend, Newton County Sheriff's Deputy Gerald Burman, pulled up in his chocolate-brown-and-tan Ford LTD cruiser. Also arriving were Sheriff Ed Madison and the county's part-time elected coroner, Pat Cardwell, a funeral home owner.

As Sheriff Madison interviewed the road workers and Deputy Burman posted himself a few hundred yards up the road to keep cars away, Bartley took pictures of the scene from various angles with his 35-mm Pentax, first in black-and-white, then in color. He also photographed the box. On paper, he diagramed the location where the box was found—the weeds had been tramped down and were dead. When he finished documenting the scene, he looked inside the box.

Pushing the matted and rolled-up blanket and clothing around, Bartley could see that there wasn't just a skull, but dozens of other bones, enough to make up an entire skeleton. With darkness approaching, Bartley wanted to get the box into a protected, lighted place. He helped Cardwell load it into the coroner's station wagon, then the pair drove separately to the Cardwell Funeral Home in the hamlet of Morocco, eight miles to the south. Bartley and Cardwell carried the box inside, placing it on an embalming table and pulling off the lid that Sam Kennedy had partially pried off with a crowbar.

Wearing rubber gloves, they removed the quilt first. Up closer, it looked more like an Army blanket, though it was badly soiled. They removed, logged and placed into brown bags a collection of women's clothing that seemed to come straight from the 60s: bell-bottom blue jeans, a turquoise hippie-type blouse with wooden buttons, a badly decomposed white nightgown, another white nightgown with a lace top, a bright red dress, a multi-colored dress with puffy sleeves, a blue dress, a black-and-white dress, a striped shirt, a plaid skirt, a blue Western-style shirt, a bathrobe and several bras. There was also a pair of blue jeans with a picture of a smiling mushroom on the crotch. Nearly all the items were size small. They also removed two rings, a gold crucifix on a chain, and strands of brownish hair.

With the clothing out of the way, Bartley and Cardwell could see that the bones were dry and stained dark, the soft tissues of the muscles, skin and organs eaten away by insects and the elements. There was the skull that had startled Sam Kennedy, along with the collarbones, chest bone, ribs, vertebrae, arm bones and the little bones of the hands. The bones appeared to be those of a woman or a small-framed male; they were too big to be those of a child.

But what was most intriguing were the bones of the lower legs. They had been cut a couple inches down from the knee. The rest of the leg bones and the feet were missing. The person in the box had had his or her legs chopped off at the shins.

Bartley and Cardwell decided to leave the bones in the box for the time being. Bartley put the bagged clothing and quilt in his car and drove home. The next day, he checked the bags into the evidence room of the Indiana State Police post in Lowell.

Over the next two weeks, the box with the bones was carted across northern Indiana in a quest to figure out whom they belonged to and what had happened to this person. A forensic pathologist at the Physicians Laboratory in Lafayette examined the bones and determined they were those of a woman between the ages of 20 and 40 years, and that it looked like the legs had been sliced off with a power saw. The bones then went to Purdue University for an examination by an anthropologist, who believed the woman was probably in her early twenties, with brown hair. The condition of the pelvis showed that she had borne no children. She may have been Hispanic, but the anthropologist wasn't sure. The bone structure of the skull and exceptional teeth suggested that she was very pretty.

Word quickly spread through Newton County about the discovery of what would be called The Lady in the Box. A front-page story in the *Newton County Enterprise* on

May 1, 1980, said "Box Lady Remains A Mystery" and quoted "one informed source" as saying that police in Indiana were pursuing "significant leads" in the case. The source told the paper that if it turned out The Lady in the Box was murdered, "This will be one of the most bizarre cases in Newton County history."

Seeking her identity, authorities put out the word over the police network systems to other agencies asking if they had any missing women fitting that description: young, brown-haired, possibly Latina, and attractive. The chopped-off legs weren't mentioned—that was supposed to be the truth test if anybody responded—but the grisly detail got leaked to the local media anyway.

Despite the optimistic tone in the *Enterprise*, the investigation was actually going nowhere. No replies had come in with anything close to a woman or girl fitting the description of The Lady in the Box. Newton County sheriffs contacted the Chicago Police Department to see if the remains matched those of any missing big-city women; it was not uncommon for the bodies of homicide victims to turn up buried in Newton County farmland. "We used to joke that they did it here because the soil was soft and sandy," Burman recalled. The size of the skeleton allowed authorities to quickly rule out the possibility that this was a missing woman in a notorious case of the time—the 1977 disappearance of candy heiress Helen Vorhees Brach, from suburban Chicago. Police combed their files for missing prostitutes or drug addicts, but found nothing.

After several weeks, the investigation had stalled and authorities were beginning to resign themselves to the possibility that The Lady in the Box might always remain a Jane Doe, and so decided to give her a proper burial. But first they kept some of the evidence in case a tip came in. The quilt, the clothing and the box were left in storage in the state police post in Lowell. Also kept were the lower leg bones in case a weapon or tool turned up that could be matched against the cut marks. Coroner Cardwell kept the skull for himself, storing it at the funeral home.

Under Indiana law, unclaimed remains must be buried in the township in which they were found. These remains were discovered closest to McClelland Township in Newton County, but the township had no cemetery. The Lady in the Box was to be laid to rest in the next closest township, Morocco, in the potter's field section of Oakwood Cemetery. The bones were put in white plastic bags, which were placed in an inexpensive, plastic child-sized coffin. It was a simple burial, attended by Coroner Cardwell, crime scene technician Bartley and a small crew from the cemetery that did the digging. No words were spoken that anybody could remember. A metal plate was ordered for a marker. Since nobody knew her name, or her date of birth or death, the marker read, "Jane Doe, 1980."

Over the years, The Lady in the Box became a local legend. Teenagers would go to Hopkins Park Road west of Route 41 to check out the very spot where she was found by Sam Kennedy that pleasant spring afternoon. Those who weren't morbidly fascinated by her grew to feel compassion, this unknown woman abandoned on the side of the road, evoking sympathy and a curious sense of protectiveness, her anonymity allowing people to create their own histories for her. Flowers would be found on the Jane Doe marker at Oakwood Cemetery. Cemetery workers tried to see who brought them, and a couple of times saw a car drive off, but they couldn't get the license plate. Thinking the flowers might have been left by the killer out of guilt, Newton County authorities set up a stake-out at the cemetery. Soon, they saw a woman leaving flowers on the marker. The woman turned out to be no killer, but a relative of somebody else buried in the cemetery. When she came to put flowers on her loved one's grave, she would save a few for The Lady in the Box because she felt sorry for her. In time, the original marker was stolen, then replaced by a New Age–looking one with a circle pattern—why and by whom, nobody knew.

As years passed, the investigation would be as dead as anybody in Oakwood Cemetery. There were no leads, no reports of missing women or girls fitting her description. There was nothing to do but to remember. Bartley, the crime scene analyst, would stop by the jail occasionally and ask Burman, "Heard anything about The Lady in the Box?" And Burman would reply, "Haven't heard a word. Nothing."

"Any open case always haunts you, for lack of a better word," Bartley would say years later. "You try to pride yourself that you're better than the average bear, so to speak, and you're going to get your man. And if you don't, it eats at you, not bad, but it gnaws."

It would gnaw at him for more than twenty years.

CHAPTER 2

"Private chalets in a rustic setting." That was the sales pitch in the brochure for the Stricklands Mountain Inn in Pennsylvania's Poconos resort. Just how rustic, John and Fran Smith were about to find out. Midway into their belated honeymoon, while Fran soaked in the ruby-red heart-shaped hot tub, their television conked out. After John called the front desk for a repairman, help arrived sooner than expected. Fran was still soaking. The tub sat in the middle of the suite, a romantically cheesy feature typical of Pocono lodgings, some of which also feature hot tubs shaped like martini glasses. When she heard the knock at the front door, she carefully stepped out of the tub and walked toward the privacy of the bathroom, dripping water as she went, being careful not to slip on the wet tile.

The Smiths had checked into the Stricklands Mountain Inn on Labor Day weekend, 1991, a year after they had impetuously married in Florida. At 49 years old, Fran, whose full name was Betty Fran Gladden Smith, was ten years older than John, her third husband. She was attractive and petite, with long blond hair and capped teeth. In her youth she had taken modeling jobs for extra money, and now into middle age she still had a taste for glamour, her most recent portraits taken in the soft-focus, boudoir style. John, by contrast, was as geeky as she was pretty. No focus was soft enough to cover his freckled face, skinny build and the perpetually bad cut of red hair. The two had met at work and married on the beach, taking their vows as their bare feet wiggled in the sand; afterwards, they had moved from Florida to New Jersey. But the romance wouldn't last and the young marriage suffered. The Poconos were supposed to help change that.

With the TV man at the door, Fran was walking halfway between the heart-shaped tub to the bathroom when she felt her feet fly out from under her. She had slipped on a wet spot on the tile and her 5-foot-2, 100-pound frame crashed to the floor, pain radiating from her hip. John called the paramedics, who soon arrived at about the same time as a security man from the inn. The paramedics examined Fran as she lay on the floor. The pain was so bad she couldn't get up. An ambulance took her to the Pocono Medical Center in East Stroudsburg, Pennsylvania, where X-rays showed she had a broken hip.

Fran would have to spend the rest of her honeymoon, and then some, not in a hot tub in a mountain inn, but laid up in a hospital bed. When she was well enough she would be sent back to her new condominium in West Windsor, New Jersey, near Princeton. She would be bedridden for weeks and then, if all healed properly, able to move around on crutches or with a walker before regaining full use of her legs. As cruel fate would have it, the New Jersey condo, which Fran didn't want to live in anyway—she had preferred staying in Florida near her family—was on the third floor, with no elevator. She wondered how she would ever leave the place. New Jersey was going to be worse than she imagined.

"I'm really frustrated about being here and not being able to move around like I want," she complained to her daughter, Deanna Wehling, in a phone call not long after she broke her hip. Deanna, 26, a single mother of two small children, ages 7 and 8, lived in Houston, Texas, and called her mother every other day for updates and to try to keep her spirits up. Other relatives, including Fran's sister, Sherrie Gladden-Davis, who lived in Indiana, also phoned, so that at least one person a day checked in on Fran. By nature a bubbly woman, Fran tried to make the best of her situation, but the pain and isolation weighed on her. She had time to think, reflect and worry about her troubled marriage to her secretive husband John. She didn't want to be divorced a third time. But it was getting tough. John was making it tough.

Fran had grown up as a military brat, her family following her soldier father from base to base before settling in Houston. Pretty and vivacious, she made the best of things in her youth, joining school clubs, modeling on the side. As a woman, she always went for military men like her father—she said she was a sucker for a man in uniform—but neither of her first two marriages lasted, the second ending in divorce in 1981. Single throughout the '80s, Fran focused her energies on her children—Deanna and her two brothers—and her grandchildren. Fran was a doting and protective mother and was always there for them.

Such was the case in 1989. One of her sons was an airborne Army Ranger sent to Panama for the military invasion to topple strongman Manuel Noriega. As her son was ready to make his parachute jump, anti-aircraft fire knocked him down. A bullet struck him in the back and came out just under his arm. He was treated in Panama, air-lifted to Atlanta, then sent by ambulance to Florida, where his brother, grandmother and great-grandmother all lived in the panhandle beach town of Niceville, thirty miles east of Pensacola.

The details of his injury and transfer to Florida didn't come to Fran all at once. After some anxious hours in which she didn't know whether her son was alive or dead, she got the word that he was safely in Florida. She rushed to the airport to fly out to see him. "There was a shortage of seats," Deanna would later recall, "and a gentleman who obviously felt he had very important business cut in front of her in line. And he was much bigger than her. My mother was only five-two, and she only weighed ninety pounds. He was well over 6-foot-4 and very big. And when he cut in front of her in line, she just reached up, knocked the hat off his head, grabbed him by the shoulders and pushed him out of the way, and said, 'I've got someplace that I have to be. My son has been shot. Just move out of my way. I can go through you or around you, and it doesn't take near as much time to go through you.' " He got out of the way, and Fran got to Florida.

She soon felt that this was where she was needed most. Not only was her wounded son there, but her mother was now ailing, and her grandmother would need care soon. Her other son had been shouldering the burden of caring for his grandmother and wounded brother, both convalescing at the grandmother's house next door. He was exhausted. Fran felt like it was her turn to be the caregiver. She stayed in Florida. It was a blow to Deanna back in Houston. She loved her mother, and her children, Nicky and Jarred, were close to their grandmother. But Deanna knew that her mother was moving to Florida for the right reasons.

Deanna and her mother kept in touch, and they found a way for Fran to be closer to the grandchildren. "My mother really wanted the opportunity to spend quality time with both of my children," Deanna would recall. "She came up with the idea while in Florida, because so much of my family was there, to send Nicky over there for a year and let her go to school there, and just be around her uncle and her grandmother and her great-grandmother. My daughter's great-great-grandmother was still alive. They lived right next door and it was just going to be a great opportunity." The plan was for Nicky to spend those months with her grandmother, then Deanna's son would spend a year with their grandmother. The daughter did go to Florida that year, and, Deanna said, "It's one of the happiest years of my daughter's life. She remembers it very clearly." The son would never go.

Fran stayed busy. In addition to caring for her mother and watching Nicky, she got a job as an executive assistant at Chromalloy Technologies in Fort Walton, five miles down the banks of the Choctawhatchee Bay from Niceville. It was there, in March 1990, that she met the friendly, if awkward, engineer named John Smith, who was at the company on a two-year contract. At the time, Fran was 48, twice divorced, and John was 38, and, he said, a lifelong Mennonite bachelor. John was outgoing enough, but many of his co-workers found him strange. He spoke too loudly, smiled too broadly, wore clothes that were a little out of fashion. But this only made him more appealing to Fran, who had a soft spot for the misfit, the underdog.

They dated for a few weeks, and it became apparent quickly that John had marriage on his mind. Although she was fond of him, Fran was leery at first, having divorced twice, but John was persistent. According to family members, Fran decided to take the plunge a third time on a whim. In May 1990, while visiting the beach in Destin, across the bay from Niceville, John told Fran that this would be a perfect place to get married. Then he suggested they do it right then and there. Fran agreed. They found a justice of the peace and they rolled up their pant legs, took off their shoes and got married on the sand. They had only been dating for two months.

By all accounts, Fran was happy at first. "Mom said they had fun together," Weiss would tell the Akron *Beacon Journal*. "He was geeky, not great looking, but funny and smart and easy to talk to. He didn't yell, curse or smoke." John made a good living, or so he told Fran's family, claiming to make $120,000 a year. He put in long hours and traveled quite a bit, including trips to Connecticut on the weekend. Fran's family didn't know much about him, other than what he said, which was that he loved Fran. Fran's family was happy for her, although for Deanna the marriage meant that her mother's roots were now sunk even deeper in Florida. "It really broke my heart that she wasn't going to come back to Houston and be near me," Deanna recalled. "I understand that's selfish, but that was it." The newlyweds built a custom house next door to Fran's mother, with only a fence between them, so that Fran could continue to care for the old woman whose health was rapidly declining from what was diagnosed as emphysema.

Not everyone in the family was happy with the marriage. Fran's mother, even in her sickness, made it clear that she never liked John. She didn't say why, except that she didn't trust him.

Nine months into the marriage, on the morning of February 5, John left their new house for work at Chromalloy, as he always did. Fran had by now stopped working so she could take care of her granddaughter Nicky, who on this morning was off at school. There was a knock at the door. Fran opened it. A sheriff's deputy handed her court documents dated the day before. They read: Dissolution of Marriage.

John wanted a divorce.

Fran called her daughter.

"I can't believe this," she said.

"Mom, what happened?"

"I have no idea." She told her about the divorce papers. There had been no argument, no warning of any kind. Fran told her daughter, "He got up and went happy as a lark off to work this morning."

Her mother cut the call short. She said she needed to call John at work. She hung up and dialed John's office. He answered. She asked him what was going on.

"I've made a terrible mistake," he said. "Can't I come home?"

Fran said yes.

She called her daughter back to recount the bizarre events of the morning.

Deanna told her mother, "Well, I guess he did make a big mistake."

"I'll listen to what he has to say," Fran said.

When John came home, Fran accepted his apologies, and two days later, on February 7, 1991, he filed a petition to dismiss the divorce proceedings. Still, Fran was never sure just what exactly had happened with John. He was so vague. But she was determined to make this marriage work.

A couple months later, in the spring of 1991, John lost his job at Chromalloy; he was either laid off or his contract had expired earlier than he had expected, the family wasn't sure which. There were job leads. He told Fran and her family that he had offers in Connecticut, upstate New York and New Jersey. Nothing in Florida.

He accepted the job in New Jersey, as a manufacturing manager at a company called Carborundum, in Woodbridge township, in northeastern New Jersey, not far from Staten Island. The company made ceramic materials for industrial use. Over Memorial Day weekend, 1991, John and Fran Smith left Florida, moving to West Windsor Township, a quiet upper-middle- to upper-class community of big houses and little crime next to Princeton. The Smiths rented a comfortable condominium at 104 Heritage Boulevard, Unit 9, in the Canal Pointe development, not far from the university. They didn't bring much from Florida. Fran took with her a few personal belongings—her sewing machine, a teacart, a cedar chest. Nearly all the furniture from their Florida home, most of it new, wasn't needed because their new home was a furnished condo. John told Fran he had put the furniture in a New Jersey rental storage unit.

The move north may have brought a change of scenery and a change in job for John, but the problems in the marriage followed the couple. John had always been strangely secretive with Fran, telling her little about his past and about his work. At some point—it's not clear when—Fran somehow found out that John owned a house in Connecticut, in Milford. It irked her that he hadn't told her about it, and his evasive and inconsistent answers to her questions about when and why he bought the place aggravated her even more. When pressed by Fran, John finally said that he was giving it rent-free to his sister, Cathy, in exchange for her taking care of his two collies, Christopher and Amanda. This startled Fran almost as much as the revelation of the house. Fran didn't even know he had a sister. Also, she couldn't understand why they had to rent a condo in New Jersey when he already owned a home in Connecticut. He had said he had job offers there. Why didn't they move to Connecticut? John told her the house wasn't yet winterized, though Cathy didn't mind.

Fran wanted to see the house and meet the sister. But John kept trying to keep her away, using a variety of excuses, the most common being that he just didn't have the time. The new job was so demanding he had to work almost every weekend and travel frequently.

Then, in August 1991, Fran came home one Friday night and found that John was gone. It was a rerun of that previous April when he filed for divorce, only this time he also took his possessions with him.

"Mom, what happened?" Deanna asked after her mother called her early the next day.

"We didn't argue or anything. I don't understand, I don't know," she told her daughter. John hadn't left a note, a message, not even divorce papers.

With her mother living so far away from family and friends, Deanna was concerned. "Mom, how much money do you have?" she asked.

Her mother said she had $50 in cash. To Deanna's shock, it turned out that her mother's name wasn't on any of the bank accounts or credit cards, and that all the cash she received came from John. He would cash a check and give her the money. John paid all the bills.

"Where are your things?" Deanna asked, referring to all that new furniture the couple had purchased for the Florida house.

"I don't know. They're in a storage room," her mother said, but she didn't know where the storage room was.

"Mom, don't you think that this is odd?"

Her mother tried to keep a clear head. "You know what?" she said. "Distrust ruined my first marriage and money ruined my second marriage, and neither one of those things is going to ruin this marriage. You either trust somebody and marry them, or you do not. And if you don't trust them you have no business being married to them."

If John returned as he had before, Fran would hear her husband out. But this time she wouldn't just believe his explanations and excuses, if they came. Realizing for the first time how little she knew about John, and how vulnerable she was financially, Fran made a list of demands that she would present to John when—or if—he returned. She wanted to know where this storage room was. She wanted her name on the bank accounts. She wanted to see the Connecticut house and meet John's sister. She wanted her name on the credit cards. She wanted to get a job, even though John didn't want her to work.

"That's it. I worked all my life, I'm going to work. I'm going to have my own money," Fran told her daughter.

That following Monday, Fran called John's workplace, finding him there.

"Hey, babe, how you doing?" he asked.

"Not too good, John," Fran said, then demanded to know what had happened.

John tried to make light of it. He explained that he had gone to the Jersey shore to cool out, to collect his thoughts. He said he had slept in his car.

Once again, Fran took John back, but she kept up the pressure. She confronted John with the list: show her the Connecticut house, show her the storage unit, put her name on the financial statements. Once again, John kept stalling, saying he didn't have time to do these things because he had to work so many weekends. Fran responded by getting her own job, as a secretary at Mazotas Associates Inc., a real estate appraisal company.

John tried to make nice. They would go away, just the two of them, not to Connecticut, but to the Poconos, for the honeymoon they never had.

And so they did go, over Memorial Day weekend in

1991. But the TV went on the fritz. Fran slipped on the tile. And the weekend that was supposed to save their marriage ended in pain and isolation for Fran. But Fran had her list and her new job. When she got better, things were going to change.

Holed up in the condo with just the goldfish and a new cocker spaniel puppy to keep her company, Fran tried to stay busy by sewing. It would keep her mind off the pain. The morning of Saturday, September 28, 1991, she spoke to her daughter Deanna on the telephone, asking her to take the grandchildren to a fabric store to pick up patterns for clothes that Fran would sew. By now, Fran could sit for short periods of time at the sewing machine. It hurt, but it made her feel productive. She had just started sewing a dust ruffle for the bed she shared with John. She spent twenty painful minutes at the sewing machine, took a break to lie down, then returned for another twenty minutes. Working in short shifts, she finished the dust ruffle.

On this Saturday, she told Deanna she was feeling well enough to leave the house for the first time since the fall, and that she planned to run some errands with John. Jarred's birthday was in a couple of days and Fran wanted to buy her grandson a present. After shopping, Fran had planned to go to a restaurant with John, another first since breaking her hip. Fran thought she could handle the car ride and sitting at the restaurant. The biggest problem was getting down those three flights of stairs. She was determined to do it. She was going to have John hold her crutches while she scooted down the stairs on her backside, one step at a time, lowering herself by her hands.

As Deanna was speaking to her mother, she could hear John talking in the background. She heard her mother say sharply to him, "John, what did you do?"

He had already gotten Jarred a birthday present.

"We were supposed to go out and do that together," Deanna heard her mother say.

"Well, I'm a man, I know better what a boy wants than

you do," Deanna heard John reply, "and I have to run into work anyway."

"No, you weren't supposed to be running into work today. We were supposed to be doing this."

Fran's voice wasn't raised, but her daughter could tell she was mad. Her mother had been so excited about finally getting out of the house, and John had just nixed that.

Fran told her daughter that she'd have to go. Just before she hung up the phone, Fran said, "I love you, and I'll give you a call Monday."

"I love you," Deanna said.

Monday came, and Deanna decided not to wait for her mother to call. She called Fran instead that morning, but nobody answered. She tried again in the afternoon, but still no answer. Deanna figured her mother was at her physical therapy session. There had also been talk of Fran visiting a lawyer to discuss legal action over the hip injury. That appointment, Deanna thought, was set for Tuesday morning, so she waited until Tuesday afternoon to call. Again, there was no answer at the condo. Deanna didn't want to worry. She thought perhaps her mother had figured out a way to get out of the house on her own, and was running the errands on Monday and Tuesday that she had planned to do on Saturday. Deanna called again on Tuesday night. There was no answer. Now the worries began. Someone should be there, Deanna thought. Where was her mother? Where was John? She called again on Wednesday morning. Still no answer.

For the first time that week, she called John at work. She had been reluctant to do so. Her relationship with John was cordial enough, though it was hardly close. She gave John the respect she felt her mother's husband deserved, but she really didn't know him well.

"John, this is Deanna. Where's my mom?"

"I thought she was with you."

"How could she be with me? Why would she be with me?" asked Deanna.

"Well, I came home to a note Tuesday night that said, 'Feed the fish, I'll be back in a couple days,' and she had talked about coming to visit you or your brother in Florida, so I thought she had come to see you."

"She's not with me," said Deanna, incredulous. She asked him just how her mother was supposed to get to Florida or Texas with a broken hip. Scooting on her butt across terminals?

"I don't know," John said. "I guess maybe she had a friend come pick her up." He noted that the airport bus did stop right in front of their condo complex.

"What do you mean, 'right in front'?" asked Deanna, becoming increasingly frantic.

"There's just a main thoroughfare that runs right in front of our apartment that the bus comes by from the airport, and you can just get on it there," he said.

Through her panic, Deanna was trying to sort this out. John didn't seem concerned. Far from it. He seemed more miffed than anything, like Fran had brought a big inconvenience upon him by taking off and leaving just a cryptic note.

And what about this note, Deanna asked John, where was it?

He said he had crumpled it up and put it in the trash.

Deanna would later recall: "I knew that something was very wrong here."

CHAPTER 3

For the next four days, from her home in Houston, Deanna pestered John to do something, anything, his words echoing in her head: "I thought she was with you." Then, on Friday, October 4, 1991, she asked John if he had filed a missing persons report.

John said he hadn't.

Deanna was beside herself. "I guess I'm going to get on a plane and do it," she told him. "I'll find somebody to take care of the kids and I will come there and do that."

Fran's sister, Sherrie Gladden-Davis, was also calling John and also threatening to fly out from Indiana and march into the police station if John didn't do it.

John acted as if this was an imposition. He suggested that Fran wouldn't have wanted her daughter and sister acting this way. He said they were being selfish and not thinking about Fran's feelings.

"You know," John told Deanna, "your mom is going to be really pissed off about this, because that's going to make her wanting to have some time off seem very public."

Deanna was having none of this. "John," she said, "I don't care whose butt this chaps, get in there, get the report done."

At last, he told Fran's daughter and sister that they didn't need to come to New Jersey. "I promise I will do it," he said, telling them that he would "call one in." But the women said that if he didn't go into the police in person to report Fran missing, then they would do it.

That Friday night, after work, John Smith drove his red Mazda Miata to the West Windsor Township Police Department station at 271 Clarksville Road, housed in the same building as the municipal court, and filed a missing persons report. The information was taken by Patrolman Tom Moody at 10 p.m.

In the two-page report, John said that he had come home from work at about 7:30 p.m. that previous Tuesday, October 1, 1991, and found a note from his wife. "I'll call you in a couple days. Don't forget to feed the fish." He told the patrolman that he wasn't worried, thinking his wife had visited family in Texas or Florida, though how she would have traveled he didn't know. He said that she had left her car, a Dodge Shadow, behind, and that she was recovering from a broken hip that made it difficult for her to get around. She only had a few hundred dollars available to her. John said that he had been with his wife the previous weekend, shopping. Although the patrolman had no way of knowing it at the time, John's account of their activities conflicted with what Fran had told her daughter—that John had gone shopping without her.

West Windsor police didn't handle too many missing persons cases, and what few they had usually involved rebellious teens running away from home, or mentally addled older people wandering off. They would always be found eventually. Betty Fran Smith's case was assigned to Detective Michael Dansbury, who had spent his entire career at the West Windsor Police Department, starting out as a patrolman in 1975. Although a veteran cop, he did not exclusively handle missing persons. West Windsor was small enough—and had little enough crime—that the four detectives in the adult-crimes bureau handled a little bit of everything, from robberies to assaults. In his years at the department, Dansbury could only remember two murder cases.

Dansbury handled Fran's disappearance like any other missing persons case, entering her name, description, date of birth and other information into the nationwide computer network that sends teletypes to every police station. There were no immediate responses, but that was not unusual. She had only been missing a few days.

Meanwhile, Deanna and Aunt Sherrie waited and fumed. Dansbury had told them what John had said to police, about him thinking Fran had headed off to relatives, and it wasn't true. They *were* the relatives. Deanna's brothers or grandmother also hadn't heard from her. Despite John's suggestions that they were overreacting, Deanna refused to believe that her mother would leave home without telling her husband or anybody in her family where she was going. Even if she wanted to, the bad hip made it almost impossible for her to move. How did she go? Her car was still there. Most important, Fran had every reason to stay in close contact with her family. Her mother's health had deteriorated to the point that she was admitted to the hospital's intensive care unit, where she was hooked up to a ventilator. Fran loved her mother too much to abandon her at a time like this, Deanna felt.

By Tuesday, October 8, with Fran gone a week, Dansbury drove his blue Crown Victoria unmarked police car to 104 Heritage Boulevard, Apartment 9, to interview John David Smith. As he pulled up to the three-story building at about 8:30 p.m., he noticed that both of the Smiths' cars, the red 1990 Mazda Miata convertible that John drove and the 1991 white Dodge Shadow that Fran drove—both with Florida plates—were parked in the residents' lot next to the condos. Dansbury walked up the three flights of stairs and met John Smith at the door. Entering the condo, Dansbury saw that it was a two-bedroom unit, nicely furnished. John sat in a chair and Dansbury took a seat on the sofa in the living room, giving John the once-over. John was pale, red-haired, looked like a bookworm. "Odd duck," was the description running through Dansbury's mind. What made him seem even stranger was that he didn't seem that worried about his wife's disappearance. But then Dansbury didn't know him, so he couldn't tell for sure if he was hiding his concern or simply didn't have any.

For the next hour-and-a-half to two hours, the detective asked John for all the background he could provide, from his marital history with Fran to their activities leading up to the day she disappeared. John told him that the couple had recently moved to New Jersey from Florida, where Fran had family. John said Fran also had relatives in Texas. The detective asked John if there had been any problems in the marriage, any fights or arguments. John said there had been none, failing to tell the detective about the two times he'd left Fran. "They had no problems whatsoever," Dansbury recalled John telling him. John did say that Fran wasn't happy about her new home, her yearning for Florida exacerbated by being stuck in the condo because of the broken hip. Dansbury noticed that the walker that John said Fran used was still in the condo, but that her crutches were gone. Asked what he thought may have happened to her, John could only guess that she went south to Florida to visit her family. Dansbury asked Smith if anything was missing—besides his wife. Smith said he went through the condominium and found that a yellow suitcase and a jogging outfit were gone.

As for the note, John said he couldn't remember exactly what it said—only something about reminding him to feed the fish. The detective saw a small tank with a couple of goldfish. He also saw a cute cocker spaniel puppy scurrying around the house. The note hadn't said anything about feeding the dog as far as John could recall. Why would she be more concerned about these fish than the puppy?

"Do you have the note, Mr. Smith?" Dansbury asked.

"Well, I guess I should have saved it, but I threw it out," John said.

All twenty-six years of his police experience told Dansbury that something wasn't right. Along with John's apparent lack of concern, some of his answers to simple questions were vague, or didn't make sense. He asked John why he thought his wife would have left her car behind. At first he said that he had taken the keys away from her so she wouldn't try to do something foolish and drive. He explained that she had been feeling cooped up because of her broken hip. But then why, the detective asked, didn't she take the Miata? John said his wife didn't have that key—not because he'd taken it away, but because she'd lost it. The couple seemed to have some trouble with keys, the detective thought. John guessed that Fran must have taken either a bus or a taxi. John also had initially said in the missing persons report that his wife only had a few hundred dollars when she disappeared, since her name wasn't on the bank accounts. But when interviewed by Dansbury, John said that it appeared she had more like $2,000 in cash, reimbursement money for moving expenses from Florida to New Jersey. He also thought she might have taken one of his credit cards.

Finally, Dansbury asked John if he had a recent picture of Fran to show around town. John said he didn't, because his wife was so camera-shy.

Leaving the interview with an uneasy feeling, Dansbury went back to the station and typed up his notes on a supplemental investigation form himself—the department didn't have secretaries for the detectives—and continued his investigation. The local bus, taxi and limousine companies had no records of picking up a woman matching Fran's description from the Canal Pointe condominiums. The Port Authority police had no sightings of Fran, and the airlines had no passengers with her name in their manifests. Dansbury talked to Fran's daughter Deanna and sister Sherrie and found that Fran had a close-knit family—and none of them had seen or heard from her since September 28, when Deanna had talked to her mother on the phone about going out shopping and buying the grandson's birthday present. The relatives also told Dansbury that John seemed hesitant to report Fran's disappearance, and that he only did so when pressed. They also expressed surprise that John would say Fran was camera-shy. She'd once modeled, they told him. She loved the camera.

The disappearance made the local papers. The *Trentonian*, the paper in the state's capital quoted John as saying he didn't know where Fran was or why she'd taken off. "From day to day I just run different thoughts through my head," he said, telling the paper that Fran had a left a note saying she would be back in a few days.

Fran's daughter and sister printed hundreds of posters, with a glamour picture of Fran baring her shoulder and sporting dark nail polish. The poster gave a detailed description of Fran, sparing no embarrassment in the effort to locate her.

MISSING PERSON
BETTY FRAN SMITH

MISSING PERSON NOTIFICATION
Born: 08/04/42; Age at time of disappearance: 49; Gender: Female; Height: 5'2"; Weight: 100 lbs; Hair: Blonde, medium length; Eyes: Blue; Race: White, light-complexioned; Identifying Marks: scar on left knee, scar from hysterectomy, pin in right hip, no bone in little toe of right foot, front teeth are temporary caps and are slightly yellowed; AKA: Fran; Circumstances of disappearance: Unknown.
MISSING: OCTOBER 1, 1991,
FROM PRINCETON, NEW JERSEY

It said that anyone who had information regarding her should call the West Windsor Township police at the number listed on the flyer.

• • •

Eight days after talking with John, Dansbury wanted a second interview. There were too many lingering questions. Dansbury arrived at John's condo at 7:30 p.m. on Wednesday, October 16, took his seat on the same sofa and asked John point-blank what he had been doing to help find his wife. He told Dansbury that he had distributed hundreds of posters with Fran's picture that her daughter had made all around Princeton, which Dansbury knew wasn't true. The family had distributed them. John wouldn't do it. Dansbury also pressed John on why he'd delayed in reporting his wife's disappearance. John never gave a straight answer.

But John did offer some new information. When asked again about his personal history, John said that Fran wasn't his first wife. John revealed that he had actually been married once before, more than twenty years earlier, to a woman named Janice. They were young and crazy and had eloped in 1969 at the City Hall in Detroit. The marriage lasted only a short time, ending amicably in a no-fault divorce. John said the last time he saw Janice, in the early 1970s, she was headed for a commune in Florida. John had never told this to Fran or her family. Dansbury wondered why.

The detective drove away from the condo with more questions than he had come with. John was looking more and more suspicious.

About a month later, in early December, Dansbury spoke with John's boss, Fred Olszankyj at Carborundum, and another supervisor, John Bowen, who had worked closely with John. Olszankyj said John had never told him about Fran's disappearance, and that the only way he'd known about it was by reading the local newspaper. Bowen was completely in the dark. "When I asked [Bowen] if he knew John Smith's wife Betty Fran was missing, he was just visibly floored," Dansbury would later recall. "He just couldn't believe it, and he did not know." Bowen said he had gone on business trips with John, spending long hours with him, and was shocked that John wouldn't have told him about something so important. The detective talked to other employees and found that John had told them a variety of stories about Fran. Some he just didn't tell. Others he had either said that she had already returned and everything was fine, or that she had suffered cancer, which wasn't true as far as police or Fran's family knew.

Dansbury returned to the Canal Pointe complex and spoke with all the residents in the twelve-unit building, most of whom had never noticed John or Fran and had nothing to say. But two neighbors told Dansbury they had seen a woman matching Fran's description struggling to go down the stairs with her crutches. The woman was not only nursing what appeared to be a bad hip, the neighbor said, but she looked frail and sickly, and had blotches or bruises on her face. The observations carried some weight. One of the neighbors was a paramedic. They believed that the time they saw her was on either September 21 or September 28—they knew it was a Saturday in the third or fourth week of the month. If it was September 28, that would have been the last day Fran had spoken to anybody—the day she'd talked to her daughter by phone.

Dansbury then spoke with Fran's employer, Nancy Mazotas, who ran the real estate appraisal firm. Fran had once asked Nancy if she could hide divorce papers that had been served on her by John earlier in the year in Florida. In his interviews with Dansbury, John had said nothing about divorce. On the contrary, he said there were no marital problems at all. Dansbury later confirmed that in February 1991 John had in fact served divorce papers on Fran in Florida, but then changed his mind and withdrawn them. Nancy described Fran as "edgy" and said she referred to her husband as a "jerk."

By now, John was becoming, if not a suspect, something very close to it, even though he continued to insist that he knew nothing about Fran's disappearance. Police asked him to take a polygraph examination. John agreed, saying he had nothing to hide. On December 3, John went to the police station, where in Meeting Room B he was hooked up to the machine and asked questions by polygraph examiner Robert Dispoto from the New Jersey State Police. Police have refused to reveal what the results were, but Deanna would later say that John told her he had, in his words, "failed miserably."

The polygraph clinched it. John David Smith was now officially a suspect in the disappearance of Betty Fran Gladden. Detectives wanted to talk to John again, this time not a chat in his home but a formal interview at the police station.

John agreed to meet with them, but not without putting off investigators for two weeks, always saying that he was too busy at work to make time for the interview. Finally, on Wednesday, December 18, nearly three months after Fran's disappearance, John walked into the police station at 9:15 a.m., posed for mug shots and was advised of his constitutional rights to have an attorney present during the questioning and to remain silent. John signed a form waiving those rights. He was brought into the interview room— a small, wood-paneled room in the single-wide mobile home next to the station that served as the temporary quarters for the detective bureau while new offices were being built.

For several hours, Dansbury pummeled John with questions. While John did not invoke his right to remain silent, for all the good the interview did, he might as well have. They went over everything again, from his story about finding his wife gone and the feed-the-fish note, to all his various omissions—significant omissions—about his first marriage and the serving of divorce papers on Fran. He was questioned about the house in Connecticut, the one that Fran had always wanted to see, and John confirmed that he did own a home on the beach in Milford, about forty miles northeast of New York. A tenant named Cathy lived there whom he had known for seven or eight years. He wouldn't give any more information about her.

For several hours, John dodged and weaved and changed his stories and then changed them again until Dansbury lost track of how many inconsistencies had piled up. But John never offered any clue as to what may have happened to Fran. He never confessed to any crime. There wasn't enough from the interrogation to arrest him. Dansbury released John into the New Jersey winter, convinced that John knew a whole lot more than he was saying.

Then the detective picked up the phone and called the Milford, Connecticut, police department. He wanted to know who this Cathy really was.

CHAPTER 4

The two-story house at 23 Point Beach Drive in Milford was on a quiet street in a middle-class neighborhood. The concrete back patio opened to a rocky beach and the waters of Long Island Sound. Beaten by the New England weather, the wood siding was in need of another coat of gray paint.

On a cold day in late December 1991, Detective Frank Barre drove to the house and left his business card from the Milford Police Department in the mailbox, asking the dark-haired woman whom neighbors said lived there to call him. Contacted by Michael Dansbury of the West Windor, New Jersey, police, Barre had been trying to keep a low profile, watching the house occasionally for signs of a red Miata, discreetly interviewing neighbors, trying to get a bead on who the tenant was.

A motor vehicle department check on the license plate of the car the woman drove revealed that she wasn't named Cathy at all, as John Smith had claimed, but Sheila Sautter, age 39, a human resources manager at Avco Lycoming, a large manufacturing company in nearby Stratford and a major employer of Milford residents. She had been seen living at the house for about five years, frequently receiving a red-haired male visitor who police assumed was John. Property records showed the house was purchased in August 1986 for $232,000 by John David Smith.

After a couple of weeks, at the request of Dansbury, Barre arranged the paperwork for a search warrant for 23 Point Beach Drive. It was a rude way to ring in the New Year. On January 3, 1992, there was a knock on the door. Sheila Sautter opened it to find detectives from Connecticut and New Jersey. They introduced themselves, and one of them had a name she recognized. She had found his business card in the mailbox, but she'd never called. She didn't know the other detective—Michael Dansbury—but she recognized where he had come from. West Windsor was where John lived during the week. Also at her door were her sister and brother-in-law. Brought by police, they had accompanied the detectives to lend moral support. Sheila would need it.

The detectives were let into the house. It was small and cozy, with a little kitchen and living room downstairs and bedrooms upstairs. They took their seats in the living room, and the detectives told Sheila why they were there. They played it conservatively. As innocent as Sheila looked—her face pale with shock at the sight of all these cops coming to her front door—the detectives had learned to always cast a suspicious eye on a witness until the evidence proves otherwise. They told her they were conducting an investigation into the disappearance of John's wife, Betty Fran Gladden Smith.

Sheila Sautter's face fell, as did her world.

She said she wasn't John's sister. She was John's longtime girlfriend—an upset and confused girlfriend, but not an entirely surprised one. Even before the detectives had arrived she was reeling from something John had told her. She had seen him on Wednesday, December 18—the same day that he was interviewed by police in West Windsor. After spending a few days there, he'd had to return to New Jersey. At about 5 a.m., as he was walking out the door, he casually told her, "Oh, by the way, I'm married and my wife is missing."

Then he left.

Sheila was stunned. He didn't tell her the wife's name, how long they had been married, or what could have happened to her. He'd just said what he'd said and walked out the door.

This wasn't the first time John had surprised her. Earlier in their relationship, she had discovered that John had been married when he was young. But that marriage was long before he met Sheila. The second one had been going on while she was with him. She had known John for almost eight years, but realized she didn't really know him at all.

Recounting her history for the detectives, Sheila told them she first met John Smith in 1983. It was what Hollywood would call a "cute meet"—she was the human resources person at Avco Lycoming, he was applying for a job. He got the job—and the girl. "We became a couple—girlfriend, boyfriend," she would later recall. They first lived in the condominium she rented in Stratford, then moved to his house in Milford, on Eastern Parkway, where they stayed for about two years. Sheila moved out of state for about a year-and-a-half, but returned. "John said to come back home, and my family and friends and my ties were in Connecticut," she said. Then they moved to the house on Point Beach Drive that John had purchased, staying there for five-and-a-half years with their two collies. It was never a clandestine relationship—they took trips together back to John's home state of Ohio, meeting his mother Grace, brother Michael and his grandparents, Chester and Ethel Chaney.

For most of their relationship, Sheila thought John had never been married before. He certainly never mentioned anything about a prior marriage. Then about five years into their relationship, she found one of John's old résumés. On the last line, it said: "Divorced, no children." Sheila questioned him about it. At first he said his secretary had made a mistake, but Sheila said secretaries don't make those kinds of mistakes. "He said that it was true, that he was married right after high school," she recalled. "He was very young and they were married for a very short time and then they both went on their separate ways. . . . It sounded like an amicable relationship to me."

Sheila continued to live in the Connecticut house while John got jobs out of state, first in Florida, then in New Jersey, but he returned to the house frequently, usually on weekends. In the last few months, he had been there almost every weekend—those "business trips" he'd told Fran about. In fact, he was in Connecticut on Sunday, September 29, 1991—one day after Fran had her final phone conversation with her daughter, and the day that John had told police he was shopping with Fran. Instead, Sheila said, John was shopping with *her*, buying curtains for the house. She provided a receipt from a G. Fox store in Connecticut.

Then there was the weekend after Fran had disappeared. It turned out that on Friday, October 4, after filing the missing persons report, John drove to Milford to spend three days with Sheila and her family to attend a birthday party for Sheila's mother. When John arrived, Sheila found him acting strangely, withdrawn, not his usual outgoing self. He looked ashen. While the party went on downstairs, John stayed upstairs, avoiding the guests, who could hear him pacing.

She had last seen him about two weeks earlier, when he'd left the house in the morning telling her that he was married and his wife was missing. At the time, Sheila didn't know what to think. When the detectives arrived, she did. John had been living a double life.

As the interview wound down, the detectives asked if she would cooperate with them—without telling John.

With resignation in her voice, she said she would.

CHAPTER 5

The nightmares would jolt Deanna Wehling awake. She would dream that her mother was lying in a trash bin, or dumped on the side of a road, or buried in a shallow grave in the woods. The nightmares would make her lose sleep and the exhaustion would cause more anxiety, and more nightmares. Deanna sunk into what a psychiatrist would later diagnose as a major and incurable depression. After each nightmare, Deanna would hear John's words: "I thought she was with you."

John had to know.

These were difficult times for Deanna's family. Along with her mother's disappearance, her grandmother—Fran's mother—was near death from emphysema. Hooked up to a ventilator, the woman couldn't talk. All she could do was write on a chalkboard as she lay in the hospital bed. When Deanna visited in January, her grandmother scratched one word on the slate: "Fran."

Deanna told her grandmother she would do whatever she could to find out what had happened to Fran. Her grandmother cried, or tried to, the ventilator preventing her from making any noises—only silent tears. Within weeks, her grandmother died at age 65.

On February 23, 1992, Deanna and her Aunt Sherrie, frustrated with the police investigation and angry with John, traveled from their homes in Texas and Indiana to West Windsor, New Jersey, to talk to Detective Dansbury. They wanted, as Deanna would say, "to humanize this person"— Fran—in the eyes of police by linking family faces with her. They also wanted to go inside the condominium to get a feel for the place, to answer at least some of their many questions, to seek the truth about Fran. Again describing himself as a man with nothing to hide, John let them stay there. One day, while he was at work, "We decided we were just going to tear that condo apart," Deanna recalled. Rummaging through the drawers and closets, the women discovered that Fran had disappeared with only a purse and the clothes on her back. They found all of her personal belongings of the sort she would have taken had this trip been planned: clothing, nylons, panties, makeup, toothbrush, razors, shampoo and reading glasses. Items of great sentimental value were still there: jewelry that had been in the family for generations, little bird figurines from Fran's children, expensive Lladro statues, and Fran's prized shoe collection, dozens of pairs of shoes she kept in labeled boxes. The only clothes that seemed to be missing, as far as they could tell, were two sweat suits, one pale blue, the other pink, and a pair of white Keds tennis shoes.

What they also found strange was that although John said he was still living there, he didn't have many clothes in the condo: just a couple of suits and four pairs of underwear. It was as if he were living somewhere else. The refrigerator was empty, save for a jar of pickles.

Outside, they searched Fran's Dodge Shadow and in the hatchback area found another item of great importance to her: a blue comb. Fran's mother had given it to her ten years earlier, and Fran was never without it. The comb didn't cost much, but it was a difficult kind of comb to find when her mother bought it, a combination comb on one end and a pick on the other. She could do her hair perfectly with it. "She swore by that comb," Deanna would recall. "She thought that was the greatest gift anybody had given her."

When John returned to the condo, Deanna and Sherrie confronted him. He pleaded ignorance, as he had so many times in the past. He didn't know where she'd gone or why these things were left behind. Again, he said he had always assumed she was with relatives. They asked John if he thought Fran had any money with her. At first, he had said he thought she had taken $200, then he changed that to $2,000, but his story strained credibility. He said that the $2,000 came from a moving-expense check they had cashed, with the money earmarked for a deposit on a little house near Princeton University. But Fran had earlier told her daughter that they had decided to *stay* in the condo and not take the house, using the money instead for decorating. While recovering from her broken hip, Fran had put all that painful effort into making the dust ruffle. Deanna figured her mother was intent on redecorating—and staying in the condo.

Pressed on these issues, John threw up his hands. How would he know? He just came home and found a wife and her yellow suitcase missing, with only a note saying to remember to feed the fish. The women asked him again about that. They'd scoured the condo and found no such note.

"Well, you know," John said, and the women sensed a lie coming on, "it wasn't a note, it was more like a nine-page letter. And I told the police I threw it away because it was just too personal for them to read it, but I'll give you a page of it."

From another room he brought out a piece of paper. The words were Fran's handwriting—Deanna was sure of it. But this note, or letter, or whatever it was, didn't seem to have anything to do with her leaving town or feeding fish. It didn't mention John or New Jersey or anything of any relevance to her disappearance. It looked like a random page ripped out of a diary.

"This is kind of out of context," Sherrie told John. "What does this have to do with it?"

"It's from somewhere in the middle," John said. "It was about nine pages. This page is from somewhere in the middle."

"Well," said Deanna, "I want the whole letter."

"The rest of the letter is at work," John said. "I don't even have it here at the condo."

John then groused that work was tough on him. "They're being so difficult because my wife is missing," he said. "They're accusing me."

The women suggested they should all visit his company, look for the note, and talk to his co-workers. Maybe that would take some of the heat off of him—and give the women a chance to check out his office.

But first, the women wanted to go to the police station, both to get an update on the investigation, and to share what they had found—and not found—in the condo. For along with all of Fran's personal belongings, two other items had been left behind—two items that proved that Fran didn't leave on her own.

Opening a storage closet on the outside balcony patio, empty boxes tumbled out. Behind them were two yellow suitcases.

Detective Dansbury welcomed the involvement of Deanna Wehling and Sherrie Gladden-Davis in the investigation, though he would later make it very clear that they had searched the condo on their own, with no prompting from police, who didn't have a warrant. He sympathized with their concerns and shared their frustrations about John. They told him about the one-page letter that John said Fran had left behind, the letter that seemed to have nothing to do with anything. They told them about all of John's crazy stories and inconsistent statements about Fran's disappearance. And they told him about the yellow suitcases, the same kind of suitcases that John had said disappeared along with Fran.

None of this came as any surprise to Dansbury, who also had been deeply suspicious of John. Then he said he had some information for them, revealing that John had been seeing Sheila Sautter before and after Fran's disappearance. He asked the women if they knew anything about her. They were flabbergasted. They knew that John had a house in Connecticut with a woman living there, but he had said she was his sister, though he'd given different names for her. He had told Deanna the sister's name was Kathleen, and told Sherrie the sister's name was Deborah. When once asked about this, John said his sister's name was Deborah Kathleen.

Dansbury then told the women that in his second interview with John, John had told him he had been married once before to a woman named Janice Hartman, in a civil ceremony in Detroit in the late 60s or early 70s. John had claimed he had gotten an amicable no-fault divorce after a few years and had not seen or heard from Janice again. This was the first that Deanna and Sherrie knew about another Mrs. Smith. They were certain Fran hadn't known about this either. John had always described himself as a bachelor, a Mennonite bachelor no less.

After the women spoke to Dansbury, they hooked up with John and went to his company to find the rest of this nine-page note that Fran had supposedly left behind. John led them through a back door and brushed past about twenty people, introducing the women to no one, then bolted for his office. There was no note. But the women did see one thing: sitting on the credenza was a big picture of Fran. They knew that police had been asking for a picture, and that John had said he didn't have one, claiming Fran was too camera-shy. After a few minutes, John then led the women out of the building, again refusing to let them talk to anybody. "Later on," Deanna recalled, "we found out that he had played us off as me as his step-daughter and my aunt as my mom. He told everybody, What did you think of my wife and step-daughter?"

Deanna and Sherrie would leave New Jersey certain that Fran was dead—and that John was responsible. Dansbury shared that view. But he told them that to make an arrest he needed evidence of the kind that investigators couldn't seem to find, physical evidence like blood, fibers, hair, a weapon, anything; or eyewitness evidence—anybody who may have seen John kidnap or harm Fran; and most of all, he needed Fran's body. Even if he had all that other evidence, he said, it was still extremely difficult to prosecute somebody for murder without a murder victim.

Frustrated but not beaten, Deanna and Sherrie continued the investigation that had started with the search of the condo. The most promising lead was the revelation that John had been married before. When she got back to Indiana, Sherrie worked the phones, searching for this Janice Hartman whom John had been married to twenty years earlier. Maybe Janice would have some helpful information; maybe John had even contacted her. Since John had said he'd married her in Detroit, Sherrie started her search on her own Midwestern turf, trying all the Hartmans in the heartland. The surname wasn't as common as John's, but the phone books were filled with Hartmans. Call after call resulted in nobody who was or who knew Janice Hartman.

Then, dialing names in Ohio's 216 area code, Sherrie reached a Garry Hartman, from Wadsworth, in northeastern Ohio near Akron. She asked him if he was related to Janice Hartman. He said, yes, Janice was his sister, a vivacious, petite young woman. He said his sister Janice had in fact married a John Smith, originally from Seville, Ohio. They had eloped in Detroit in the late 1960s. And she had divorced him in the early 70s.

Sherrie asked the brother how she could reach Janice.

"My God, lady, you've got a problem," he said, and the reason would take Sherrie's breath away.

Shortly after divorcing John, Janice disappeared—without a trace, never to be found again.

Just like Fran.

Sherrie told Garry that her sister was married to John,

and that she had disappeared without a trace.

Gary would later recall: "The hair on the back of my neck literally stood up, and I literally couldn't speak for several seconds."

Two wives, two disappearances, one husband. The women thought John had to have killed Fran, and probably Janice, too. It was too much of a coincidence. Maybe now, Sherrie thought, they had the evidence they needed.

She thought wrong.

CHAPTER 6

One day in March 1992, Detective Brian Potts was at his desk in the five-member detectives' division of the Wayne County Sheriff's Office when the phone rang. The sheriff's office is located in Wooster, a pleasant town of Victorian houses in northeastern Ohio about forty miles south of Cleveland. Wooster is home to the College of Wooster and is the middle of Amish and Mennonite country; it's not uncommon to hear the clip-clop of an Amish horse-drawn black wagon going down Liberty Street. Potts picked up the phone. It was a Detective Michael Dansbury from the police department in West Windsor, New Jersey. Dansbury said he was trying to locate a Tim McGuire, who in the early 1970s was a young detective for the Wayne County Sheriff's Office. Potts explained that McGuire still worked for the office; he was now Potts' supervisor. Potts asked if there was anything he could do to help.

Yes, Dansbury said. The New Jersey detective explained that for the last six months he had been investigating a missing persons case that appeared to have a link to an old case in Wayne County—a case that Tim McGuire had investigated in 1974. Dansbury said his investigation focused on the suspicious disappearance of a middle-aged woman named Betty Fran Gladden. Her husband, John David Smith, had emerged as the only suspect. The case had begun petering out when Fran's sister, doing some amateur detective work, discovered that John's first wife, a Janice Hartman, had also disappeared, back in the early 1970s, shortly after getting a divorce from John. Both Janice and John had lived in Wayne County—Janice in Doylestown after their split, John in Wooster, in a mobile home. According to members of Janice's family, Sheriff's Detective McGuire had investigated Janice's disappearance. Like Fran's family, Janice's family had suspected that John was involved. But for some reason the investigation was abandoned. Janice was never found and John drifted out of the family's lives, until this week—when Janice's brother had received the call from Fran's sister.

Listening to Dansbury, Potts was struck by the startling similarities between the cases, and agreed with Dansbury that this couldn't be explained as coincidence. If the account given by Janice's family was correct, this John Smith might well be a double-murderer. Potts told Dansbury he'd dig through the department's files and get back to him.

Potts went to a drawer holding the blue index cards that recorded all the old cases. There it was, under "H", a missing persons case involving Janice Hartman Smith in November of 1974 in Wayne County. Using the reference number on the card, Potts scrolled through microfilm until he found a copy of the original paperwork. He made a printout and sat down to absorb the information.

The initial report was case number C-2133-74, written on a standard, pre-printed "Missing Person & Runaway Case Report." According to the report, the sheriff's office had received a call at 6:28 p.m. on November 19, 1974, reporting that a woman had disappeared. Deputy Thomas L. Gasser was initially assigned the case. He drove to a location—it wasn't clear where, but it appeared to be the mobile home of John David Smith. The address was Lot

#167 in the Melrose Trailer Park, Wooster. The trailer park still existed on the edge of town. According to Gasser's report, John was listed as the husband of Janice. Her address was also said to be the Melrose Trailer Park. Her occupation was "housewife."

Some of this information, Potts noted, conflicted with what Janice's family had told Dansbury. They said John wasn't Janice's husband at the time the report was taken, because the couple had recently divorced, and that Janice was not living in Wooster, but in her father's mobile home in Doylestown, fifteen miles to the north.

Potts read on. In the report, Janice was described by John as 5-foot-4, 115 pounds—petite, like Fran. Janice had blue eyes and blond hair in a "middle back" style, the report said. Her complexion was fair, her teeth and physical condition both good, except for the "bruises about face and arms." Potts wondered how she'd gotten those and whether they were linked to her disappearance. According to the report, Janice was last seen wearing a blue top with red stripes, blue jeans and black shoes "that lace up the front." She was wearing a wedding band and engagement ring— odd, thought Potts, for a divorcée—and a diamond watch. She was carrying nine dollars in cash.

Providing additional physical details, the report said that Janice's nose, ears, mouth, teeth and speech were all "normal," her neck was "skinny," her posture was "erect," her complexion was "fair" and her hair was "straight." The report said she did not chew tobacco, snuff or gum, drink wine or use marijuana, LSD or heroin. Under identifying traits, the officer had checked the boxes for "bold," "boisterous," "friendly," "smiles," "jokes" and "happy." Under mental condition, a box was checked for "forgetful" and the officer wrote in "upset"—why, it wasn't said. For habits, the report said "smokes," "frequents bars," "frequents taverns," "drinks beer," "drinks liquor" and is a "light eater." Her favorite bars were Albert's, the Sun Valley and Kippy's, all within a half-hour's drive from Wooster. She was said to be drinking before her disappearance.

In the section reading "Who last saw missing person," the name Kathy Paridon was provided. Kathy was described as a white female, age 18, of 188 Howard, Doylestown. Paridon had last seen Janice "in front of Paridon residence," with Janice headed to a place marked "unknown."

The person to be notified if Janice was to be found was listed as Nonda Paridon, a "friend," who also lived at 188 Howard in Doylestown. Potts wondered about this a moment. Why wouldn't the contact be John Smith? And what was Nonda's relationship with Kathy? Sister? Mother?

In the box for "person last seen with missing person" was the name John Richardson, preceded by the notation "possibly" of 31st Street in Barberton, about five miles from Doylestown and twenty miles from Wooster. His age was listed as being possibly 27.

The narrative section of the report, handwritten by Deputy Gasser, described an evening that had begun at a Doylestown bar and ended with Janice driving off with a man to places unknown, leading John Smith to call the sheriff's office.

Complainant [John Smith] advised that he was with Janice at Sun Valley on 11/17. Comp. advised she was with another friend at that time, but he can't advise name. Only description is stocky man with mustache. Comp. advised his wife was to meet a John Richardson there at 2200 hours. Comp. then left Janice. Janice later took Kathy Paridon home. Kathy advised a man was with Janice at that time, but she did not know who the man was. Comp. advised that Janice must have returned home sometime Monday, 11/18/74, in early morning hours as her car was back at Lot 167 Melrose when he got up. He advised that he didn't think much about her not being there because he thought that someone had picked her up to take her into Wooster to file charges against Ron Paymer and several others Ref: C-2061-74. She has

*not been seen since taking Kathy Paridon home. Ka-
thy advised male in car when she went home was
w/m, dark hair, beard, medium build, bad case of
acne. T/U attempted to contact John Richardson. No
phone listing. Neg. with Barberton P.D., contacted
James Richardson of 31st St., Doylestown, does not
know a John Richardson or Janice Smith. County
alert was given.*

It was not the clearest of narratives, and it required some
thought to sort things out. Reviewing the narrative and the
rest of the information in the report, Potts had a number of
questions:

- John Smith claimed to be Janice Hartman's husband, even though her family said they were recently divorced. Why would John say this?
- John Smith said that Janice lived in his mobile
  home in Wooster, even though they were supposed
  to be divorced. Why? Was her family wrong about
  the divorce?
- The two of them were at the Sun Valley bar in
  Doylestown, apparently together, the night of November 17, 1974, even though they were supposedly divorced.
- Janice was also with "another friend," a stocky man
  with a mustache, but John doesn't have his name.
  Who was he?
- Janice was to meet a man named John Richardson
  at the bar at 10 p.m., but the report is ambiguous
  as to whether she did or whether this stocky man
  was John Richardson. Did she meet this man? Who
  was he?
- John left the bar at some point; Janice and Kathy
  Paridon stayed behind. Where did John go? Why
  did he leave?
- Kathy saw Janice at the bar with an unknown man.
  This information must have come from Kathy since

John had already left. This meant that the investigating deputy was getting some of his information from Kathy and some from John. Which information came from which person?

- Janice later took Kathy home to Doylestown. This information had to have come from Kathy. Or did it?

- In the car with them on the way to Kathy's home was the dark-haired man with bad acne. Elsewhere in the report a John Richardson is described as "possibly" the last person to see Janice. A check of the phone directory by the deputy turned up a James Richardson on 31st street, but in Doylestown and not Barberton. James claimed not to be the man with Janice, or to know either the dark-haired man or Janice. But to Potts it seemed to be too much of a coincidence that there would be two men named Richardson, both with first names starting with "J," and both living on 31st Street. Was James really the man with Janice and was he lying? Did he abduct and/or kill Janice? Why did the deputy take James' word for it? Or, Potts wondered, was John Richardson an invention of Kathy Paridon and John Smith?

- John had awakened the next morning, November 18, to find Janice's car parked at the mobile home in Wooster. Unconcerned, he'd assumed that someone had taken her to Wooster, where the county courthouse was located, to file charges against a man named Ron Paymer and several others. This was the most disturbing piece of information of all: Janice had disappeared right before she was to file criminal charges against some men. If that didn't point to a motive to kill her, what did? What were these charges, and who were these men? And were the injuries on Janice's body related to case? The missing persons report contained a reference number for another case, C-2061-74, the last two numbers meaning it was a recent case, in 1974. Potts would look at that report. But first, he would go through the supplemental reports to the missing persons report to see if Detective McGuire answered any of these questions.

The first supplemental report, dated November 21, 1974—two days after the missing persons report was taken—was written by McGuire, who had been assigned to follow up on the information taken down by Gasser. McGuire had first gone to John Smith's trailer in the Melrose Trailer Park at 11 a.m., but didn't find him. McGuire had seen a gray Mustang II parked in the driveway. A check of the license plate came back with the car belonging to what McGuire wrote as "Janet Smith, missing person, who used to live on Hubbard St., Columbus." Potts paused. Where did this Hubbard Street address come from? Investigators now had two addresses for Janice: the Melrose trailer and this one in Columbus.

McGuire's report went on to say that he'd left Smith's trailer without talking to him and gone to the residence of Kathy Paridon on Howard Street in Doylestown. She was there and, the report said, "stated that victims [sic] husband, John Smith, was at the Paridon residence last evening and they discussed the situation on where she might be. At this time they could come up with no known location." It would occur to Potts that he may have been wrong in assuming that the original report was taken at John's trailer. It never says in the report where Deputy Gasser was; it only gave a time of arrival. Potts' assumption was based on the entries of John as the complainant. But John could have been at Kathy's trailer when he spoke with Gasser. This would account for why Kathy was providing information, and why Gasser made no note of the Mustang.

In any event, the report quoted Kathy as saying there had been some trouble between John and Janice at the time of her disappearance. "It is the understanding by this officer from what Kathy Paridon had stated that John Smith and his wife have not been getting along and she has been seeing other men, but to her knowledge the names are unknown," the report said, now providing another motive for killing Janice. That would throw suspicion on John, though McGuire didn't make any mention of considering this.

According to the report, McGuire had asked Kathy about this John Richardson of Barberton, the man whom Janice was supposed to meet at the bar, and who may have been the last man with her in the car after Kathy was dropped off. Kathy said that she knew a John Richardson who worked at the chemical plant in Barberton. She didn't have the name of the plant, but McGuire assumed it was the Pittsburgh Plate Glass Company. McGuire had finished his interview with Kathy and spoken with the head of security at Pittsburgh Plate Glass. The security man knew of only two Richardsons there: a Clarence Richardson, age 50, and a James Richardson, age 54. James was the man who had already been contacted by deputies and who denied knowing anything about a John Richardson or Janice Smith, and was far too old anyway. Clarence also was too old. James Richardson was described as being about 27. McGuire contacted another company in Barberton, Babcock & Wilcox, and found no Richardsons on the payroll. The report ended, "Investigation continues."

That same day, November 21, McGuire had looked into the John and Janice relationship, checking divorce files, since, he wrote, "they were recently divorced." How he got this information, he didn't say; presumably it came from Kathy. He'd found no records of a divorce.

McGuire had then decided to try again to speak with John. He said he'd gone twice to the trailer but had had no luck finding him. McGuire had written that he asked Unit 5—the sheriff's office's designation at the time for Sergeant James Gasser—if he had time to interview Smith. James was the brother of Thomas Gasser, the deputy who'd taken the original missing persons report. "Unit 5 did so," McGuire wrote. "It is this unit's understanding that according to Mr. Smith her red suitcase is gone."

Potts wondered why John hadn't mentioned the suitcase before. Did he just notice it gone?

Smith had also told Gasser that he thought that "Janice could possibly be with a guy named Sunshine" at a house on 11th Avenue in the university section of Columbus. The report offered no more information on Sunshine—who he was or why Janice would be with him. Smith then was quoted as saying he and Janice had been married four years ago and gotten divorced on November 14, 1974. When they got married, John was quoted as saying, "She was pretty heavy on alcohol. She left several prescription bottles behind." The drugs had been prescribed by a Dr. Avery of Seville and a Dr. Ross of Columbus. McGuire would finally find the records: divorce finalized in the Medina County, Ohio, court on 11-14-74—just three days before Janice disappeared. McGuire had found that Janice and John had canceled their bank accounts and credit cards back in August "when they divided up the property." All this raised the obvious question in Potts' mind: Why had John claimed on the missing persons report to be Janice's husband, living with her in the trailer and hanging out with her in a bar, when they were divorced and had split up their property?

Or maybe the question wasn't so obvious. The report made no reference to Unit 5 or anybody else confronting John with this.

The next report, dated the morning of November 25, 1974, had McGuire getting information that John had moved out of the trailer in Wooster and into his grandfather's house in Seville. John at the time was said to be working at the Flxible Co., a Loudonville, Ohio, bus manufacturer. The grandfather was identified as "Mr. Chaney," who ran a small Marathon gas station on Route 3. The information McGuire received was that Chaney also hadn't seen Janice. The report also had information about Janice attributed to John: "Mr. Smith stated that while they were married, she just packed up and went to Florida three separate times." How McGuire had gotten all this information, he didn't say. Had he talked to Chaney? To John? McGuire wrote that he would try to get the address of Janice's brother in Florida and talk to Janice's doctors. "Investigation continues," it said.

A report filed later that day included the results of the doctor search: Dr. Avery had last seen Janice on November 10—a week before her disappearance—and prescribed birth-control pills and ten Phenobarbital pills—barbiturates—"for her trying to get to sleep. She had been having problems." McGuire had written. "This is all he knows about the girl and stated that she was very nervous and seemed to be very mixed up. She has not since then been in or called about her prescription." This meant that Janice had been popping barbiturates for emotional problems just days before her disappearance. What was worrying her? Potts wondered. McGuire had also tracked down the wife of Janice's father working at the Post House Restaurant to see if she had the address of Janice's brother in Florida. The woman said that Janice's father did, and that he would call the sheriff's office. The report ended, "Investigation continues."

Two days later, according to a November 12 report, McGuire got a hot lead on the location of John Richardson. The security man at the Pittsburgh Plate Glass Company had called to say that there was an employee named John Richard Lower, nicknamed "Spitz," who worked the 4 p.m.-to-midnight shift. Lower was known to "hang around" the Doylestown area and did live on 31st Street. McGuire wrote that he would try to find this "Spitz."

The investigation then appeared to have stalled; if McGuire had ever found "Spitz," the paperwork didn't reflect it. Lower was never arrested, charged, or even considered a suspect. The next report wasn't made until March 7, 1975—almost four months later—and focused not on the search for Janice, but on the reaction of Janice's mother, identified as "a Mrs. Lipencott," the surname misspelled (it was actually "Lippincott"), to the pace of the sheriff's investigation. McGuire had updated the mother on the course of the investigation, and, "She stated that she has not heard anything from Janice since she left and has not received any letters or a phone call." The report said, "She believes that there may be fowl [sic] play because she [Janice] was to visit out at their residence the following Sunday to return some clothes of her younger sister and she did not show up." Janice's mother then pointed a finger at John. "Mrs. Lipencot [sic] feels that John Smith, who lives at Melrose Trl. Park, knows more than what he is saying because he was the last one to see her and that ever since the divorce, John felt that if he couldn't have her, no one could." The mother had ended by saying she appreciated what deputies were doing and that if she heard anything she'd call them.

McGuire apparently took seriously that provocative statement about John. Three days later, on March 10, the detective had gone to Chaney's gas station, where he spoke to John's sister-in-law—the wife of John's brother, Michael. "Mrs. Smith stated that John is very concerned about the whereabouts of Janice," the report said, not giving her first name. "She stated, in her opinion, he would not be the type to do anything drastic to Janice for he loved her too much." She'd also said that Janice was very close to her brother Ross, who lived in Florida, and that "if she requested him to keep her whereabouts secret, that he would." McGuire had asked the woman to tell John that if he had any more information, to call the sheriff's office. McGuire never spoke to John. Meantime, Janice's Mustang had been repossessed and auctioned off, according to the report. If McGuire had ever had any thoughts of searching it for trace evidence—and there is no notation that he did—it was too late now. "Investigation continues," he wrote.

Two days later, on March 12, McGuire had called Janice's mother back to tell her that Janice's car had been repossessed and that he had talked to John's sister-in-law at the Chaney residence. He noted that John had brought Janice's remaining clothes to the house, and her mother asked to have them sent to her. The detective had said he would do what he could. The mother also gave the detective two phone numbers that Janice had called while she was staying with her mother before the disappearance. He wrote that he'd try to find out what these numbers were. "Investigation continues," the report said.

McGuire wrote in a report the next day, March 13, 1974, that he'd checked on those phone numbers. One was disconnected, the other belonged to the Buckeye Mart discount store in Columbus; police there would look into it. Also, McGuire had followed up on the suggestion from John's sister-in-law that Janice's brother in Florida may be hiding her. A check by St. Petersburg, Florida, police found that the brother had married "a girl named Debbie" and moved away. About a week later, Columbus police got back to McGuire about the Buckeye Mart connection; it turned out that Janice had once worked there, but as far as the Buckeye people knew, Janice and John had left Ohio for somewhere in California.

"Investigation continues," the report said.

But it didn't.

Not a single report could be found after March 1974 about the disappearance of Janice Hartman Smith. No word on whether anybody had pressed John on his mother-in-law's claim that he once felt, "If he couldn't have her, no one could," or whether anybody found it strange that Janice had disappeared just three days after divorcing him, or why John had spent time with her at a bar and described himself as her "husband" and given the same address for the two of them when they were divorced. In fact, there was no record that McGuire himself ever spoke to John, or had ever visited the other address for Janice, in Doylestown, to see if her—or her body—was there.

Also, there was no indication of whether this man named Sunshine or the other man named Spitz had ever been found or questioned, or whether Spitz was in fact the man with the bad case of acne who was in the car with Janice when she drove off. There was no indication of what detectives had done to find out why Janice was feeling "mixed up" and needed barbiturates to fall asleep shortly before her disappearance and divorce. There was no word on what they'd done to investigate Kathy Paridon's claims that the couple "had not been getting along," an incongruous statement since the "couple" were divorced because they weren't getting along.

As Potts reviewed the supplemental reports, the mountain of unanswered questions was daunting—and disappointing. Why hadn't his department followed up on these questions? Why did the investigation die?

Most incredible to Potts was the apparent lack of attention to one of the most important details in the missing persons report. Mentioned in passing, it was noted that just before her disappearance, Janice was about to file charges against a Ron Paymer and other men over something involving case number C-2061-74. A woman is about to file charges against somebody, then disappears? It would seem that this somebody would be, if not a key suspect, then certainly somebody high on the list of those to be questioned. But his name never appears in any of the follow-up reports.

Going through the blue index card drawer, Potts found case number C-2061-74. It was right behind the one for the Janice Hartman Smith missing persons case. He looked up the report on microfilm, and by the time he was done reading it, he had formed an opinion as to why the missing persons investigation had been allowed to peter out.

According to the report, a woman identified as Janice E. Smith had come into the Doylestown police station early the morning of Sunday, November 10, 1974, wearing a green pullover sweater, a gray-and-white fuzzy jacket, light blue checked pants and gray moccasins, beads around her neck and a gold crucifix. Her body was a mess. Scratches covered her hands, arms and stomach. Her ankles and knees were bruised. The left side of her neck was scraped. Her lip was cut.

Janice Hartman told police that the night before, she had been attacked by several men who had tried to gang-rape her.

The alleged assault had occurred just days before Janice disappeared. What's more, the assault report was taken by Sergeant James Gasser—the same man whom McGuire said had spoken with John Smith days later about Janice's disappearance. And yet, to Potts' amazement, the documents showed no sign that authorities linked the assault with her disappearance.

Why?

Potts began reading through the assault report. It said that Sergeant Gasser had been sent to the Doylestown station to talk to Janice, who gave her address as 653 South Portage Road in Doylestown, a different address, Potts noted, from the one John Smith would provide on the missing persons report. Janice said that the night's activities had begun at the Portage Pub in Doylestown with her date, a Leonard Bennett, at 2 in the morning, November 10, 1974. Another man, whom she described as 5-foot-7 to 5-foot-10, 160 pounds, with ash-blond hair, came up to her and asked if she wanted to party at a nearby home. Janice said she would come by, but not until she ate. This sparked an argument—why, it isn't spelled out—but it was determined that she would eat.

At about 2:40 a.m., Janice and Leonard had gone to a house at 950 Clinton Road in Doylestown owned by a Larry Swain. They were let in and Janice got two beers from the refrigerator, one for her and one for her date. They took a seat in the living room. A brown-haired man, about 5-foot-6 to 5-foot-8, 165 pounds, asked Janice to get up and dance. Janice said she hadn't been paid to dance; the man agreed to pay her. The amount wasn't noted. Why the men would think to pay her to dance—and why she didn't see this as unusual—was not spelled out in the assault report, Janice was described as a "housewife" in the missing persons report. In any event, the assault report had Janice telling the man she couldn't dance because a table was in the way. The man had said he'd move the table. Janice said he couldn't do that. The man said he could because it was his house, too, and he could move the table if he wanted to.

After the man and another man had moved the table, Janice danced to music apparently coming from a hi-fi or radio. As a second song began, one of the men asked Janice to take off her top. "He stated that if she would take off her top, all of them would strip completely," the report said. Janice said she would do it, but then got scared, and agreed to take only her pullover off. Underneath, she was wearing what was described as a "small go-go type top." Potts had his answer to the dancing question: the "housewife" also apparently worked as a go-go dancer.

When the second song finished, Janice had sat in Leonard's lap, while the other men passed around a marijuana cigarette. Janice didn't want any, but took two puffs because she was scared. As the third song began, Janice danced again. Halfway through the song, the brown-haired man had tried to grab her, but she pulled back and told him to stop it. A minute or two later, the man threw her down. Janice tried to push him away, while the man called her a "bitch" and pulled off her remaining clothes. As he grabbed her arms, Janice broke free, crawling away on all fours. But two men dragged her by the feet into the bedroom, where she was forced onto a waterbed. A man got on top of Janice and, the report said, "attempted to have intercourse but was unable to gain penetration" because Janice kept struggling. She kneed him in the groin. He choked her and said, "Bitches like you don't deserve to live."

Two more men had then come into the bedroom and held down Janice by the legs. Then two more men came in and held down her arms. Four men were now pinning Janice while the brown-haired man put his finger in her vagina.

Then Janice's date, Leonard, came into the bedroom and tried to have sex with her, but he couldn't because she kept moving. Leonard left and yet another man tried, but also couldn't. Janice had then bit one of the men on the thumb. She was struck back in the face. She wriggled free. She got to the window, broke it and tried to get the neighbors' attention. She was thrown back on the bed and struck again. Two men entered the bedroom. One of them was the man she had bitten. He now carried a shotgun, which he aimed at her and said, "Narcs always have an easy way out." What that statement was supposed to mean wasn't explained.

"God, don't kill her!" somebody shouted from the living room.

One of the men grabbed the man with the shotgun. The man opened the shotgun and a shell fell out onto the floor. A dark-haired man with a mustache told everybody to leave the room. Janice found a hunting knife on the nightstand and plunged it into the waterbed. One man returned and gave Janice her clothes. She got dressed and left the house for the police station.

After telling the story to the sergeant, Janice had provided a written statement, the tone much lighter and flightier than the narrative in the report. Penned in cursive, her statement looked like a girlish letter to a friend, filled with exclamation points, rough language, grammatical errors, misspellings. It also betrayed her youth, as she referred to a man of 25 to 30—just slightly older than she—as "elderly." She also made reference to another woman at the house. It's not spelled out what she was doing, apparently either dancing or having sex with several of the men in the bedroom. Janice had written:

1:55 at pub—ask to go to Larry Swain's house to party—said OK! Drank their to 2:30—went to Larry's house then! 8 guys taking turns on thin blond about 5'2. Elderly guy about 25–30 wanted me to dance so I started to dance—then when they all took their turns—deal was I took off my top if everybody got naked. I said O.K.! So that was smooth and easy! Then the blond girl come out of the bed room and sat on the couch and I sat over by Lenord! They ask me to dance again—as they past some joints [marijuana]. So I danced! Elderly man about 25–30 grabbed me and place me on the floor—said I was a [illegible, but could be "whore."] I said what! And wanted up—he threw me down and started to take my clothes off! (The more I fought the more I get beat!) The next thing I knew I got drug to the bedroom! He wanted me to be nice and I refused and said let me go—he said no! I was held down and still didn't give in. A blond guy about 25 to 27 was holding my arms—I bit him and got smacked in the mouth—twice after that I kicked the one guy on top of me in the balls and got hit in the face again—this getting to be serious. I told them I was not going to let in and to let me go—blond dude ask why [illegible] or what! Then he put a shot gun to my head and said I wasn't leaving alive and said go ahead—I bullshitted them and finally after getting beat got to get up—I grabbed hunting knife on the bed stand and slashed the water bed and finally confinced them of my clothes I wanted—dressed and started walking up the street—Lenord picked me up and went to the police.

So summed up Janice's night of beer, dancing and attempted rape. According to the missing persons report, it was later that day she had gone to the doctor to get the birth-control pills and barbiturates to help her sleep, the events of the previous twenty-four hours explaining why the doctor observed her to be "very nervous and very mixed up."

Sergeant Gasser had tracked down the owner of the Clinton Road home, who provided the names of four other men, including Ron Paymer. That was the name of one of the men who, according to the missing persons report, Janice was going to file charges against before she disappeared. According to the assault report, Gasser searched the house for the shotgun shell that Janice had said was ejected from the gun, but couldn't find it. He did confiscate a 20-gauge shotgun and photographed a hunting knife. Gasser had gone to Janice's residence on Portage Road to show her the shotgun. "She said the shotgun could've been the same one but she wasn't sure," the report said. Asked to describe the knife she'd plunged into the waterbed, she said it was ten to twelve inches long. The deputy later tracked down most of the men, who gave statements and were photographed. One man didn't give a statement except to say, "I don't know anything, I didn't see anything." The pictures of the men were shown to Janice, who identified Paymer as the man who'd ripped off her clothes and put his finger in her vagina. Paymer was never arrested or charged in the case, and Janice's allegations may be totally unfounded.

The deputy had written that he would contact the prosecutor the next day. But Potts could find no indication that any arrests had been made or any charges ever filed.

Why the case was dropped wasn't explained in the paperwork. But Potts had an idea.

Although Janice had obviously endured a traumatic experience, her statement and the circumstances of the night didn't paint her in the best of lights. It was an after-hours party of sex, drugs, music and dancing that she seemed to willingly and happily take part in until it took a violent turn. The detective speculated that in conservative Wayne County in the early 1970s, the problems of a foul-mouthed go-go dancer party girl who put herself in dangerous situations likely ranked low on the priority list. That she would have disappeared one day probably didn't surprise anybody in a position of authority.

After reading the reports and speaking with Dansbury, Potts decided to take action. He suggested to his superiors that the case of the missing Janice Hartman Smith should be reopened eighteen years later, particularly in light of what had happened in New Jersey. Two wives of the same man had disappeared, under many of the same circumstances—cars left behind, suitcases taken, families of the missing women suspicious of the husband—it was all too much to ignore, he said. It was a delicate situation. Those who had taken part in the investigation were still at the department; the Gasser brothers both were on the force, and McGuire was now their boss. All three said they remembered nothing of Janice Hartman or John Smith or either of the investigations.

After debate behind closed doors, the Janice Hartman case was reopened—and assigned to Potts.

He called back Dansbury. They laid plans to conduct a joint Ohio–New Jersey investigation. Two murders, nearly two decades apart. The target: John David Smith.

CHAPTER 7

As strongly as Potts felt about giving the Janice Hartman cases the attention he felt they deserved, he knew that reopening them posed awesome challenges. Witnesses could have moved, or died. Memories could be clouded or erased. Key pieces of evidence could be long gone. He didn't even know if the trailer where John Smith had lived was still in the Melrose Trailer Park. The investigations in New Jersey and Ohio threatened to strain the tight budgets of the two little police departments. And, from the Ohio standpoint, it could all be a wild goose chase. What if Janice Hartman had just taken off one day and found trouble somewhere else?

In March 1992, New Jersey Detective's Dansbury and Dave Mansue drove seven hours to Ohio in an unmarked Crown Victoria, their department unable to spare enough money for airline tickets and a rental car. When they arrived in Wooster, they met up with Detective Potts and other investigators, then fanned out across the state to track down and re-interview as many of the people from the original Ohio investigations as possible, putting an emphasis on friends and family members of John Smith.

Although so much time had passed, detectives were encouraged to find that John's family wasn't as itinerant as he was. His grandparents, Chester and Ethel Chaney, still lived in the Pleasant Street home in Seville that McGuire had written about in his supplemental reports. But when investigators got to their house, they found the couple's hospitality didn't live up to the street name. Told by detectives that they were investigating the disappearance of their grandson's former wife, the Chaneys refused to answer any questions and told the investigators to go away.

John's mother, Grace Malz, also still lived in the area, and she was no more forthcoming than her parents, evoking this "feeling of extreme indifference," as Mansue later recalled it, acting as if she were too busy with her family's real estate business to worry about such things as ancient missing persons cases that she didn't know anything about anyway.

Detectives had more luck with John's brother, Michael Smith, a forklift operator from Wadsworth. After driving to his house, Potts and Mansue were met at the door by a man of medium height with straight red hair like his brother's—just a "regular blue-collar guy," as Mansue recalled. They questioned Michael for nearly three hours, going over the family history, his relationship with John and the brothers' relationships with their mother Grace, their late step-father Sam Malz—who had done very well in real estate—step-brother Stephen Malz and the grandparents. The family dynamics played this way: John and Michael loved their grandparents dearly; were a little more distant from their mother, Stephen and Sam; and in recent years didn't speak much to each other. The brothers had drifted so far apart that, when told that John's wife had disappeared, Michael said that was a shame, he had always liked Sheila, the woman in Milford. The detectives did a double-take. When they told Michael that John had married a woman named Fran—and that she was the one who was missing—Michael said he didn't know anything about her. The detectives were skeptical that Michael was telling the truth—John was known to keep secrets, but from his own brother? They couldn't test Michael on this further because the interview would end abruptly.

Michael's grandmother burst into the house—"like a tornado," Potts recalled—and shouted, "Don't tell them anything!"

The detectives were told to leave, shaking their heads as they went to the car.

Although rudely sent away, they were encouraged that these and other witnesses were still available, even if their cooperation was not. Maybe they'd reconsider after hearing about the disappearance of another Mrs. John Smith. The only key witness they couldn't talk to was Larry Swain; he had died. Other witnesses seemed willing to help, but said they only had sketchy information. Leonard Bennett, still living in northern Ohio, recounted some of the details from the night Janice was attacked, though what he said largely mirrored the police report. He said he didn't know anything about Janice's disappearance. Another friend, Dennis Evans, a schoolmate of John's who also knew Janice, provided details of John and Janice's elopement and marriage, along with some of John's actions after Janice disappeared, but he too pleaded ignorance on what had happened to her.

Potts and Mansue got more information from Kathy Paridon, the woman quoted about Janice's disappearance in the original report. Now a clerk in a department store in Wooster, Kathy told the detectives that she had had great affection for Janice. At first Kathy said she couldn't remember anything about the last night she was with Janice. Then, when Potts showed Paridon a picture of John Smith, she claimed she didn't remember anything about him. Potts and Mansue didn't believe this. How often in a lifetime does a woman file a missing persons report and not remember the details of the disappearance, or the man with whom she filed it? When pressed about this, Kathy said the missing persons report was wrong. She said she didn't think there was a man in the car with Janice when she drove off. Kathy didn't know how that information got in the report. If Kathy's second version was right, that meant the search for John Richardson—or Spitz—was a worthless endeavor, possibly set in motion by John. What's more, no John Richardson was ever arrested, charged or even questioned.

The teams of detectives returned from the interviews and compared notes. They found Bennett and Evans credible and Paridon helpful, though they felt she still knew more than she was saying. As for John's family members, detectives couldn't decide whether they were hiding something. Mansue recalled them as "an odd, protective family"—but protective enough to cover up a murder? That would take time to find out.

In the meantime, investigators accumulated enough information from these witnesses, along with members of Janice's family—who gave full cooperation—to reconstruct the story of John and Janice. It was, investigators found, a story of young and forbidden love, two Ohio kids from similar backgrounds whose lives took dramatic turns after a night at a Doylestown bar.

For John David Smith, growing up in his grandparents' home on Pleasant Drive in Seville, Ohio, death was never far away. Literally. Next door was the Armstrong Funeral Home, owned and operated by the Armstrong family since 1918. If this bothered the young John, it never showed. Like most children, he seemed to take things as they were. He and his brother Michael would play ball with other neighborhood kids in a field behind the mortuary. The brothers fought, as brothers do, then they would make up and go about their lives. John would grow into a skinny, awkward-looking teen who loved riding his motorcycle and working on car engines in the garage of the gas station his grandfather operated. The brothers were, as funeral home owner Richard C. Armstrong remembered it, seemingly normal all-American Midwestern boys. "They were just boys running around their grandma and grandpa's house," he said. "Pretty good kids." John Smith was born on April 2, 1951, to Grace Chaney Smith and Carl Smith, within a year after they married in Homerville, Ohio. Three years later, John's brother, Michael, was born. Their parents separated soon after Michael's birth, and Grace filed for divorce on the grounds of gross neglect of duty and extreme cruelty, boilerplate terms of the day that could have meant anything from wife-beating to simple incompatibility. The three of them—mother and two sons—moved in with Grace's parents in Seville, then a community of 3,500 people. Seville was an agricultural town, with grain operations and big dairy farms, and a few small shops. The Chaneys lived in a white house with green trim behind the two-pump Marathon gas station that they operated on Route 3, or Pleasant Street, as this section of the highway was called in town. After a few years, Grace bought a house two doors down from her parents.

The Chaneys were well-liked pillars of the community, with Chester joining the Masonic lodge, serving as a councilman and working for the volunteer fire department. In the 1950s through 1970s, he also volunteered for the town's ambulance service, which was operated by the Armstrong Funeral Home—it was common in small rural towns in those days for the local funeral director to also have an ambulance service. Chester's Marathon gas station was the local gathering place for friends and cronies. If things were slow with the business—and they often were—Chester would join his friends around a table and chat. The gas station sold soda, candy and ice cream, and children would often be seen there, talking with the old man. And while Chester was always friendly enough, and never seemed to get angry, he could also be quiet and reserved, even secretive. He would tell people only what he wanted them to know.

Chester's wife Ethel Chaney was another upstanding member of the community who would volunteer for local causes. When Seville started its first police department in the '50s, she was the dispatcher. She was a homemaker and assisted Chester at the gas station. Friends described her as a pleasant lady, a local girl who lived in Seville her entire life. But Ethel had a tough streak, and there were signs of strain between Grace Smith and Ethel Chaney. Arguments could be heard between mother and daughter.

For John and Michael Smith, their grandparents were as much their parents as their mother was. With their natural father out of the picture, the boys would call Grandpa Chaney "father" and even Ethel would refer to him as "your father" before correcting herself. Chester would take the boys hunting or sit with them while watching sports on television, a favorite pastime. The boys' relationship with their mother was a little more complicated. By all indications John was the apple of his mother's eye. Michael would later say that, while he looked up to his older brother, he resented his mother's attitude, as he saw it, that John could do no wrong. Michael knew this wasn't true; he had seen John's occasional temper tantrums.

John grew into a rail-thin, pale, redheaded teen-ager with big ears and a bad bowl-type haircut. He had a crooked smile with a chipped front tooth. He never had any girl-friends at Cloverleaf High School that anybody knew. But he was no recluse. He ran track and received ribbons and trophies in competitions. He had a mind for mechanics, and could be seen in his grandfather's garage late at night tinkering with a truck or van that he had bought.

He also loved his motorcycle. It was loud and powerful and he drove it fast over the country roads, sometimes with Michael clinging on for dear life. John bought it when he turned 16, and it became an important prop in his effort near the end of high school to look James Dean–cool and dangerous. He'd don a leather jacket and motor at top speeds to parties after school. But the leather look was just that—a look—and not a very good one. The motorcycle and tough-guy jacket clashed with his Howdy Doody face and common-as-common-gets name. And everyone knew that he was a good kid, in school and at home. He never got into any scrapes with the law. Nobody ever saw him drink too much at parties.

It was at one of these parties where he met her. It might have been the high school graduation party, though friends couldn't remember precisely. She was a pretty, petite teenager from Norton High with light brown hair who just happened to have a thing for guys with fast motorcycles.

From a very early age, Janice Hartman loved to dance. A girl described as sweet and bubbly, little Janice would prance through the house to the music from her record player. Janice and her two older brothers, Garry and Ross, played on the swing set and on the teeter-totter, in the sandbox and the kiddie pool, in the shade of their back-yard oak and maple trees, which they loved to climb. Their house in the little farm town of Doylestown had a big garden—Janice's mother Betty canned vegetables—and a bunch of animals: rabbits, pigeons, ducks, geese, dogs and cats. In the hot summer months, the family would go twice a week to Royal Oak Lake Park's swimming beach to beat the oppressive Ohio heat. In the winter, Janice and her brothers would ride sleds or go ice-skating on a frozen pond.

But Janice wasn't all sweetness. Growing up with two older brothers taught her from a very young age how to hold her own. One day, Janice's mother got a call from a neighbor lady complaining that the neighbor's son was getting beat up. "What guy is it?" asked Janice's mother, thinking it was one of her sons who was in trouble. Instead, the neighbor said it was 8-year-old Janice. "She beat the crap out of him," Betty recalled years later. "I had to punish her. Girls don't go around beating the crap out of boys. But it tickled me. I had to laugh."

Janice Hartman was born March 2, 1951—exactly one month before John Smith—the third child to Betty and Neal Hartman. Her sister Lodema came ten years after Janice. A photo taken at Christmas captured a 9-year-old Janice well.

Wide-eyed with a big smile full of mischief, she stood front and center clutching a handbag, a Christmas tree in the background. Next to her are her brothers Garry, then 12, and Ross, then 10, and two girl cousins. Janice is wearing a dress right out of the 50s, with pictures of sombrero-wearing bongo players on them, and a cut white blouse, white bobby socks and black Mary Janes. It was a scene out of a Norman Rockwell painting, but the situation at home was hardly that perfect. When Janice was young, her parents split—angrily and bitterly—and her mother returned to work, raising the children on her own. It taught Janice independence, self-reliance and toughness. It may also have fueled her rebellion.

After leaving Royal Oak Elementary School, Janice attended Norton High School, getting, her mother said, good grades, especially in math. She never had any serious boyfriends, but did go to parties and had lots of friends. She grew into an attractive woman with wholesome Midwestern looks: bright smile and eyes of the same twinkling gray-blue from the Christmas picture. Her high school graduation photo with blondish-brown hair cut in a fashionable short 60s style.

Always spirited, Janice was developing a rebellious streak, and had taken up smoking. She and John were both 19 years old when she met him at the party, though she looked older than her age, and he, with that awkward, boyish face, could pass for years younger. John could be quiet around people he didn't know, but when he opened up, he couldn't stop talking, particularly about his plans: college at Ohio State, a career as an engineer.

Janice's mother was asked years later what the attraction was between her daughter and John. "Beats the heck out of me. I guess it was the motorcycle." Her brother Garry was equally perplexed, later telling *The Daily Record* of Wooster that John was a "foul-mouthed, hot-tempered person . . . I think she married him for his fast motorcycle." Others said it could have been that Janice saw John as an intriguing outsider—the dorky looks only adding to his unique allure.

John may just have been the right guy at the right time. He was gentle with her, paying her the kind of attention she didn't get growing up with a single parent and three siblings. He spent money on her and showed her a good time.

After graduation, Janice went to St. Louis, Missouri, to train to be a stewardess. She and John wrote to each other frequently. Her mother kept in touch with her by phone. Then, one day, her mother couldn't find her. She called and called and Janice never answered.

Her mother called the police.

She didn't find out Janice's fate until several frantic days later when a friend who owned a local motel called.

"Did you know Jan's here?" said the friend.

"No, I didn't," said Janice's mother.

"Well, she's married."

Betty nearly burst. "Are you sure?"

"Sure." The friend wouldn't let them check in until she saw the license. The couple had eloped at City Hall in Detroit.

Janice's mother reached them at the motel and convinced them to come to her house. It was the first time her mother had ever met John Smith. "I had a good talk to them about running off," Betty recalled. "A mother usually wants their child to get married at home. Jan just thought it was a big adventure. John said he loved her and would take care of her. But," added Betty grimly, "that never happened." Betty did make one demand: she wanted a wedding photo. She got two, one she took herself, a Polaroid of John carrying Janice across the threshold of her mother's house. John had to be begged to pose for the picture; he didn't like to be photographed, camera-shy in the way he would later say Fran was. The couple then sat for a formal portrait, Janice in a white cotton dress, John in a shirt and tie.

From the very start, Janice's mother was leery of John.

"He did talk a lot. He liked to hear himself talk. He was the biggest bullshitter you ever saw," she said. "He was going to build bridges. He had it all planned out," she said.

John's family wasn't any happier about the marriage than Janice's mother was. His mother Grace was so mad, she locked him out of the house. The boy who could once do no wrong was now not even allowed to come in to pick up his clothes and personal effects. John's grandparents also didn't like the marriage, worrying that John was too young and the future too bright—with college coming up—to take on the responsibilities of marriage. The family was concerned that his life was ruined.

Under these less-than-ideal circumstances, John and Janice Smith began life as newlyweds. They moved to Columbus, eighty miles southwest of Seville, to a small second-floor apartment on Hubbard Street. Jan managed a gas station while John attended classes at Ohio State University, studying engineering. John also did odd jobs around the apartment to get a reduction in their rent. Money was tight. "They argued sometimes, once in a while," recalled John's high school friend Dennis Evans, who lived with the couple for several months. "It would either be money, or not enough money." Janice complained that John wasn't doing his share of the wage-earning. He would instead spend his spare time driving up to Janice's mother's house in Doylestown for free meals. Janice's mother would give him food and then ask where Janice was. John would say she was working. When asked what he was doing so far from Columbus, he would say something about having to meet a friend in the area and that he thought he'd just stop by. Janice's mother became even more leery of John, wondering why he couldn't spend some of that time at a job to help take the load off Janice.

Not long after the wedding, Janice's mother, her sister Lodema and a friend of her mother's came down from Doylestown to the state fair in Columbus, staying in a motel because there wasn't enough room in the apartment. Jan visited them in the motel and went with them to the fair. John was nowhere to be found.

When asked why, Jan snapped, "He's an asshole."

After the fair, they all returned to the motel for a night-time swim in the pool—"the last time I swam with both my girls," her mother recalled.

When Janice's brother Garry visited them he also picked up on the tension. "A buddy and I were going to go to my grandmother's that lived in Florida. We stopped by because I wanted to see Jan," Garry recalled. "And we got to the apartment, and found the apartment. And John was at work at the time, and Janny was ironing. I remember exactly what she was doing, ironing clothes.

"We said, 'Hey, we're here, let's go out for dinner.' She said, 'Well, we'll wait for John to get home from work.'

"We waited around about an hour-and-a-half, two hours. We went out to eat. And everything changed as soon as the door opened."

John had come home.

"It was like a whole new atmosphere, it was a domi-neering kind of situation, and caught both me and my buddy by surprise," Garry said. "We planned on spending the night there . . . We actually left because we were un-comfortable with the situation."

The next time Garry Hartman saw John and Janice, it was at their mother's house. Garry still didn't know John very well and it was the first opportunity for them to spend time with each other and talk. "We got into a chess game," Garry recalled. "I was a big chess fanatic when I got out of the service. We were playing chess on the living room floor, and I won the game. When I called checkmate, there was this boom. The chessboard went up against the wall, pieces were everywhere. John jumps to his feet and walks out the front door. He says to Jan, 'We're leaving.' And I hear the motorcycle—they rode a motorcycle a lot, she liked that—rev up in the driveway. I thought he was going to leave without her. Then she comes through the living room, and I'm picking up the pieces. She said, 'Oh, you must have won.' And they left."

Another visit by John and Janice to her mother's home was just as unsettling. "I had put my younger daughter to bed," Janice's mother recalled, "and I was getting ready for bed, and I think it was about 10, maybe 10:30 that they came in. And I asked if they wanted anything, that I could get them anything, and Jan said, Yes, she would like to eat something. So I said soup and sandwiches. And John flared up like a firecracker and pounded my cupboard, stomped his foot and says, 'Don't you people know how to fix anything else but soup and sandwiches!' I told him at that time of night there wasn't much of anything else."

The marriage was falling apart, though Jan tried to keep her best face on, especially for her family. Her sister Dee said that even during the tough times Janice had a good sense of humor and showed her gentle, caring side. Dee recalled one evening with her sister. It was Easter, 1972—Dee was 12 at the time, Jan was 22—and both sides of the family had gathered at the home of John's grandparents. "We were watching a late movie and just sort of making comments on the movie because it was . . . a really old one that was really bad, B-movie type," Dee said. The two girls were laughing. They performed a skit. "We were up in the bedroom and we actually spent the night there. It was just a skit about shopping for, like, Easter bonnets and Easter shoes and that type. Like one person was a sales clerk and the other was a customer." They tape-recorded their silly skit. Dee never got rid of that tape.

John also seemed to be trying to make it work. During a school break Dee visited John and Janice in Columbus. While Janice was working, John and Dee went shopping for a watch. John wanted to buy his wife something special. "He had in mind like a watch with diamonds all around it," Dee said. "I suggested something different. You know, maybe something with gemstones." Janice liked to be different. They went into a Service Merchandise, a large retailer, where they narrowed the search down to two watches with gemstones, ruby and emerald. Dee suggested emerald because green was Janice's favorite color. John bought the watch.

But things only got worse between John and Janice; no watch was going to save this marriage. Janice would call her mother from Columbus, collect so John wouldn't know, and talk about the fights that had started to go beyond verbal sparring. "He was knocking her around," her mother recalled. "But she hit back. She had a couple of brothers who taught her how to fight." It never got so rough that either one had to go the hospital, as far as her family knew. Janice's brother Ross would later say that he saw John slap Janice across the face. "I told him if he ever did it again, I'd whup his butt," Ross would later tell the *Trentonian* newspaper. Janice's friend, Kathy Paridon, would say that she too saw John slap Janice. The fights would start with money, then John would start complaining about everything she did, from her smoking to her cooking. "He was such a pill," Janice's mother remembered.

But it was worse than that. John's attitude grew increasingly frightening, the fights more and more intense. The tension was taking its toll on Janice, her personality growing darker. When she called her mother, her voice would quiver and she would cry out of depression and anger. The transformation from the Janice everybody knew—happy-go-lucky, carefree, a little rebellious and reckless, but always sweet-natured—was unsettling. Then came the most disturbing call of all. Janice told her mother that John had warned her, "If you ever leave me, I'm going to kill you."

Her mother told her daughter to get away from him as soon as possible. It wasn't worth it.

In July 1974, just weeks after the alleged threat, Janice called her mother to say that she was getting a divorce from John. The next month, on August 17, 1974, Janice and John signed a legal separation agreement, and Janice moved out of the Columbus apartment.

Now on her own for the first time in her life, Janice found that her mother was much more sympathetic to her marital woes than to other aspects of her life. Janice planned to move back in with her mother, but found her house rules too constricting: in bed by 11, no smoking in the house, no people her mother didn't know stopping by. So Janice moved in with her father, in his mobile home behind the Far West Lounge, a bar, in Doylestown, near her friend Kathy Paridon's trailer. Janice dropped by her mother's house frequently for meals and company. There seemed to be a cooling-off period with John. Relations with him appeared cordial enough while the two were proceeding with a divorce. When Janice's mother remarried, to a man named Ed Lippincott, John was at the wedding along with Janice's family.

Soon, though, John dropped out of school—and out of touch. Janice and even John's own family didn't know where he had gone. All they knew was that he wasn't in the Columbus apartment anymore. Unknown to his own family, he had moved into the mobile home in Wooster. Soon, he would start showing up at places where Janice was. One hot day over the summer, Dee recalled, John dropped by unannounced at Janice's father's mobile home. Dee was going to go out and greet him, but Janice said, "No, you stay inside." Janice then went outside, talked with John briefly, and came back in—without John. This sort of thing happened at bars and restaurants. Janice would be drinking and dancing with friends, and there would be John.

It was a confusing time. While Janice seemed irritated by John, there were some indications that she would be with him by choice. One night, Janice shocked her mother by stopping by the house with him. "They came in and stayed about a half an hour or so. They were going to celebrate their [upcoming] divorce. He wanted to take her out one last time," said her mother, who recalled thinking that none of this made any sense, but that Janice was in a happy, loving mood. "Jan came over and sat on my husband's lap and told him that she loved him, then she sat on my lap and said she loved me and would be here for to help with Thanksgiving," her mother said. "I said, 'I love you, too, and I'll see you.' " Her mother stole a glance at John. Her take on him: "He was quiet as a mouse and just as white as a sheet. I thought he wasn't feeling well."

Dee also recalled Janice visiting the house with John. It may have been that same night, or another night within days—she wasn't sure—but it was around the time of the breakup. They drove up in Janice's silver-and-black Mustang and stayed briefly, with Janice dropping off some clothes she had borrowed from Dee and then taking other ones. The two—although ten years apart—were the same size because Janice was so small. From Dee, Janice took a pair of Earth Shoes—popular at the time—and a blue nylon coat with quilted lining and fake fur around the hood. Before she left the house that night, Janice hugged Dee. Then she said something strange. "[She] whispered in my ear that she would see me at my graduation," recalled Dee, who didn't understand it. Dee was just starting high school; graduation would be four years away. Dee would never figure out what her sister had meant.

Around this time Janice had befriended Leonard Bennett, who would go drinking and dancing with her, and was rather fond of her. He gave her a gold crucifix, which she wore all the time. Janice seemed to enjoy her newfound freedom. She had bought that Mustang II, used, but precious to her. It was the first thing of any value she had purchased on her own and she was protective of it. She had one key and wouldn't let anybody else drive the car. She also got a new job. Always fond of dancing, Janice would strap on white high boots, short-shorts and a frilly, glittery top, and shake what she had at a bar as a go-go dancer. She never took her clothes completely off, but those few members of her family who knew about it—and her mother did not—expressed concern. Her brother Garry, recalling he was "a little skeptical," visited the bar once with his wife one evening in the fall of 1974. "We stopped by the bar to see exactly what was involved," he recalled. "But we were surprised. It was a nice place and they served dinner. If I remember right, we didn't eat anything. But the bottom line was that we sat at the table, she got up and did about three minutes of dancing, and she was free for about thirty minutes and then she'd go up and dance some more. Not on top of a bar or anything. She was pretty good." During that visit, Janice and her brother made plans to attend Thanksgiving at their mother's house.

It was a weekend not long after her brother came to see Janice that her dancing, late-night drinking and partying with Leonard Bennett would spill over from a Doylestown bar to the house on Clinton Road, where she was attacked in the early morning of November 10, 1974. She filed the police report, went to the doctor for birth-control pills and barbiturates and moved on with her life.

Four days later, on November 14, the marriage between John and Janice officially ended with the filing of a Decree of Dissolution of Marriage. As divorces go, this one did appear as amicable as John would later describe it to Detective Dansbury. They used the same lawyer and easily agreed on how they'd divide up their few assets. Janice got the 1974 Mustang II titled in her name, and agreed to make the rest of the payments. She also got a General Electric black-and-white portable television. John Smith kept his 1974 GM van in his name, bedroom furniture and three stereos. Each kept personal effects. Janice kept the jeweled watch that John had bought her. The whole settlement only added up to a few thousand dollars.

Although still scratched and bruised, and suffering sleep problems that required drugs, Janice now had her freedom from John Smith—or so she thought. In the last night she would ever be seen, Janice went with her friend Kathy Paridon to the Portage Pub in Doylestown. John was there.

• • •

One day in November 1974, Betty Lippincott got a phone call. It was a man identifying himself as an officer from the Doylestown Police Department saying that her daughter Janice hadn't shown up for her scheduled testimony in court in a drug case. The caller wanted to know where she was. She said she didn't know. (There is no reference in any of the Wayne County sheriff's reports that Janice was to testify in Doylestown, and investigators had questioned whether it really was a Doylestown officer.)

Betty immediately called John Smith.

"Do you know where Jan's at?" she demanded.

"No, I have no idea," said John, in a tone that didn't sound too concerned. She said he told her that all he knew was that Janice's car had been found on the road to Columbus with the door open, even though the car was parked in front of his trailer.

"Why didn't you call me?"

"I didn't want to worry you."

"Hey, I'm her mother!"

Betty would have to get all her information from the sheriff's office—and that wasn't much. "I couldn't sleep for weeks," she recalled. "I had nightmares. I even dreamt she was in a ditch. I woke up in a cold sweat, hollering. It was a sad time." When the calls didn't get her anywhere, she wrote letters "to anyone who would listen"—the mayor, the U.S. senators for Ohio, congressmen, the missing persons bureau, the FBI, but, "Nobody would help," she said. She spent $2,000 on a private investigator to look for Janice. The letters came back. They all said the same thing: there was nothing they could do.

John, meantime, seemed to be suffering no such grief. His behavior after Janice's disappearance eerily mirrored what he did—and didn't do—after wife Betty Fran disappeared. By now gainfully employed at Flxible, he never called Janice's family to see if she had turned up, and apparently never spoke to sheriff's deputies except for the evening he filed the missing persons report and the follow-up interview with Gasser. Instead of being concerned about his missing wife, John worried more about his missing wife's car. His friend Dennis Evans recalled John complaining that for some reason the bank wouldn't let him drive Janice's beloved Mustang, even though he had co-signed the loan. "I mean, he was upset that he was paying for a car, he had to pay for the car, but he couldn't have it," said Dennis. John did eventually tell Dennis that Janice wasn't around anymore. "She was supposed to have been testifying for some drug case and she didn't want to, or she took off," said Dennis, though there would be no mention of this in the missing persons report and Potts never found any evidence of it. John moved back in with his grandparents in Seville and eventually bought another Mustang, this one a brand-new black 1975 model that Dennis helped him customize. The men spent a lot of time with each other in Grandpa Chaney's garage working on the car. If Janice's disappearance worried John, he never mentioned it.

In the summer of 1975, while Betty Lippincott was suffering nightmares over her daughter, John was working on his love life. Dennis introduced him to a woman named Sandi Norwood. The two became close friends—"very close friends," Sandi would say later, close enough that they moved in together in a place in Delaware, Ohio, outside Columbus. John was driving that black Mustang that he and Dennis had modified, making it "loud and fast," Sandi recalled. Though living together, Sandi described their relationship as one of convenience to help John's career at Flxible. "John was a young executive and he was up and coming—very, you know, very professional young man and he wanted to appear to be settled and stable," she would recall. "And we had talked about marriage for that reason."

While she was fond of John, she found him to be a "very high-strung type person, lots of energy, a lot of energy, very busy. He seemed to be troubled sometimes, sometimes anxious." In a day that Sandi would never forget, John told her what was weighing on him: memories of his first wife. Her name was Janice, but he called her by the nickname Tiger. "He told me they got married out of high school and that he loved her very much, that they were very good together, they had a wonderful marriage, and that he would always love her," she said. But he said that Janice had created problems in the relationship. "He told me that Jan started hanging around with a rough group of people, that she began using drugs and doing things that were counterproductive to marriage, and the stress was bad on both of them because he was very career-driven and he didn't really like that type of atmosphere," she said. "And they agreed to mutually sever the relationship."

But the story only got stranger. According to John, Janice's lifestyle wasn't just counterproductive to marriage—it was counterproductive to living. Her drug problem was so bad that she owed money to dealers, money she couldn't repay. John knew this, he said, because he'd received a phone call from an anonymous person asking him to go somewhere—Sandi couldn't remember where he said it was. At this location John said he found Janice's body. She wasn't bloodied or bruised, but she was clearly killed—in an awful way. "It could have been some kind of a kinky sex thing that was going on," Sandi said, recounting what John had told her. "He said that there was visible semen in her perianal area and that she was lying there and she was dead." John said that he pulled the wedding band and engagement ring from his dead wife's finger, and took off, leaving the body behind. Sandi asked him why he didn't call police. He told her that he thought he would be killed if he did.

He showed rings to Sandi. They were white gold. The engagement ring had a large center diamond with smaller diamonds surrounding it.

"Well, I was a little shocked by it, frightened," Sandi recalled, but she stayed friends with John and continued to live together. They stayed together for about three months, during which time he only occasionally mentioned Jan. "The only things he would say later were things like he still loved her," said Sandi, "but we never discussed the scenario again."

These memories of Sandi's, related to detectives, ranked among the most significant information investigators would find after re-opening the Janice Hartman case in the spring of 1992. The work of Detectives Potts, Dansbury, Mansue and others had unveiled a series of events in Ohio chillingly similar to what had later happened in New Jersey. But as compelling as this information was, it didn't help Potts accomplish his task: solving the Janice Hartman missing persons case.

The detective didn't buy the stories that John had told to Dennis Evans or to Sandi; if anything, the very outrageousness of the tales only suggested he was hiding something. But if Janice didn't somehow meet her demise at the hands of murderous, sexually perverted drug dealers, as John had told Sandi, what did happen? Despite better detective work and the advantages of additional time and manpower, the Wayne County Sheriff's Office still could prove little more about John's possible involvement in his ex-wife's disappearance than it could in 1974. Like the New Jersey investigation before it, the work in Ohio uncovered suspicions, but no hard evidence.

Disappointed, Potts considered his options: lean on Michael Smith and Kathy Paridon some more, go back to the grandparents and hope they'd open up, re-interview the men involved in the attack on Janice, scour official archives for any unclaimed Jane Doe bodies. Maybe he had missed something or had failed to ask the right question of the right person that would shake everything loose. Or maybe, he feared, he had all that he was ever going to get.

Potts thought about the two Mrs. Smiths, and the seventeen years between them, and wondered: were there more

Mrs. Smiths? And did any of them disappear, too?

At the very least, the Ohio investigation gave the New Jersey detectives more to work with. Maybe, he hoped, they would have better luck.

CHAPTER 8

Detectives Michael Dansbury and Dave Mansue returned from Ohio in the spring of 1992 with a long list of questions for John David Smith. They wanted to press him on all the inconsistent statements and wild stories that he had told about his first wife Janice: Killed by drug dealers? Off to see John Richardson or Spitz or Sunshine? They wanted to know why he showed the same apparent lack of concern over her disappearance as he did over Fran's. Why hadn't he called Janice's mother? Why hadn't he ever followed up? They wanted to know where had he been all those years between Janice and Fran. Was there a wife or wives between Janice and Fran—and were they missing, too?

Whether John would ever answer any of these questions remained to be seen. But Dansbury and Mansue knew they now had new ammunition to use against him.

On April 9, 1992, West Windsor police served search warrants on Smith's condominium, car and office. The information from Ohio, combined with the evidence from the New Jersey investigation earlier, provided sufficient probable cause. In the third-floor condominium unit they found many of the same items that Deanna and Sherrie had discovered a month earlier: several pairs of glasses, drawers full of women's clothes and sweaters, a lady's hair curler, makeup and the two yellow suitcases. John didn't seem to have moved a thing. In John's private office at Carborundum, officers recovered from the credenza the five-by-seven framed picture of Fran—the sort of picture John had claimed that Fran wouldn't sit for. In one of John's briefcases there was a package of fifteen five-by-seven—professionally taken modeling-type photos—of Fran looking anything but camera-shy. Also in the briefcase were $900 in large bills and two keys for a Mazda Miata. John had told Dansbury that Fran couldn't drive the Miata because she had lost her key—and here were two extra ones in John's suitcase.

That same day, John was invited to the police station to explain all this, plus answer questions about the Ohio revelations. Again, as he had before, John agreed to talk to police without a lawyer. He was placed in Meeting Room B, where he had taken—and reportedly failed—the polygraph exam, and was grilled for twelve straight hours. Detectives Michael Dansbury and Chris Pukenas took the first nine hours, hammering John with questions, demanding explanations. It was the same old John: dodge and weave, plead ignorance, make up one story to cover for another, with no apparent regard for whether detectives believed him. No matter, for instance, that when asked about Janice's disappearance, he told the New Jersey detectives that her Mustang was found abandoned on a highway 100 miles away, even though the police report stated that an investigator had found the car parked in front of John's mobile home. It just didn't seem to matter to John; nothing did. He sat there, Dansbury would recall, "like a sponge," absorbing everything the detectives could dish out, cool as can be. He didn't take off his topcoat until nine hours into the interview. He never went to the bathroom. He never ate. Sitting without a lawyer, in a police station, he couldn't be rattled, not by the interview, not by the fact that his wife had now been missing for seven months and he was obviously the subject of the investigation. Finally, Pukenas had to ask him: How do you feel about Fran's disappearance? In typical John fashion, he twisted the question around. John said *he* was the real victim during their marriage. "I've learned about a totally new Fran," he said. "I feel emotionally and sexually abused." For the final three hours, one more detective had his crack at John, and he had no more luck than Dansbury and Pukenas. John had defeated them. "Basically after twelve hours we had three police officers that were just beat," Dansbury recalled. As for John: "It's like he stopped into the police station to ask directions." He was sent home.

As eerily calm and composed as John was during the marathon session in Meeting Room B, he would ultimately make a mistake that day—not a big one, but a mistake nonetheless—that would be used against him years later: He took a phone call from longtime love Sheila Sautter. John apparently didn't know that Sheila had not only been contacted and interviewed by police, but had agreed to work with investigators out of her feelings of betrayal, anger and hurt. She called him from the little kitchen of John's Connecticut home at 7:55 p.m. Sitting in the room with her were police detectives, including Frank Barre of the Milford Police Department and Mansue of West Windsor. The RECORD button was pushed on a West Windsor Township police tape-recorder hooked to the phone. The law in Connecticut and New Jersey allowed a phone call to be taped as long as just one party knew about the recording.

"Hello? Hello? Hello?" said John.

"John?"

"Yes. Sheila?"

The detectives had asked Sheila to engage him in idle conversation, then build up to what they really wanted her to ask him about. But in all her excitement and anxiety, she dove right into it.

"What is going on?" Sheila asked.

"Well, let me tell you what's going on, babe," he said.

"Let me ask you this, OK?" she said.

"OK."

"This is really, really so upsetting to me," said Sheila.

"All right," John said. "Yeah."

"I went to the police department and they showed me pictures of Janice."

"Janice, that's correct," replied John.

"Who's Janice?" Sheila asked.

"Janice Hartman," he said.

"Who is Janice Hartman?" she asked.

"Janice Hartman was my first wife when I was nineteen years old."

"What happened to her?"

"Janice Hartman and I got divorced. I left the area. I have not seen Jan since I left and I reported her missing. I found out today that in all these years that she's never been found and that she was declared legally dead. . . . That's it point-blank, simple facts."

"Do you know her family?" Sheila asked.

"No, I don't know her family," John said, "and no, I haven't talked to her family."

"How could you not talk to her family?" Sheila asked.

"We were divorced. I thought that she was headed her way and I headed my way. I mean, I didn't know she was missing all these years, you know."

"How could you not know she was missing?" Sheila asked. "Did anyone—No one told you she was missing?"

"No one told me she was missing all this time," John said. "I thought she was back with her family by now. I hadn't maintained any contact. I didn't know it. I didn't know—I didn't know that—I didn't know that she was missing all this time until today. I didn't know she was still gone until today. I didn't know that she was declared legally dead until today."

Smith told her that an investigation surrounding Janice's disappearance had begun. "And they called up everybody ever associated with it, as far as I can know."

"Well, let's get real simple here," Sheila said.

"OK," John said.

"I mean real simple."

"OK."

"Let's just start with honesty, right?" Sheila said. "You have got to start with honesty. You've just got to lay it on the line."

"I have started with honesty," John said.

"Start with me."

"But the thing I'm worried about, Sheila, is I think it's too late. Maybe not. I don't know, but this is going to be tough."

"How can anything be too late?" Sheila asked.

"Well, I guess it is," John said.

"This is the worst thing that could happen, you know, by lying and lying, I mean, life doesn't have to be this way," Sheila said.

"Right, right," he said over her words. "No, it doesn't."

"It shouldn't be this way," she said.

"No," he said. "It shouldn't be this way either."

Smith told her he was sitting in his condo.

"Yeah," she said. "Here you are in your condo. This is totally—Everything is just falling to pieces because you're lying to everyone around you."

"That's correct."

Authorities now had John Smith on tape lying through his teeth. Of course he knew that Janice was missing; he was the one who had reported her missing. More than that, he said it was "too late." Too late to do anything. Too late for Janice.

As detectives reviewed a tape of the phone call, they knew it was good stuff—just not good enough to arrest John. And that was the problem, as it has always been. As far as authorities in New Jersey and Ohio were concerned, John Smith looked, sounded and acted guilty; everything they heard from his friends, family and lovers made him sound guilty. But there was still a lack of hard physical evidence of the kind a prosecutor would need to bring the case before a jury. No blood, no hairs, no fibers, no bodies of Janice Hartman or Fran Smith. There were no witnesses to kidnapping or murder, no confession from John. Just strong suspicions—and that wasn't going to do it.

By the end of 1992, after fifteen months of intense investigation in Ohio, New Jersey and Connecticut, the John Smith case was fading. In New Jersey, police focused their time and efforts on the other crimes in West Windsor, waiting for a break to come to them. In Ohio, Detective Potts was feeling equally stymied. He was running out of people to interview and leads to follow. The entire investigation, not to mention simple common sense, dictated that Janice Hartman, who had a large and close family, didn't one day take off, change identities and start a new life—just as the investigation and common sense dictated that Betty Fran Gladden Smith didn't do the same. That meant that Janice and Fran had died or, more likely, were killed. Either way, they were probably dead, which meant there would be bodies.

Bodies.

That would be the evidence that would hang John. The bodies may be impossible to find. They could have been buried, burned beyond recognition or dropped to the bottom of a lake with weights on the feet. But there was also the very real possibility that one—or both—of the bodies could already have been found, and nobody had been able to identify it. Potts had already sent out scores of teletypes for Jane Does. But the teletypes went to police stations, not coroners, and in busy police stations teletypes had a way of not getting read. So he sat down at the typewriter, and on the official stationery of Wayne County Sheriff Loran D. Alexander, wrote:

Dear County Coroner:

   In November, 1974, John Smith reported his ex-wife missing. They had been divorced three days. He had stated if he couldn't have her, no one could. She has never been heard from since. Her family had declared her legally dead.

In October, 1991 John Smith reported his wife of one-and-a-half years missing in West Windsor, New Jersey. She has never been heard from since. We feel Mr. Smith was probably involved in both disappearances. We are asking you to check your files for any W/F, unidentified bodies that would fit the time frame above.

First Wife: Janice E. Hartman Smith, W/F, DOB 030251, 5' 4", 115 lbs, blonde hair, blue eyes.

Second Wife: Betty Fran Smith, W/F, DOB 080442, 5'0", 100 lbs., blonde hair blue eyes.

Thank you for your time and trouble. We would request you contact us either way so we can verify for our records that we checked each Coroner's office.

                                         Sincerely,
                                         Brian Potts
                                         Detective

The letters were sent to every coroner in the state of Ohio. Quickly, one promising lead emerged, with Cleveland police telling Potts they had unidentified skeletal remains that may match the description of Janice Hartman. Potts sent Cleveland authorities Janice's medical records, but the lead went cold. The Cuyahoga County coroner would determine that there wasn't a match.

The rest of the responses from other Ohio coroners' offices were like this one:

Dear Brian:

   We do not have any unidentified W/F at this time.
The one we had for 6 mos last year was finally pos-
itively identified.

                                    Sincerely,
                            Hockney Co. Coroner.

   Potts had cast a wide net and come up empty. The investigation in Ohio, like the one in New Jersey, was on
hold, and starting to look hopeless.

Janice's mother, Betty Lippincott, had that hopelessness for
years. She'd once tried to remain positive, even buying
Christmas presents for Janice, jewelry usually—a necklace,
bracelets, little rings with daisies on them. "She loved daisy
rings," her mother said. She couldn't give them to Janice,
of course, so she held on to the presents with the hope that
one day Janice would return. Christmases came and went,
and at last, Betty gave up. She put up a tombstone with Janice's name in the family's plot in a cemetery in Killbuck,
Ohio. She tried not to think about it, but every time she heard
a news report about the discovery of a body somewhere, all
the sadness, pain and anger came flooding back.
   Meanwhile, the family members of Betty Fran Gladden
Smith were also coming to terms with the realization that
she was probably dead. But Fran's daughter Deanna and
sister Sherrie weren't ready to stand by and do nothing but
grieve. The amateur detective work that had found Janice
Hartman's brother, and expanded the John Smith investigation from one to two missing persons, proved to them
that regular people could make a difference. They tried a
new tactic.
   In January 1993, Deanna and Sherrie went public, speaking to any media outlet that would listen about their suspicions that John David Smith was responsible for the
disappearances of Janice Hartman and Betty Fran Gladden
Smith. The tale of the two Mrs. Smiths was gripping copy,

and the local media in New Jersey and Ohio jumped all over it. The *Trentonian* in New Jersey was the most aggressive, trumpeting the story with such headlines as "New evidence points to murder in posh suburb" and "Husband matches psycho profile." It quoted Mercer County First Assistant Prosecutor Kathryn Flicker as saying of John, "We have looked at him, and we are looking at him," and scoffing at the idea that Fran may have committed suicide. "Normally," she said, "suicide victims don't hide their own bodies." As for the disappearance of Janice Hartman, the paper quoted her brother Garry as saying, "John killed them. He killed them both."

Confronted with the publicity, John made rare statements. He told the *Trentonian* that he didn't know where Fran was. "The feeling is one of disappointment. I would have hoped [Fran] would have been home by now." And to *The Daily Record* of Wooster, he rejected the accusations of Sherrie and Deanna as the kind of remarks that come about "when you don't know what happened. You just have to look at all the angles." Of the disappearances of two of his wives, he said: "I think it's one of those strange coincidences." These were the last public statements he would make. He hired a lawyer, Arthur Lash, who after a few brief remarks of his own would also come to refuse to talk to the media.

But that didn't stop the story from being reported. In one *Trentonian* article, Garry Hartman said that investigators had told him John fit all the characteristics of a sociopath: he lies pathologically, manipulates people and shows little remorse or empathy. "They said he fit the profile to a T," Hartman told the paper. Then came news in another *Trentonian* story of John's "double life," revealing Sheila Sautter as John's "former fiancée" and reporting on the birthday party he'd attended at the Connecticut house the weekend after Fran's disappearance.

Soon the papers and television stations in Connecticut picked up on the two Mrs. Smiths story because of the Milford angle. *Hard Copy* and *A Current Affair* would come to West Windsor to conduct interviews. If Deanna and Sherri, who'd triggered the media onslaught, thought it would turn up the pressure on John, they were right. His Carborundum co-workers began tormenting him with gallows humor, hanging crude caricatures on bulletin boards of him carrying a knife and a body. Once, John was summoned to the locker room, where he found a mannequin covered in ketchup. The black humor got so out of hand that members of a plant union, the Oil, Chemical and Atomic Workers International Union Local 8-490, circulated a petition calling on management to put a stop to it. John seemed to be holding up, though some employees privately said they feared he would snap. But by the end of January 1993, John quit his job, getting ninety days' severance pay, and moved to the Connecticut home, which had been vacated by Sheila.

In addition to driving John out of New Jersey, the publicity gave police a new lead. With some embarrassment, a man came forward to say that the previous summer he had picked up a prostitute in Connecticut. After they did their business, he offered to drive her home. She accepted, directing him to a beach house in Milford, Connecticut, where he dropped her off. The man would then see a picture of that house in the local paper in a story about John Smith. He contacted police, and Detective Barre tracked down the prostitute. She was a familiar face in the area, a drug addict named Janice Miller, who shared more than a first name with John's first wife. Petite and blond, the hooker looked hauntingly like Janice Hartman.

Janice Miller would tell detectives that she had met John Smith in the summer of 1992 when he picked her up one night in Washington Park, a popular spot for drug dealers and prostitutes in Bridgeport, Connecticut. This was about two months after the tape-recorded phone conversation with Sheila, who by now had ended her long relationship with John and moved out of the Connecticut house. John was still working at Carborundum at the time, apparently spending his weekends in Connecticut, as he often did even while married to Fran.

After picking Janice Miller up in the park, John brought her to his Milford home for a couple of hours, then drove her back to the park. The next night, John returned to the park and picked her up again. This time they got something to eat, then went down to a seaside area called, appropriately enough, Pleasure Beach. "I think we sat there and talked maybe an hour or so," Janice Miller would recall, and said that John returned her to the park afterwards. This went on for the next several nights. John gave her money, which she used to buy drugs to support her four-times-a-day cocaine and heroin habit.

One day, John asked Janice Miller to travel with him to Atlanta—she didn't know the reason. She considered going, but at the last minute decided not to. "I got nervous," she said. "The night before, he told me about his first wife." It was, she said, a crazy and scary story. John had said that his first wife was a drug addict like she was. He said she would go out at night, but come home every morning to fix him breakfast. One morning, she didn't come home. John said that the FBI had come to his house to explain that the wife was a snitch for drug dealers and that a murder contract had been put out on her. The contract was carried out, and the wife was murdered. John told Janice Miller that he never saw his wife's body, and it was never returned to him.

"Guess what her name was?" John asked the prostitute.

"What?" she said.

"Janice."

A weird feeling came over Janice Miller. She wouldn't travel with John—this time. But this eerie story wasn't enough for her to sever her relationship with him. Her addiction wouldn't let her. So in August or September of 1992—she couldn't remember which—she moved out of her apartment and into John's beach house, where she stayed for about a month. John provided her with money for drugs, along with clothes, jewelry and cosmetics. As much as she needed John's support, she often felt uncomfortable around him, "creeped out" in her words. He would at times yell at her for things she never did. "I got the feeling he wasn't talking to [me]," she would recall. "He was talking to somebody else. He was confusing me with somebody else."

Janice Miller finally did agree to go on a trip with John, traveling—of all places—to his mother and stepfather's house in Ohio over Labor Day weekend, 1992. They'd had dinner together, with John's family apparently having no clue they had just been introduced to a drug-addicted hooker John had found in a park. John and Janice returned to Connecticut the following Monday so Janice could make a court appearance on Tuesday for an earlier prostitution bust.

The relationship broke off in October 1992. John stopped giving Janice Miller money for drugs and wanted her to return the clothes and other belongings. "We got into an argument," she said. "I threw a pumpkin at him." She called a "friend"—actually a boyfriend she'd continued to see while living with John—and he picked her up. That was the last she had seen of John Smith.

From the day Janice Miller walked out of John Smith's life, four years would pass, with police having only sketchy information about John's activities. They knew that after the Janice Miller relationship, he'd left Connecticut for New Hampshire, where he worked at a label-producing company and began a relationship with yet another woman, this one a co-worker. She would later tell police that in the few months she was with John she'd known nothing about the two Janices, Sandi, Fran, Sheila or any other women in his life. After several interviews, police believed her.

After this relationship ended, John returned to his home state of Ohio, in about late 1993 or early 1994, to help run the family's lucrative real estate business with his mother and stepfather Sam Malz. Although the financial data was sparse, Detective Mansue would estimate that at the peak of the family's real estate success the business was worth $28 million. Staying with his mother and rich step-father in their large new house in Medina, about five miles north of John's childhood home in Seville, John lived the good life, spending weekends with his mother and Sam on his step-father's cabin cruiser on Lake Erie. In 1994, Sam Malz died, and John's role in the business increased substantially. Now the business was being run by John and his mother. John's brother Michael also was on the family payroll, though in a much lower capacity, doing handyman work on the apartment complexes.

John had been in Ohio for about four years before he crossed paths with authorities again. In March 1997 the Ohio Bureau of Investigation found reports indicating that John had been involved in a car accident. The paperwork was forwarded to Wayne County Sheriff's Detective Potts, who pored over the documents and found that John had given a false Social Security number. A search of the number found that it belonged to a stripper who had once lived in Milford, Connecticut. Potts tracked the stripper down at her new home in Florida, but she claimed not to know any John Smith and to have no idea how this man had gotten her Social Security number. Potts had his doubts, but there was no more information he could get out of her. Still, the Social Security lead gave authorities an opportunity to go after John again. The state of Ohio suspended John's driver's license for providing a fake Social Security number, which meant that he was now driving illegally.

Potts alerted police in West Windsor, New Jersey, and detectives Dansbury and Pukenas drove out to Ohio. They staked out Grace Malz's house, and when John came out of the driveway in a Dodge Shadow, he was pulled over, arrested for driving with a suspended license, taken to the police station and placed in an interview room. Two teams of investigators—Brian Potts and Charlie Snyder of Ohio's state police, and Dansbury and Pukenas—took turns interrogating John, who once again didn't ask for a lawyer. Potts and Snyder played good cops, trying to engage John in conversation, while Dansbury and Pukenas played the heavies. It was afternoon when the interrogation started, and the four detectives went after him for ten long hours, once again going over every aspect of the case. Dansbury hadn't seen John since the last interrogation, five years earlier, but it was the same old John. He dodged questions, invented stories to explain other stories—cool, nonchalant, never seeming to care whether police believed him or not. And exactly as he had in that twelve-hour interrogation in West Windsor in 1992, John kept his topcoat on, never asked for anything to drink and never asked to go to the bathroom—for the entire ten hours. At one point, he acted so bored with the questioning that he rested his head on his hand and pretended to sleep. "John, wake up!" Potts snapped, and John opened his eyes to dodge and weave and invent stories some more.

Finally, Potts tried to appeal to something deep inside John.

"John, this is bothering you," Potts said. "Some day you're going to kill yourself. Write me a note and tell me where the bodies are."

Potts thought he saw some glimmer of contrition in John's eyes, but he couldn't be sure. At 2 a.m., the interview ended, the investigators exhausted, John looking no more tired than he did the day before when he was pulled over outside his mother's house. He was put in the jail for the night on the suspended license charge. John had beaten them again.

"This has been a roller coaster," Potts recalled thinking. "There's been so many times that we thought we had him: 'We got you, you son-of-bitch.' Then he would just slip through our fingers."

Over the next year, John would slip out of the state, and authorities didn't know where he went. There wasn't much point in finding out; what would they do if they found him? John had now been interviewed twice informally and interrogated three times, and it had gotten detectives nowhere. Potts went back to his other cases in Wayne County, Dansbury to his other cases in West Windsor, frustrated as always, hoping that somehow a break would come their way.

As it turned out, help did arrive, from an unlikely source—a man Dansbury had known for years.

CHAPTER 9

In his eight years with the West Windsor Police Department, Patrolman Robert Hilland, a local Jersey boy who had grown up in adjacent East Windsor, handled the crimes typical in this affluent suburb: burglaries, carjackings, traffic accidents, the occasional runaway kid. There was also one stubborn missing persons case. Each day at roll call, officers would be told to be on the lookout for a 5-foot-2, 100-pound white female with blond hair and blue eyes who had been reported missing by her husband—and eventual suspect—John David Smith.

In May 1997, Hilland left the small department for the law enforcement big-time, joining the FBI office in New York City. There, he landed a position in the Cold Case Homicide unit, where he and seven other agents re-investigated unsolved murder cases, usually involving drugs or organized crime, that other agencies had given up on. About six months into the job, Hilland had to return to West Windsor to testify in a drunken driving case left over from his patrolman days. After the court session, he paid a visit to former police colleagues. Among them was Detective Michael Dansbury. Over coffee in Dansbury's office, the two caught up, with Hilland talking about the FBI and his work with Cold Case Homicide, and how the unit surprisingly was able to close some of the most hopeless cases. As he spoke, Hilland noticed a collection of binders on a shelf behind Dansbury's desk—the voluminous paperwork from the John David Smith case.

"Dead in the water," Dansbury told Hilland when the agent asked about the status of the case, explaining that after years of police work, the leads had dried up, no body was ever found and John Smith's whereabouts were now unknown—all of which drove Dansbury crazy. The detective said he feared that John was going to get away with two murders.

The case intrigued Hilland. He knew the budgetary limitations of the department and thought the FBI might have better luck cracking the case with its additional manpower, money and expertise. Dansbury readily agreed. Hilland explained that the bureaucratic FBI didn't just investigate cases whenever he wanted it to. There were procedures that had to be followed. So at Dansbury's desk the two drafted a formal letter to the FBI requesting the assistance of their Cold Case Homicide unit New York.

Hilland returned to New York promising to do everything he could to help Dansbury and his old department.

It wasn't going to be easy. Even as he encouraged Dansbury to seek help from the FBI, Hilland knew it was going to be a tough sell at the Bureau. Cold Case handled drug- and organized crime–related homicides in New York. This was a missing persons case in New Jersey. Even if the FBI were to investigate, protocol called for the case to go to the Newark, New Jersey, office, whose territory covered West Windsor. But Hilland pushed ahead, lobbying his supervisors.

He was turned down flat. His superiors told him he had enough work to do and that the case was outside of the jurisdiction of the New York office. Hilland pressed on, going up the ladder. He had worked out a solution to the jurisdictional problem by arguing that the body of Betty Fran Gladden Smith *could* have been dumped in New

York's territory; New Jersey was adjacent to New York, and bodies have been known to be dumped in the Arthur Kill between New Jersey and Staten Island. He also stressed that the New York office had expertise in cold cases, and noted that, based on some phone calls to the Newark office, the agents there were extremely busy with their own caseloads.

This time, he got the OK, though he'd be on a tight leash. He'd have to work on his own time and not spend too many tax dollars.

In the beginning, Hilland was the only agent on the case. Although he knew the basics of it from when he was a patrolman, he had to bone up on the details. He began with the long and winding paper trail, gathering all the information available on John Smith from the New Jersey, Ohio and Connecticut investigations. Hilland read through thousands of pages of police reports and interview summaries. As he did with other investigations reopened by Cold Case, he tried to look at the Smith cases from new angles and spot any lost opportunities or overlooked leads.

As Hilland went on with his reading, he considered the basic facts. Shortly after John David Smith· had been divorced from Janice Hartman in 1974, his newly ex-wife had disappeared, never to be seen again. Although she'd vanished just days after an attempted gang-rape, her family suspected John was involved in her disappearance, but the investigation came up with no evidence. Over the years, John would tell conflicting and increasingly outrageous tales about what had happened to her, everything from claiming she had taken off for a Florida commune, to suggesting she was bumped off by sex-crazed drug dealers. Not long after Janice disappeared, John had embarked on a series of relationships with women: Sandi, Sheila, Fran (whom he married), a prostitute also named Janice and a co-worker in New Hampshire. John's last known wife was Fran, who, just as she was taking a stand against him, disappeared. As with Janice, Fran's family suspected John, but again police didn't have enough evidence.

Reviewing the paperwork, Hilland realized that the task ahead was more daunting than he had imagined. There was no physical evidence or any eyewitnesses in either woman's disappearance, and there were no bodies. In John Smith, Hilland saw a formidable foe: a master manipulator and compulsive liar, who could charm women and toy with police. John had survived lengthy police interrogations by admitting nothing, changing his stories to fit the circumstances while never breaking a sweat.

Women, money and manipulation. Hilland wondered how far it all went. The more he read, the more he thought about those largely unaccounted-for years between missing wives. As Potts and Dansbury had before him, Hilland asked: Could there be more victims?

Finishing his reading, Hilland decided everything should be re-started—and in the Janice Hartman case, re-re-started. He compiled a list of everybody in Smith's life, from his earliest years to the present day, and ordered up a psychological portrait of John by the FBI's profilers in Quantico, Virginia. Hilland believed that to begin again from square one he needed to have everybody who had investigated the Smith cases gathered in one room to map out a strategy, then covertly go out into their jurisdictions to re-gather evidence and re-interview witnesses. This would require money and manpower. Hilland was about to violate both the conditions his superiors had placed on him.

In looking at the reports of the stalled investigations, Hilland realized a troubling fact: nobody knew where John Smith was. By this time, March of 1998, Ohio investigators hadn't seen him since the ill-fated interrogation a year earlier. The New Jersey investigation was, as Dansbury had put it, "dead in the water," and the little department couldn't keep up with Smith, who traveled extensively for business and pleasure.

Hilland believed that even before holding the summit meeting it was critical to find John. The agent tapped into every resource the FBI had to offer: computer databases, credit records, banking information, motor vehicle records, police and prosecution records. He sent teletypes to police stations across the country and mailed out scores of requests for public documents. As other investigators had discovered before him, digging up information on a man named John Smith was overwhelmingly difficult. The problem wasn't a lack of data. The problem was too much. The country had so many John Smiths that dozens of mailbags were dumped on Hilland's desk every week filled with forms and letters and official documents about men by that name. Hilland read through each one, comparing dates of birth and Social Security numbers with John's, hoping for a match, looking for clues as to where he was.

Hilland wouldn't be the only one looking for John. In Ohio, where John's relatives claimed to have no idea where he'd gone, Detective Potts went through a computer database that tracked new job hires. The database seemed promising because John seemed to have no trouble finding employment. Meanwhile, Fran's daughter and sister, who had beat police in finding Janice Hartman's brother, continued to work the phones and go through court and business records.

It's a matter of some dispute over who found John first: Hilland, Potts or Fran's relatives. But the fact was that John was located. He was in Southern California, working at a business called LaForza Automobiles Inc., which customized high-end Italian cars. The business was in Escondido, northeast of San Diego, and John was renting a room in the guesthouse of a co-worker named Trevor Haywood. The San Diego FBI office was contacted to keep tabs on him, discreetly, and to quietly investigate. It turned out that John, now 47 years old, didn't just have a new job; he had a new love, a 49-year-old Oceanside woman named Diane Bertalan. A high priority was placed on watching John while the investigation came back to life. Nobody wanted a third missing Mrs. Smith.

In August 1998, representatives from every agency that had been after John, including West Windsor Township police,

New Jersey State Police, the Wayne County Sheriff's Office, the Wayne County prosecutor, the Ohio Bureau of Criminal Investigation, the Milford, Connecticut, police department and the Connecticut State Police, gathered in a conference room at the FBI's offices in Quantico. Also on hand were members of the FBI's profilers and Hilland's colleagues from New York's Cold Case Homicide unit. The purpose of the meeting—and a second, smaller meeting later in New York—was to generate new leads, review leads that already were out there, fill in the gaps, and, most important, ensure that all the investigators were going after a common aim: amassing evidence for prosecutable case against John David Smith.

At the meeting, Hilland stressed that investigators may be dealing not just with a double-murderer, but with a serial killer. If John could have killed two wives, he might have killed more women. He traveled a lot and never seemed at a loss for female companionship. Hilland wanted investigators to go over other missing persons cases in places where John had been to see if there were any unsolved disappearances of women, including—in light of the Janice Miller relationship—prostitutes. He also wanted to re-interview everybody who had been involved with John Smith over the last twenty years, not only to make sure that no lead was overlooked, but also to locate the weakest link, the person who not only had damaging information on John, but who could turn on him.

The consensus was that the most promising witness in this regard was John's younger brother Michael. When Detectives Potts and Mansue had interviewed him six years earlier, they'd had that nagging feeling that he was hiding something. Also, of all the members of John's family, Michael seemed to be the most likely to respond to an appeal to his conscience. "He was the most level-headed," recalled Jocelyn Stefancin, a Wayne County assistant prosecutor—and the one who would likely have first crack at trying John—who attended the Quantico meeting. "He had been interviewed before. There had been some surveillance. They understood from the family background that he was the person who always helped Mom, who was always around. Michael was just a plain, ordinary guy, married, works a blue-collar job. They just got the impression if anybody would ever talk to us, it would be Michael."

Over the next year, the investigation proceeded steadily while the FBI in San Diego maintained surveillance on John and interviewed people who knew him there. Agents found that John wasn't just an employee of LaForza, but a major investor in the company. It also turned out that the investigation wasn't as discreet as Hilland had hoped. Informants told the FBI that John knew the feds were on his tail and that he wanted to shape his life so that he looked as innocent as possible, developing relationships with people who would vouch for him if need be. The most important of these people was Diane Bertalan.

As with his relationships with Sheila and Fran, this one had begun at the workplace. The sheet metal company for which Diane worked did business with LaForza, and a mutual friend of John's and Diane's introduced them. Diane wasn't impressed with John at first—she thought he was ugly—but he hounded her for dates and she finally gave in. After a three-month courtship, in which he picked her up in fancy sports cars, they were married on September 5, 1998—just a month after the law-enforcement summit meeting in Quantico. Diane would later say she didn't marry John out of love. "When he asked me to marry him, I said, 'OK, why not?' " she would tell *The San Diego Union-Tribune*. "It was a good way for me to get out of a situation where I was living paycheck to paycheck." They settled into a condominium in the Quail Ridge development in Oceanside, north of San Diego, and John lavished his new wife with fancy toys, including a yellow Ferrari. Always secretive, the only thing he told her about his history was that his previous wife had died of cancer and that he kept their wedding rings in his pocket. "He never talked about their past," Diane told the *Union-Tribune*. "Any time I brought up subjects on his past, I was being 'nosy.' "

• • •

While John was being watched in San Diego, investigators in Ohio, New Jersey and Connecticut interviewed witnesses whom they felt wouldn't go to John. Much of the work covered old ground and yielded nothing more than what investigators already knew. But the effort wasn't a total waste. In Seville, Ohio, detectives discovered some information about John's brother Michael that could prove helpful later on. While doing maintenance work on the Malz family condominiums, when John was living in Ohio in the mid-90s, Michael warned women tenants not to get involved with John because he might be dangerous. This alleged statement told investigators that Michael did have suspicions—or more— about his brother, supporting the idea that Michael knew more than he was saying, and more important, that he had a conscience to which they could appeal. It was appearing that the Quantico profilers were right: Michael was the most likely family member to turn on John.

In the spring of 1999, after eight months of investigation, Hilland had all the information he felt he needed before taking the operation to the next level. He arranged an ambitious—and expensive—interview blitz of a dozen key witnesses, mostly John's family members, co-workers and friends—the kinds of people who weren't interviewed in the new investigation because of fears that they would alert John. The plan was to send teams of investigators across the country to interview these witnesses on a single day.

And John would be at the top of the interview list. Hilland would take this one himself. The date set for the interviews was May 5, 1999.

CHAPTER 10

From his research, and the picture of John developed by the FBI profilers, Hilland was certain that John would sit for yet another interview without any coaxing. John had sailed through lengthy interviews in Ohio and New Jersey, getting more information out of the interviewers than the interviewers got out of him. Smith would doubtless feel confident that he could manipulate his interrogators again. Hilland also believed that John knew the FBI was investigating him, and that he'd be hungry for what they had on him. John couldn't resist the challenge. So certain was Hilland that John would agree to be interviewed, that he reserved a suite at the Holiday Inn Express Hotel and Suites on West Valley Parkway, near LaForza, for the interrogation, and another room for two FBI profilers to view the interrogation on closed-circuit monitors.

It was 7 a.m. when Hilland and a second FBI agent, Marry Galligan, saw a red-haired man in a T-shirt and tight jeans arrive for work at LaForza at 2037 Michigan Road in Escondido, California. The agents met John at the front gate to the business. Introducing themselves, they told John they were conducting an investigation into his possible involvement in the disappearances of Janice Hartman Smith and Betty Fran Gladden Smith. They asked if they could speak with him.

Just as Hilland had expected, John agreed to be interviewed—without a lawyer. It was to be the most important interview on the most important day of the new FBI-led investigation. As John was arriving at work, dozens of detectives across the country were approaching his friends and family for the last major round of interviews. Hilland knew that his credibility was on the line. If it didn't yield results, his supervisors' leash—loosened as his investigation heated up—would be yanked tight.

They drove in separate cars to the hotel, Hilland taking the lead in his rental, John following in his car with Agent Galligan in the passenger seat. The agents wanted John to have his own car so that if he felt like he didn't want to continue with the interview he could leave. They didn't want him to feel trapped. They wanted him comfortable.

After arriving at the Holiday Inn Express, John was offered food and something to drink. He took a cup of coffee, but turned down a sandwich or donut. This was the first indication that this interview would be different from the other interrogations in which he didn't so much as take a sip of water. They got to the room and he sat down, their actions all being watched by FBI profilers huddled over closed-circuit monitors in the other room. As he had before, John waived his rights to remain silent and to have an attorney present.

The interrogation, which was not recorded on audio or video tape, began with the agents telling Smith they wanted to talk to him about what had happened to Janice and Fran. John repeated his contention from all the earlier interview sessions: He didn't know. Then the dodging and weaving began. How could he not know, they asked him, when he was in possession of Janice's 1974 Ford Mustang after she disappeared? He first denied that he had the car. Hilland showed him the Wayne County Sheriff's Department's original missing persons report from 1974, along with follow-up reports. The paperwork said Detective McGuire had seen the Mustang, with license number N 2524, registered to Janice Hartman Smith, parked in front of John's mobile home at Lot #167, Melrose Trailer Park. John changed his story. He told the agents that although he and Janice were divorced at the time, they were still living together in the trailer—and that's why the Mustang was there. He said that on the morning he woke up to find her missing, he'd seen the Mustang in the driveway and assumed that sometime the night before she had returned home, parked the car, then left before he got up. This was how John had responded to hours and hours of questions years earlier: tell one story, then change it when faced with facts that contradicted it, and not worry about it a bit.

Hilland had suspected that John would do this. The agent wanted him to continue to do it—for a time.

Hilland and Galligan pressed John some more on details of Janice's disappearance. They showed him statements by Kathy Paridon, Janice's friend. In the 1974 report, with information largely provided by John, Paridon is said to have last seen Janice driving off with an unidentified man after being dropped off at home. The agents then told John that in 1992, Kathy was re-interviewed by detectives and had changed her story to say there was no man in the car. John insisted that Kathy was lying, and he didn't understand why she would say such a thing. He said that the original report was right—that it was taken at Kathy's house right in front of her mother. That was strange, Hilland told John. Why was he filing the missing persons report from Kathy's home when he and Janice lived together in his trailer? John was silent a moment. Then he said he couldn't remember.

Dodge, weave and forget—John was acting as if he were back in the West Windsor police station breezing through twelve hours of questioning. The agents were going over old ground and they knew it. John had been confronted with these contradictions before and admitted nothing. He'd change his stories as he was doing this time, but he'd never lose composure, never get angry, never offer any information of value. And that was OK with Hilland and Galligan. They simply wanted to lull John into a false sense of security.

That's when the agents threw John the first curve. They asked him about Sheila Sautter, his longtime girlfriend in Connecticut. John had been confronted about Sautter before—but this time there was a twist. The agents asked Smith if he recalled that day in April 1992 when he gave the formal statement to Detective Dansbury in West Windsor, that day when police also searched his home and his storage facilities and cars and office. He said he remembered that. They asked him if he recalled at the end of the day receiving a phone call from Sheila. He said he remembered talking to her, but didn't recall what was said. They asked if Sheila was a good person. He said yes. They asked if she would have any motivation to lie. He said no. Then they asked him if he'd ever told Sheila "I think it's too late" to find Janice and Fran, and "That's correct" when asked if he was lying to police. John insisted he'd never said that.

"You're sure?" Hilland asked.

"Absolutely positive," John said.

That's when Hilland got out a tape-recorder. He played a portion of that phone call which had been secretly recorded. Smith heard his own voice saying the very things that he had denied saying.

"John," Hilland asked, "when you told Sheila that you lied to police, what did you lie about?"

John didn't answer. Instead, he shrugged his shoulders and then let out a high-pitched squeal, like a woman's shriek. Hilland and Galligan didn't know what to make of that, except that all of a sudden this wasn't the same John Smith of the other interviews, who could keep his topcoat on and wore out the cops questioning him. They increased the pressure.

They pasted photos and pieces of paper with names on them on the wall—friends, co-workers, lovers—and revealed to John that they were all being interviewed as they sat in that Holiday Inn. They were, the agents told John, all like spokes in a wheel, all pointing directly to him. They told him the FBI knew everything about him, that he was being closely watched everywhere he went. They showed him surveillance photographs of him and Diane in San Diego and even photos of them from a recent trip to Rome.

"John, your life as you know it is over," Hilland said. "This is not the minor leagues. This isn't West Windsor, or Ohio. This is the FBI."

Then they moved on to the most sensitive subjects of all. The agents asked him about Michael, about the things Michael had said to others: how Michael had warned women to stay away from John. They asked him to think of his grandparents, now both dead. They told him that his grandparents had to live with his dark secrets their entire lives, taking these secrets to their graves. They told him to think about his grandmother, who had died just three months earlier, watching over him, listening to John's lies.

John started to fall apart. His face turned bright red, voice started quivering, almost shaking. He came close, the agents thought, to breaking. But then he collected himself. He posed a hypothetical question: If two people had an argument, and one of them ran off and was hit by a bus and died, would the other person be responsible?

"That would be an accident," Hilland said. "Is that what happened to Fran?"

John didn't answer. Instead, he cried. Hilland thought he finally had him.

In a weak voice, his face wet with tears, John said: "I'm tired of lying. I don't want to lie anymore."

Then don't, Hilland said.

John said he didn't know how to begin. "My life is a nightmare," he said. "I am tired of living this nightmare." He said he was tired, and, "I want the nightmare to end."

Hilland felt he was almost there. If John didn't give a confession right now, at the very least he would provide crucial information that could be used against him—that could help authorities find Janice and Fran's bodies. John looked like every inch a broken, helpless, vulnerable man.

They had him in their grasp, at last, after all these years of chasing him.

And then, as he had so often before, John slipped away.

He stopped talking about lies and nightmares, and began complaining of a headache. He said he suffered migraines. He asked for an Aleve tablet. Hilland and Galligan looked around the suite. All they could find was Tylenol in a first-aid kit. Somebody was sent out to get Aleve. Keep John there, Hilland thought. Give him what he wants. Let him pick up where he had left off. Don't let this be the end.

The agents offered Smith a cold washcloth for his head, which he turned down. John swallowed the Aleve. He got out of his chair and lay on the couch and continued crying and complaining about his headache. Then he curled up into the fetal position. He asked for a blanket to cover his head, but the agents refused to give him one. He said he wanted to lie on the couch forever. He stayed there for fifteen to twenty minutes, then complained about a pain radiating to his arms and chest, like a heart attack. The agents thought he was faking. No, John said, the pain is real. It's excruciating.

The agents couldn't gamble. They wanted to break John, not kill him. They had no choice but to offer medical assistance. They dialed 911 from the hotel room, and paramedics came. John was hooked up to an IV and wheeled out of the Holiday Inn on a gurney toward an ambulance and a ride to the hospital.

The interview was over.

Now it was Hilland's heart causing the problems. It sank. He had gone into this interview determined to stay there as long as it took. Instead, the critical interview with John Smith, on the biggest, most important and most expensive day of what had blossomed into a major, multi-state, multi-agency investigation, ended with John pulling the oldest trick in the book—something a child would do to stay home from school. He'd played sick. And it worked.

Interview over. No confession. No clue as to where the bodies were. Just provocative and suspicious—but also vague and ambiguous—statements to the FBI.

Hilland wondered how the other interviews had gone, and desperately hoped they were more revealing. Hilland was particularly concerned about the interview with Michael Smith. They couldn't break John, but maybe they could break his brother.

Michael Smith was at work in Ohio on May 5, 1999, when Sergeant Dave Mansue of West Windsor police tapped him on the shoulder.

"Remember me?" Mansue asked.

Michael turned around and looked at Mansue in surprise. They hadn't seen each other in seven years, since the day Mansue and Detective Potts had interviewed Michael in the session cut short by his grandmother bursting in. Though taken aback by seeing the officer again after all these years, Michael agreed to sit for another interview with Mansue and his interview partner, FBI Agent Bob Drew of the New York office.

Michael left work early and drove to the Medina Police Station, with Drew's rental car leading, and Michael in his car with Mansue in the passenger seat. Once at the station, Michael was taken to an interview room.

"Mike, there's more we need to talk to you about," Mansue said.

At first, Michael said he resented being treated this way, and was particularly upset at Mansue for catching him by surprise at work. "You could have picked up the phone and called me," Michael said. He had never been very fond of Mansue anyway—he would later refer to him as "a little short arrogant guy"—and the circumstances of this interview did nothing to change Michael's low opinion.

Mansue didn't take it personally. Rather, he sensed there were other reasons for Michael's anger. Much had happened since the last interview. Michael worked for the family, doing handyman chores at the apartment complexes.

The investigation had found that the job may have exacerbated Michael's lifelong feeling that his older brother was his mother's favorite. Michael had complained to people about toiling for low wages and no benefits while John enjoyed those yachting trips on Lake Erie.

As he was questioned, Michael showed a range of emotions, from shouting to crying. He told them that he felt like he had been treated like dirt—that the family had taken advantage of him. But as for details of the Janice Hartman disappearance, Michael had little to say. John, he said, had moved out of state, but Michael didn't know where. When he was told that John had made a major investment in a foreign car business and was working in sunny California, Michael again became angry—and more talkative. He spoke in more detail about himself and John than he had in the first interview, giving the detectives a better picture of the family history—and the events leading up to Janice's disappearance.

Mansue held his breath. Maybe Michael would turn on John.

The family history, as Michael related it, had its first milestone when he was 6 or 7 years old. "My mother and my dad got a divorce when we were young," he said. He and his older brother moved with their mother to the white, wood-frame house on 17 Pleasant Street in Seville, two houses down from Michael's grandparents, at 21. He liked living near his grandparents. "Our relationship was close," he said. "I guess my grandfather, you would consider him my dad. My grandmother would always, she would say it like: 'Your dad is this.' And I'll be confused and say, 'Who?' She'd correct herself by saying, 'Our grandpa.' "

The first time Michael met Janice Hartman was in 1974, when Michael was 17 and his brother and Janice were 19. They were all at a motel on Greenwich Road just outside Seville, and John and Janice weren't yet married. That was all Michael could remember. "I was just with my brother and we went out to visit her, and we just stayed and visited her for a little bit and we left," he said. Michael said he didn't attend the wedding of John and Janice in Detroit. Nobody did. It rankled some in the family, particularly their mother, who refused to see John after the elopement. When John came to pick up his clothes, "I was not allowed to let him in the house," Michael said. "I picked it up and I carried it out to the porch and handed it to him over the porch."

The couple moved to Columbus, while Michael stayed in Seville with his mother, who had remarried, to real estate man Sam Malz, but life at home was far from peaceful. "I got into a fight with my parents and they kicked me out of the house," recalled Michael, and he moved in with John and Janice for two weeks in their little apartment in Columbus. "I don't know that much about their relationship," he said. "I know when I got there Jan did not like me. She did not want me there. She was acting very clear." Living conditions were cramped, too, because John and Michael's friend Dennis Evans was also there. Michael stayed away from Janice and spent much of his time with Dennis.

While with his brother and sister-in-law, Michael saw them argue, though he portrayed the fights as nothing more than the usual marital spats. It was often over money and Janice's smoking. "We went somewhere," Michael recalled, "and Jan and I was standing outside, and John went inside for some reason. As soon as he walked around the corner, she pulled out a cigarette and said, 'Don't tell your brother.' She started smoking it, and John came back and she threw it down. He started yelling at her for smoking, and I told . . . him, 'John, it was me.' That was the end of that, so he stopped . . . I just didn't want to listen to him yell at her."

By the fall of 1974, John and Janice had split. Janice was living in Doylestown with her father and Michael couldn't remember where John was, but seemed to recall spending time with his older brother. "I'm sure we did stuff," he said. "Couldn't tell you exactly what we did." Some of this "stuff" included John's impromptu visits to places where his estranged wife was hanging out, but Michael saw what he considered an amicable post-split relationship. "She said they were getting along better now than what they were when they were married," he said.

One evening, in November, John asked Michael to drive him to the Sun Valley Lounge in Doylestown. Michael had no idea why John wanted to go there. He had no interest in hanging out at the bar, so he dropped John off.

Unknown to Michael at the time, this was the night that John joined Janice and Kathy Paridon, the last night that Jan would be seen alive.

Michael insisted he didn't know anything about Janice Hartman's disappearance. All he knew was what John told him. "[He said] something about Jan was gonna go into a relocation program for drugs," Michael recalled. "She was turning in some people that was supposedly selling drugs. A witness relocation program."

Mansue pushed Michael hard, telling him investigators had information that Michael suspected his brother was involved in Janice's disappearance. Mansue told Michael that people had said Michael warned female tenants of the family's apartments to stay away from John because he was dangerous. Michael became angry at the question, but he didn't budge. He wouldn't talk about that. He didn't know anything about why Jan had disappeared.

The detectives turned to the subject of Fran's disappearance in New Jersey. Michael also claimed, once again, that he didn't know anything about that, either. He said he didn't know that John had married Fran, and that when he was told that John's wife had disappeared, he had just assumed it was Sheila Sautter. On this subject, Mansue now believed Michael. John had told so many lies to so many people, it stood to reason he would have withheld this information from his brother, Mansue thought.

But while Michael seemed to be telling the truth about John and Fran, Mansue couldn't shake the feeling that Michael was holding something back about John and Janice, just as he had in 1992. After Michael would claim ignorance about Janice's disappearance, he'd complain again about John. He couldn't believe John was living the good life in San Diego while he was still working hard at a blue-collar job in Northeastern Ohio. Just the right kind of prodding, Mansue thought, and Michael would turn on John.

The interview would last three hours. But no matter how Mansue and Drew approached it, Michael wouldn't say anything more about Janice's disappearance. Still, even when the interview was over, the investigators thought Michael might open up. As Mansue and Drew walked out of the station to the parking lot, they noticed that Michael was following them. They paused and talked some more with him in the parking lot. Michael would answer a few questions about his family, walk away, then turn back around and talk to them some more. This went on for about an hour. Each time Michael came back, Mansue thought he would open up.

But it never happened. Finally, Michael and the investigators parted for good that day. While driving away from the police station, Mansue and Drew asked each other what they had missed. Which of Michael's buttons did they fail to push? They thought about giving Michael a couple of days to cool off, to think, then approaching him again.

That night, in San Diego, Hilland got the update on the interview with Michael Smith and the other important people, including John's co-worker and former landlord Trevor Haywood and John's current wife, Diane. The news was the same: nothing major had come out of the interviews. Hilland returned to his hotel room. All the work, the travel, the expense, the meticulous planning—and nothing. This was the day that everything was to come together, and it didn't. His credibility had been on the line—and it had taken a big blow. The mass interviews consumed resources he knew his supervisors wouldn't free up again unless there was a break—a big break. He'd have to go back to New York empty-handed.

The next day, May 6, 1999, all the investigators flew

back to their respective homes—all but one. Hilland stayed an extra day in San Diego. He talked to some of the local people who had been interviewed the previous day. He wasn't expecting to get anything new. He just wanted to put a face on the FBI, to show them Agent Bob Hilland in the flesh, so that when John Smith tried to demonize him— as Hilland knew he would—they'd know that Hilland was no monster.

The agent spoke with Haywood and found him a basket case, shaken by the knowledge that he may have been renting a room to a multiple murderer. He hadn't known about John's marriage to Janice or about Janice's disappearance. But Haywood had nothing more to report to Hilland, who moved on to talk to John's latest wife, Diane. She was in worse shape than Haywood, still trying to cope with what the investigators had told her the day before: John had had not one, but two previous wives, and both had disappeared. Fran had not died of cancer as John had told her; she may have been murdered by him, the investigators said. This was the first Diane had heard about the missing persons cases and she struggled to believe it. They showed her news clippings about the two Mrs. Smiths. Hilland spent three hours with Diane, who didn't seem to know who or what to believe. Hilland urged her to listen very carefully to everything John said—then she would know. Hilland told her he figured that John would leave the hospital the night before with a story about how the evil FBI agents were harassing him for events that had happened years, and even decades, in the past, events that he wasn't responsible for. And, in fact, Diane said that was exactly what John had claimed. Hilland asked her to think about who she should believe.

"I don't want you to believe me because I'm Bob Hilland from the FBI," he told Diane. "I want you to take the facts and sit and think about them, form questions and confront them."

He gave her his card and said she could call any time.

. . .

After Michael Smith got home to Wadsworth, Ohio, he reflected on the interview and searched his soul. He thought of his grandparents, now both dead, and how they had raised him, steering him through difficult times. He thought of how his grandfather had been the father he never really had. He thought of John and how he had loved, respected and looked up to him from the time he was a kid riding on the back of John's motorcycle down those country roads.

And he thought of the nightmares—the nightmares that never went away, even after all these years. In his sleep he would see Janice Hartman, young and alive. But in this nightmare, Janice came to him, legless. The legs were in her hands. She was hitting him with them.

"I had to talk to my wife," Michael recalled. "I told her there is something I need to tell her." Michael collected his thoughts. "I needed to think about the truth, you know," he said. "I buried it and covered it up. And it almost killed me once. I had nightmares for years. I needed to get it as straight as possible, which, after I thought for a while, wasn't a problem, because, man, this burnt a hole in your brain. I mean, this is something you don't forget."

Over the years, he had tried to cope with what he knew by inventing stories to explain Janice's disappearance. One was that Janice was buried under 200 Grace Lane in Seville at the apartment complex. He didn't know if that was true or not, but that's what he would say. Another story was that Janice was stuffed up a tree at his Aunt Verne's house. "I mean, these stories were so ridiculous," he would recall. "One time I think [I said] she was in a trash bag on my back porch. Just stop to think, it's ridiculous. I think another story was she was buried under the railroad tracks at Sterling. It was just my way of dealing with, just dealing with this."

The stories gave him an alternative ending to the real story—a story too painful to think about. Now it was time to face facts. Michael had promised his grandparents he would some day tell the truth.

Michael had a heart-to-heart talk with his wife Tanya, then he went to a lawyer, Ronald Spears, of Medina.

When Spears heard what Michael had to say, he contacted the FBI.

It was mid-May 1999 when Michael Smith and his lawyers flew to New York to talk to Agent Bob Drew, and only Drew. During the interview in Medina, Michael's loathing for Mansue was offset by his growing respect for Drew. Mansue, Michael would recall, was "not someone that I needed to trust." Michael said he observed that when Mansue would "lie to [him]," Drew seemed embarrassed by his interview partner's actions. "The FBI agent would look down or look to the side," Michael observed. "I felt this was the guy I could trust."

And so, he had another meeting with Drew. Only this time, Michael said to take everything he had talked about in the previous interview and "throw it out the window."

"You are not gonna like what I tell ya," Michael said.

The real story, Michael said, began in 1974, in the weeks after Janice's disappearance. One day, Michael went with John to John's mobile home in Wooster. The trailer was a mess. "Things were just kinda scattered everywhere, like anyplace when you're getting ready to move people," he said. "Just helter-skelter everywhere." Michael was in the trailer for maybe twenty seconds, just long enough for John to hand him boxes, bags of clothing and "God knows what else." The clothing, he noticed, was for a woman. They took the bags and boxes to their grandparents' house in Seville and stacked them in the unused garage against the northeast wall.

Shortly thereafter—Michael thought it was Thanksgiving weekend—he went to his grandparents' house to watch the Ohio State–Michigan college football game on television. "It was fun because my uncle and my grandfather would get upset and throw hats and newspapers at the TV. It was always exciting," he recalled. A couple of John's friends, Dennis Evans and a man named Stanley, stopped by later. Michael recalled that John had driven there in his fancy, customized van with a big mural on the side and shag carpeting, chairs and cabinets inside—"Pretty cool for that time period."

At some point, Michael, John and the two friends went into the garage to talk. Around noon, Michael then went back inside to watch the game with his grandparents. John didn't join them. In the middle of the game, "I went out to the garage [to] find out why my brother wasn't in watching the football game with us," said Michael.

John had a project going: "He was working on building a wooden box."

Sherrie Gladden-Davis (facing camera) embraces Deanna Weiss. After 49-year-old Betty Fran Smith disappeared from her Princeton, NJ, home in 1991, Gladden-Davis, her sister, and Weiss, her daughter, began checking into the past of Smith's husband, John:

"Dialing names in Ohio's 216 area code, Sherrie reached a Garry Hartman, from Wadsworth . . . She asked if he was related to Janice Hartman. He said, yes, Janice Hartman was his sister, a vivacious, petite young woman. He said that his sister Janice had in fact married a John Smith, originally from Seville, Ohio. They had in fact eloped in Detroit in the late 1960s. And she did in fact divorce him in the early 1970s.

"Sherrie asked the brother how she could reach Janice.

"'My God, lady, you've got a problem,' he said, and the reason would take Sherrie's breath away . . .

"Shortly after divorcing John, Janice disappeared—without a trace, never to be found again.

"Just like Fran." (*Photo by Bill Kennedy* © 2001 The Plain Dealer. *All rights reserved. Reprinted with permission.*)

"For John David Smith, growing up in his grandparents' home on Pleasant Drive in Seville, Ohio, death was never far away. Literally. Next door was the Armstrong Funeral Home." (*Michael Fleeman*)

Janice Hartman "wearing a dress right out of the 50s" with brothers Garry and Ross and two female cousins, Christmas, 1960: "It was a scene out of a Norman Rockwell painting, but the situation at home was hardly perfect." (*Courtesy Betty Lippincott*)

Janice Hartman: "She was a pretty, petite teenager from Norton High with light brown hair who just happened to have a thing for guys with fast motorcycles."
(*Courtesy Betty Lippincott*)

A photo snapped by an insistent Betty Lippincott after learning her daughter had eloped with John Smith. "Others said it could have been that Janice saw John as an intriguing outsider—the dorky looks only adding to the allure."
(*Courtesy Betty Lippincott*)

"'I went out to the garage [to] find out why my brother wasn't watching the football game with us,' said Michael. John had a project going on. 'He was working on building a wooden box.'" *(Courtesy Wayne County, Ohio, District Attorney)*

John Smith's black Corvette: "The box was placed on the passenger side with one end up against the dashboard and the other against the rear window, lying over the folded-down passenger seat. It was a tight squeeze, but it fit." *(Courtesy Wayne County, Ohio, District Attorney)*

The Box, discovered by a Newton County, IN, Highway Department crew in April, 1980. "As an object appeared, he gasped. Sam shouted to the other workers to stay right where they were until he called for help . . . the old quilt in the box was covering a human skull." *(Courtesy Wayne County, Ohio, District Attorney)*

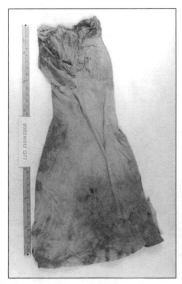

"Wearing rubber gloves," Indiana examiners "removed, logged and placed into brown bags a collection of women's clothing that seemed to come straight from the 60s." *(Courtesy Wayne County, Ohio, District Attorney)*

2000: "Potts focused on the road and the work that still had to be done, reviewing for the millionth time the facts of the case. He had been working it so long the details were branded into his brain. Then another thought occurred to him. It was March 2. They had dug up the bones on Janice Hartman's birthday."

"Standing back, the men in the room saw a skeleton—a skeleton with the legs cut off just below the knees." *(Courtesy Wayne County, Ohio, District Attorney)*

Dr. Frank Saul "could say little more about her identity. His visitors placed the skull next to a picture of Janice Hartman and 'tried to get me to say: That's her. That's her smile,' recalled Saul." *(Courtesy Wayne County, Ohio, District Attorney)*

"Murder doesn't come very often to the courthouse in Wooster, Ohio . . . That this trial followed by 27 years the alleged crime made the case all the more special."

Judge Mark K. Wiest. *(Courtesy Judge Mark K. Wiest)*

Assistant Wayne County Prosecutor Jocelyn Stefancin. *(Michael Fleeman)*

Wayne County Sheriff's Detective Brian Potts. *(Michael Fleeman)*

Wayne County Courthouse. *(Michael Fleeman)*

"John—the man they never really knew, the Mennonite bachelor who turned out to have been married at least once before and had girlfriends all over the country, the John Boy Walton-type with the potential for rage, the husband who never really seemed to care when his wife disappeared one day." At his bail hearing. (*Bill Kennedy* © 2001 The Plain Dealer. *All rights reserved. Reprinted with permission.*)

"While he's serving his time, investigators will wonder whether John killed anybody else, those tooth fragments found under the apartment garage and the skull fragments found in the storage facility left as two huge unresolved pieces of evidence." *(Michael Fleeman)*

CHAPTER 11

The box was being made of plywood. John had propped it up on an old car hoist. He had constructed the bottom of the box and one side. Michael asked his brother why he was making it. John said the box was for Janice's belongings, though Michael thought it was a strange shape: long and skinny.

"Why are you building such a shit box? Why don't you build it more like a chest?" Michael asked.

John took offense and snapped at Michael.

Michael didn't remember his exact words, "But they were angry, nasty."

Michael told his brother, "OK, fine, I'm gone," and went back to watch the rest of the Ohio State–Michigan game, then started watching the UCLA–USC game that followed.

At about 7 p.m., he returned to the garage to find his brother still there. "He had this box built," he said. "It was on the other end of the hoist. It was turned sideways. And I never seen anybody do this before, but he was picking up clothes and he was kinda rolling them up. I have never seen anybody roll clothes up. He was taking these clothes, rolling them up, putting them around the edge of this box."

There was no lid on the box at this point. By Michael's

estimation, the box was about eight inches high, about sixteen inches wide and about four feet long. Michael couldn't remember what his brother said, if anything. "We would've had a real short conversation," he said. "He was visibly upset, and I already got yelled at once." Michael felt uncomfortable. "He was almost to the point of crying," Michael said. "So I decided, OK, this is it. I'm out of here."

Five years went by, and Michael and John never spoke of the box, even though it was never far away. It sat in the garage of their grandparents' gas station along the eastern wall next to a weight-lifting bench that a neighborhood kid used. Boxes and garbage bags, apparently containing more of Janice's clothing, were stacked on top of it. Eventually, the box was moved to the south part of the garage by a window and a double-door, beneath a shelf holding oil cans and funnels.

In April of 1979, Michael married his second wife, Tanya, and they honeymooned in Florida for a week. When they returned to Ohio, they moved into his mother's old house two doors down from his grandparent's—his mother and step-father were by now living in the big house in Medina. Michael was doing handyman work and painting at a three-building apartment complex his stepfather was building outside of Seville, off of Greenwich Road on the newly created Grace Lane, named after Michael's mother. The first building had been completed, and workers were completing the second one with plans for a third. Because the complex was only a couple of miles from his house, Michael would go home for lunch.

It was during one lunch break shortly after returning from his honeymoon that something happened—"something I will never forget."

Michael was at his house eating when his grandfather walked in, panic on his face.

"There's something wrong, you gotta come quick, there's something wrong," he said. His grandfather led him to his house and into the garage. His grandfather had rented half the garage to a neighbor named Jack Bistor, who planned to use the space to repair small engines. Michael's grandfather explained that he and Jack had been cleaning the garage when they came across the box that John had built five years earlier. They had pried the lid partially off—why, Michael didn't know.

"Look at it," his grandfather said.

It was a surreal scene. His grandfather was upset, but Bistor was giggling. "There's an old dead turtle in that box," said Bistor, as Michael pried the top of the box farther up. "Watch out, it'll bite you."

Michael looked inside the box. He couldn't figure out what was in there, but it was no dead turtle. All he could make out were circular objects. Wanting to get a better look, Michael carried the box down the street and placed it behind his house. "My curiosity got the best of me," he would later recall.

Using a hammer and crowbar, Michael took the top of the box off completely.

"I got a stick and I started poking it around. I had no idea what was in there. Could have been a rat, could have been anything. I don't know," he recalled. "So I'm poking around, and what I found was what appeared to be legs. You know, it was just—it appeared to be human legs that had been cut off just below the kneecaps. I'm like, Woa."

Then he saw something else, he said. "I think I lost it."

"It was wavy, brown hair, except—except that it was real weird," he said. "It was blue and it was blonde, you know. It was just multi-colored, strange-looking hair."

He poked around some more.

Then he saw it. "The face." The skin was gray and mummy-like, he said, but the face was recognizable: "It was Janice Hartman."

Dazed, he got his grandfather. "You need to come look at this," he told him, and his grandfather went with him to the box and also jabbed around with the stick, while Michael paced. Finally, he told his grandfather, "We got go call the police."

With a pained expression, his grandfather looked at him and said, "We can't call the police. It will kill Ethel"— Michael's grandmother. She had recently suffered a heart attack and was in delicate health—or so she claimed. ("My grandma played it for all it's worth," Michael would recall.)

His grandfather began to cry. He walked up the street. Michael nailed the lid back down on the box and put the box in his garage. He went to his grandparents' house, where his grandmother was at the table. She was breathing heavily, acting like she was still suffering the effects of a heart attack.

Michael couldn't tell her about the box.

"I did not want to kill my grandmother," he recalled. "Unfortunately, there was nothing I could do for her—the person in the box. I did not want to kill my grandmother."

He and his grandfather decided they had to call John and tell him to pick up the box he had built. And then, the two decided somberly, after John picked up the box, "He was never, ever to be allowed back at their house again," Michael said.

He called his brother from his grandparents' house—the phone at Michael's had been disconnected—using a number provided by his grandmother. He reached John at a work number in Hammond, Indiana, outside Chicago.

Michael told John that they had been cleaning up the garage, throwing away some of the stuff, and found the box.

"Yeah, OK," John said.

"John, you know, we moved the box and we opened the box," Michael said.

John asked if they'd looked inside.

"Yes," Michael said.

"I'll be right there," John said.

Michael hung up the phone, drove downtown, bought a 12-pack of beer and guzzled it down, all of it.

"I was pretty shook up," he recalled. "I was like dazed, confused. I was in shock. I was supposed to be working. I went up to work. I know I didn't do anything that day. I was just there. I went home that night, waited for my brother to get there."

Within hours, Michael got word that John had arrived at his grandparents' house in his new, souped-up black Corvette. He must have driven fast. Hammond was some 350 miles away. He was talking with his grandparents when Michael arrived. Michael took him into the kitchen.

"John, I think you owe me an explanation here," he said.

John sat down. He had something to tell Michael—a story so incredible it would leave Michael's already dazed and confused head spinning. John told him the story of how Janice came to be in the box.

It all started, John said, when two guys came up to him and either drugged him or blacked him out somehow, Michael couldn't remember all the details. These guys, according to John, were an FBI agent and a Wayne County sheriff's deputy. When John came back to consciousness, he was in a warehouse. Next to him was Janice, dead on the floor. The men were laughing at John, telling him they were going to frame him for murder. They then knocked him out or drugged him. He next woke up in a trailer in Wooster, Ohio. Janice's body was now on the floor of the trailer. John picked her body up and ran outside to his van and put it inside. He drove away just as a Wayne County sheriff car pulled into the driveway with its lights on.

As outrageous as this story was, Michael said he wanted to believe it. "You know, you grow up with somebody, he's your brother. He could have told me a rock from the moon came down and cracked her on the head and I—I wanted to believe it," he said. "Given the choices: Do I want to believe this or do I want to believe my brother killed his wife? I mean, he really loved her. I mean, he loved her more than me."

Michael told his brother he had to get rid of the box. Michael suggested bringing it to the construction site for the Grace Lane apartments, where workers were about to pour concrete floors in the garages.

"No," John said, "This is my problem. I'll take care of it." And that was the end of the discussion.

By now it was after 9 p.m. Michael got the box from his garage and set it on the grass between their grandparents' house and the gas station.

Michael recalled: "I went in the house and probably grabbed another beer and went to the bathroom. And when I came back out, the box had been moved. It was put in the Corvette, which was parked out front of the gas station."

The box was placed on the passenger side with one end up against the dashboard and the other against the rear window, lying over the folded-down passenger seat. It was a tight squeeze, but it fit.

Michael asked John what he intended to do with the box. John said he was going to take it back to his place in Hammond. He was thinking of burying it in his basement or burning it in the garage where he worked on his Corvette.

John then drove off.

It was a cliffhanger that would haunt his dreams for the next two decades.

About two weeks later, Michael Smith went to his grandparents' house and saw his grandmother talking on the phone.

"Oh, it's Johnny. Here, talk to him," she said to Michael.

"OK," said Michael, and he picked up the phone and asked, "Did you make it home all right?"

"Yeah, sure," John said. "No problem."

"Oh, OK," said Michael.

No problem.

Michael didn't speak with his brother for the rest of the year.

Michael didn't call the police.

"I was scared to death," he recalled, "because now I'm . . . I'm . . . I was, you know, I am part of what I believed would be part of a murder. And I did nothing, but I covered it up, and so I was—I was scared to death. I did not want to go to jail."

And so, when anybody asked about Janice, Michael either said he didn't know or made up stories about how she could have been buried or stashed up a tree. And with that, the interview with FBI Agent Drew—the first man Michael would trust enough to share this secret with in twenty years—came to a close.

The case against John Smith had just been blown wide open.

Drew gave Hilland the news. Just two weeks after he'd thought the investigation had collapsed, Hilland was now once again hot on the trail of John Smith. There was work to be done—and fast. Hilland needed to corroborate everything that Michael Smith had said. It was an incredible statement, and a jury would want proof that he was telling the truth—*if* he was telling the truth. That meant more interviews, search warrants, perhaps even excavations for Janice and the box. It meant more time, money and manpower, at a time when Hilland's bosses wouldn't let him have all three. But with a break this big, the brass couldn't refuse.

One of the first phone calls Hilland made was to Detective Brian Potts in Ohio.

"This is bullshit," Potts responded. "Cuts her legs off?"

As fantastic as Michael's tale was, Potts knew in his heart that it was true.

For Hilland, Potts and everyone else who would be back on the case, the major question of the moment was: What did John do with the box? Michael didn't know, but his statement provided enough clues to keep investigators busy. For starters, there were the Grace Lane Apartments. Although according to Michael's account, John seemed to have rejected the suggestion of taking the box there, Hilland could think of no better place to dispose of a body than under the garage floor just before concrete was poured. If not at the apartments, there was also the possibility that

John had returned to his grandparents' house nearby and buried the box there; or, perhaps, there were other remains on the property. Michael had said the legs were cut off below the kneecaps. Maybe the feet were buried somewhere beneath 17 Pleasant Street.

Another important lead was Michael's account of John heading back to Indiana. To date, the investigation had focused on Ohio, New Jersey, Connecticut and California. Now there was another state: Perhaps John did bury the remains at his Indiana place, wherever that was. Investigators had to find this home—not to mention friends, coworkers and anybody else in Indiana who might have known him.

Then there were the problems in Michael's statement that might never be solved. The account of the rainbow-colored hair, for instance, simply didn't make much sense. Also troubling was Michael's claim that he'd seen Janice's face. After five years in the box, that face would have decomposed down to the skull, making it unrecognizable. Could John have somehow preserved, even embalmed, Janice? Hilland knew that John wouldn't have had to go far for the chemicals: the Armstrong Funeral Home was next door.

But while Hilland had nagging questions, he was pleased that once again there *were* new questions. The interview blitz of May 5 had been a success after all.

Within days of Michael giving his statement to FBI Agent Bob Drew, Hilland was on a plane to Ohio. He didn't want to give Michael any time to reconsider. On May 26, 1999, he met him in a motel. They sat down and Michael went over the story again, with Hilland writing it down and Michael signing each page.

It was a slightly different version of the events than Michael had given Drew, leaner in some areas, more detailed in others, but it captured all the critical facts. The statement said:

Approximately 1 month after Jan disappeared John was in my grandfather's garage building a wooden box out of plywood. The box was approximately 8 inches high, 16 inches wide, and approximately four feet long.

I believe he was crying.

I asked him why he was building such a storage box and he got upset and said he was putting some of Jan's things in there.

When he got upset I left because he was angry.

I lived in Medina at the time.

Sometime shortly after that the box appeared in my grandfather's garage. It was on the floor in the North East corner along with some other things [on] top of it.

The box stayed there for years.

Somewhere over time the box was moved to the South End of the garage, east of the back doors just below the windows.

I think it was the Spring of 1979 when I came home for lunch. I was living two houses down the street from my grandfather's house at 17 Pleasant Street. When I came home for lunch my grandfather came to my house, was visibly upset, and told me I had to come up to his garage right now.

When I got to his garage, Jack Bistor, my grandfather and I were in the garage together.

I believe Jack told me there was something in the box that looked and smelled like an old dead turtle. He was joking when he said that.

I went over to look at the box, the one end was opened. The one end piece, approximately 16 inches by 8 inches was partially opened.

I pulled the end down to get a better look inside. When I looked inside I saw four round things. I wasn't sure what it was. I got a scared feeling. After I looked in the box I picked it up, put it on my shoul-

der and walked down the sidewalk to my backyard and sat the box down the sidewalk [sic] on my backyard and sat the box on the ground. I opened it but I don't remember with what. A hammer, crowbar or something. I pried the top of the box open enough to look inside. I started at the end that was already loose. The box was filled with rags or clothing. I think it was clothing. I picked up a stick from the yarde and started moving some of the clothing material out of the way. I found something that was grayish in color and was hard. I then came across what I later realized where kneecaps. There was no doubt in my mind they were kneecaps. The legs were cut completely off just below the knee. I don't remember seeing feet. I went up to the other end of the box and started moving the material around with the stick. I found wavy hair.

The hair was different color and wavy. I had a very bad, scary feeling. I was scared to death. I saw the side of Jan's face.

I knew it was Jan but I didn't want to believe it. I went and got my grandfather, brought him down and showed him what was inside the box. Grandpa took the stick and was poking around in the box. I'm not sure, but I believe a conversation took place between my grandfather and I. We decided we weren't going to call the police. I think grandpa was concerned that this was going to hurt his business. He had a gas station. I nailed the top of the box back down and put the box in my garage. I went to my grandparents' house and called John at his work. I think he was working in the Chicago area.

I told him he needed to come home right now. I told him that I had found the box and we had opened it. We didn't find the box. The box was always there in the garage. John said he would be right home and John showed up at around 8 o'clock of night. I be-

lieve I told him he owned me an explanation: John started telling me a story that he winds up in what could have been a warehouse with Jan dead on the floor. There were other details but I can't remember them right now. John said next, his next story, that he was at his trailer in Wooster and "came to." When he looked up Jan was lying dead on the floor next to him. I think John told me that he took her body, put it in the car and was driving to the hospital. I'm not positive but I think he told me as he was pulling out on the road, out of his driveway the police were pulling in. After John's story, I went and got the box out of my garage and put in the area between my grandparents' house and garage. I told John that at the apartments being build in Grace Lane that in the next few days that they were getting ready to pour the garage floors and he could put the box there. John told me that he was going to take the box and take it back to where he was living in Hammond, Indiana and bury it out there. He also told me he was going to burn it up in the stove while he worked on his car in the garage.

John took the box and put it in the passenger side of his car and left. That was the last time I ever saw the box or its contents.

Following the statement were a series of questions and answers. Michael initialed each answer, scribbling in "m.s."

Q: When you refer to "John" who are you talking about?
A: My brother John Smith. My older brother.

Q: What is the name of your grandfather and where did he live?
A: His name was Chester Chaney and he lived at 21 Pleasant Street.

Q: The box you lifted was kept at 21 Pleasant Street, is that correct?
A: It was actually the garage next to 21 Pleasant Street.

Q: Did John ever tell you where he put the box?
A: No.

Q: Where do you think he put the box?
A: I'm not certain but I believe Hammond, Indiana. I believe this because that is what John told me.

Q: Could Janice be buried beneath the Grace Lane apts?
A: Anything is possible. I don't know.

Q: Did you kill Janice Hartman?
A: No, I did not.

Q: Do you know who killed Janice?
A: I believe it was my brother John.

Q: Did John ever tell you he killed Janice?
A: I don't think so.

Q: Do you know where Janice is buried now?
A: No, but I believe either in Hammond or at Grace Lane.

Q: Why do you think John killed Janice?
A: Because of what I found in the box and that John came home immediately to take the box.

Q: Do you have any doubt in your mind that Janice Hartman's body was inside the box?
A: No, no doubt.

Q: Do you have any doubt in your mind that John is responsible for Janice's death and ultimate disposal of her body?
A: No, no doubt.

Q: Did you help the disposal of the box?
A: No, I didn't.

Q: Does anyone else know about what happened to Janice?
A: My grandfather, grandmother, and my grandmother didn't see it but I think she knew what happened.

Q: Did you ever know or meet Betty Fran Smith?
A: No.

Q: Did John ever discuss Betty Fran's disappearance with you?
A: Yes. He told me that she left a note and never came back. One day I got a phone call from John between Thanksgiving and Christmas of 1991. John told me that he was married, his wife was missing, and that the police from New Jersey would be coming to talk to me. John also told me to tell my grandparents. I was shocked because John had just been home for the Thanksgiving holiday with Sheila. When John had called me that was the first time I ever knew he was married again, and the first time I ever heard of Fran.

Q: Is the information you have provided accurate to the best of your knowledge?
A: Yes, it is.

Q: Has anyone forced you to provide the information and answers to these questions?
A: No.

Q: Have you voluntarily provided this information?
A: Yes.

That concluded the formal statement, now memorialized for a jury to see. Even as Michael was putting his initials on the document, authorities were trying to corroborate details in his statement, digging for more information, witnesses—and the body of Janice Hartman.

CHAPTER 12

Sandra Anderson pulled her white Dodge pickup up to the Grace Lane Apartments outside Seville, Ohio, on Wednesday, May 26, 1999. A strong wind hit her face as she got out of the truck. That could be trouble; it could cause a confusing scent. Anderson was accompanied by her partner, Eagle, a 9-year-old Doberman–German short-hair mix. Extensively trained since he was a pup, Eagle specializes in sniffing out human remains, from entire bodies to the tiniest fingernail clipping. By disposition and training, Eagle is obsessed with the hunt for human remains, to the point that he never takes a break. Anderson has taken Eagle out for walks, only to have him detect a crime scene. He is trained to find almost anything that comes from a human, with the exception of urine, saliva and sweat—liquids that wouldn't necessarily point to the presence of a dead person. He is also trained to differentiate between human remains and those of animals. Certified by a number of forensic organizations, and approved in courtrooms in over twenty states, Eagle has conducted thousands of searches and, Anderson claims, "hasn't been wrong to date."

That was exactly what authorities were hoping for when they brought Anderson and Eagle into the John Smith case at the recommendation of a local police officer who had met Anderson at a law-enforcement seminar, where she was putting on a demonstration of Eagle's talent. Anderson and Eagle, who work through a private consulting company called Canine Solutions International, were summoned to the Grace Lane Apartments because Michael Smith had recalled recommending to John that a good place to bury the box would be under the floor of one of the garages before the concrete was poured. Since nobody knew which of the dozens of garages to dig up, the hope was that Eagle's nose would narrow down the search. Anderson unhooked Eagle from his leash to let him do his traditional "hasty search," scoping out the scene and getting his canine bearings.

Within ten minutes he keyed in on one garage door. Eagle announced he had picked up a human-remains scent by going bananas, barking incessantly, jumping up and down and throwing himself at the wall. "We should search this garage," Sandra told the FBI agents on the scene who were accompanied by local authorities and two forensic anthropologists, Dr. Frank P. Saul and his wife/professional partner Julie Mather Saul, who would help identify whatever was dug up.

Before Eagle was let in the garage, the FBI sent in a two-man team that used a ground-penetrating radar, a lawnmower-looking device that glides across the surface peering for underground abnormalities. When they finished their work, Anderson freed Eagle, who went through a side door to the garage. The big garage door wasn't opened because the wind would rush in and possibly throw off the scent. Anderson didn't want to know what the radar team found; she typically wants as little information as possible about a case so that Eagle can do his work independently.

Inside the garage, Eagle darted for a spot in the middle of the floor and lay down, his signal that he had located the exact place of the human-remains scent. While Eagle gets excited when a scent is near, he is trained to use a passive response to identify the exact spot so that he won't do anything to disrupt a crime scene.

Anderson reported Eagle's results. The radar men told Anderson that the spot Eagle had found was exactly where their radar had picked up an underground abnormality.

The next day, Thursday, a county road crew used a large concrete-cutting saw to slice away a section of the garage floor. FBI evidence recovery technicians, working with the Sauls, then carefully dug with small trowels into the hard, clay-like dirt beneath the slab. The dirt was hauled outside the garage and dumped into sifting screens.

It wasn't long before discoveries were made about two feet down: a piece of one tooth and two fragments that appeared to be parts of a second tooth.

From the shape of the cusps and the thickness of the enamel, the Sauls could easily identify these as permanent teeth from a human, the larger one a canine, the other two fragments from an incisor. The Sauls couldn't say how long the teeth had been there; the dental fragments could have been hundreds of years old for all they knew. But the fragments were definitely of human origin.

Expectations ran high. "Oh, my gosh," Stefancin recalled thinking. "She's going to be here. I really thought that we were going to get her."

More digging turned up some fibers that also gave off a human scent to Eagle. The crew dug some more. But by day's end, all they found was more dirt—no more remains, no plywood box with Janice Hartman inside. Still, the discovery of the teeth and fibers may have been enough. If investigators could identify the tooth fragments as coming from Janice Hartman, authorities would have enough evidence to try John for murder.

CHAPTER 13

In biology, the mitochondria are the little organelles known as the powerhouses that energize the cell. There are a lot of mitochondria and, like the nucleus of the cell, they contain DNA, the building blocks of life. The mitochondria are a forensic scientist's best friend, because there are so many of them, compared to just one nucleus. This is beneficial when having to extract DNA from very small pieces of biological evidence.

Like tooth fragments.

At the FBI's laboratory in Washington, analyst Alice Isenberg was able to extract mitochondrial DNA, called mtDNA in shorthand, from the tooth fragments dug out of the ground beneath the Grace Lane Apartment garage. The next step was to determine whether the DNA sequence in the teeth matched that of Janice Hartman. Since there was no known DNA sample from Janice—who'd disappeared without a trace and left behind no blood or hairs from which to get a sample—Isenberg would compare the tooth DNA with that of Janice's mother's DNA.

Another benefit of using mitochondrial DNA in criminal investigations is that exact segments of it are passed down from mother to child. If a particular segment of the mitochondrial DNA in the tooth is the same as the comparable segment of Betty Lippincott's DNA, there would be an extremely high likelihood that the tooth came from a descendant of Betty's. Since all of her children were alive and well except one, it would mean the tooth had almost certainly come from Janice.

Without being told why she was doing it, Betty Lippincott provided blood samples to FBI agents who came to her home in Florida. Mitochondrial DNA was extracted from Betty's blood and compared to the DNA from the tooth fragments.

Negative. The DNA sequences didn't match. The teeth had not come from the mouth of Janice Hartman.

It was a blow to the investigation. But the lack of a match also raised an unsettling question. If those weren't Janice's teeth buried under the Grace Lane Apartments, whose where they? Although the concrete had been poured long before John ever met Betty Fran Gladden, the tooth DNA was compared to mtDNA from Fran's daughter, Deanna. Not surprisingly, it also wasn't a match.

Authorities now were looking at a potential third victim.

With the excavation of the Grace Lane Apartments turning up no evidence that could be used against John, Hilland focused on the Indiana angle. Along with Michael telling the FBI that John had lived in the state—and was headed there with the box—authorities found an old résumé of John's listing as a reference a man named Scott A. Mintier of the Pullman-Standard company, a railroad car manufacturer in Hammond, Indiana.

When Scott and Eileen Mintier of Munster, Indiana, next to Hammond, were contacted by Hilland, the couple were "in total shock," Eileen recalled. John, she said, may have been "a little different," but he never struck them as violent. When she thinks about John now, and all the time he spent with them—and their daughters—she shudders.

Scott Mintier had met John in the mid-1970s when they worked at the Flxible Company in Ohio. This likely would have been shortly after Janice had disappeared and while Detective McGuire was investigating. As manager of manufacturing engineering, Scott supervised John for about a year and a half. As he would with all his employers, John had impressed his boss with his hard work and positive attitude. After Scott moved to Pullman-Standard to direct manufacturing and engineering, John contacted him in 1977 and asked for a job. Scott enthusiastically took him on again, and over the next two years Scott was both John's boss and friend.

"He would stop by and talk about work. He'd be invited for dinner," recalled Eileen Mintier. "I always got the impression John's parents were dead and that he was raised by his grandmother. He seemed very devoted to his grandmother. He said he lived with her and that she had done a lot for him. My impression was that he went home to her and sent her money."

The Mintiers remembered him as socially inept. He dressed to excess, in colorful shirts with wide ties and at times a velvet jacket. He explained to people that he used to play in a band and that's where he got his colorful wardrobe. He was skinny, with freckles and a bowl haircut, and was always smiling a bit too wide, a grin that was so big it was half gums. But behind the smile, something seemed sad about him. "I felt kind of sorry for him," Eileen said. "He didn't seem to have a lot of friends. I thought this kid has had maybe a tough life. He was outgoing with us. He was loud, he smiled a lot, but was fidgety; he never seemed to stop moving, even when seated at the table. When he spoke, it was often in a voice that was just a little too loud."

Still, the Mintier family found something endearing in John. A sports car enthusiast, John was always heard before he was seen, roaring up to the Mintiers' house in a customized black-and-silver Indianapolis 500 Pace Car Corvette. He also drove a turquoise Mustang. All he seemed to talk about was either work at Pullman or his cars. He had good manners, helping clear the table and washing dishes. And he got along well with the two girls, Scott Mintier's step-daughter Kathy McDonald, then 18, and her half-sister Theresa, 8. John would horse around with Theresa in the back yard and help her with her math homework. Once, Theresa's family offered an incentive to help her pass a test on multiplication tables: a concert by Shaun Cassidy, a teen heartthrob of the day. With John's help, she did pass, and it was John who took her to the concert.

As nice as he was to Theresa, it became clear that 27-year-old John was particularly interested in Kathy, nine years his junior, who worked at Pullman with her father and John. "He followed her around like a puppy dog," said Richard Anthony Gromlovits, a manufacturing engineering consultant at Pullman-Standard.

"I know he was sweet on Kathy. Scott and I talked about it," said Eileen Mintier. "That's probably why he hung around the house so much." Kathy shared John's interest in sports cars, and he would help her repair her car. "They did go out, not really on dates, maybe just to grab something to eat," said Eileen. "He never did anything aggressive. He did once try to make it into something more, but Kathy quelled that right away. It wasn't that she disliked him. She just didn't like him that way."

"He was a friend of the family and a friend of mine," Kathy would recall. "We both had family in Ohio, so on the weekend he would drive to Ohio and we would go visit family and friends. We would go roller-skating. He tutored in accounting."

During one outing, John and Kathy went to a family friend's house—an artist—where John bought an oil painting that Eileen had had her eye on for $700. John gave it to Eileen and Scott on their wedding anniversary. When the couple thanked him for such a generous gift, he responded, "No, thank you, for how nice you've been to me."

But of all the things that people remembered about John, one stood out. Even though he seemed to have a crush on Kathy, he struck many as feminine. It wasn't just his personality; it was his clothes, the colorful outfits and wild ties. And he wore a women's watch—a small, delicate thing with a green face surrounded by gemstones. At work, employees began calling John "homo" and "fag," forcing John's friend/supervisor Scott to call John into his office and tell him to stop wearing the watch. "Some of the other guys were making fun of it, and also his job required that he provide liaison activity between the people on the floor, which were basically mechanics, welders, typical factory workers, and the engineering department upstairs," said Scott. "And the people on the floor can be a little rough."

John agreed to remove the offending timepiece, which took some of the heat off him at work. But that didn't end the story of the watch. One day in 1978, Kathy told John that she had seen a green Seiko watch that she wanted to buy.

"Don't purchase one," John told her. "I have one I will give you."

Several days later, while standing in front of his Mustang parked at the Mintiers' home, John pulled a watch out of his pocket and handed it to Kathy.

"Here," he said, "this is for you."

It was a silver women's Bulova watch with a jewel beveled "J" and diamonds. Although Kathy didn't know it at the time, it was the watch her father had told John to stop wearing at work.

"It's beautiful. Thank you very much," she said. "Where did you get it?"

The watch wasn't in a box and appeared to have been worn. Smith hesitated. She asked him again.

"It belonged to my wife," he said.

"I didn't know you were married," said Kathy, surprised. She asked him if he had any children as a result of the marriage, and he said no. She asked him if he was still married, and he said no.

He said his wife had died.

Hilland had gotten this information from Kathy during an interview at her home in Connecticut. He finished by asking her if by any chance she still had that watch. Kathy said that her home had been broken into and that everything was stolen.

Except the watch.

On July 23, 1999, Hilland took custody of the green Bulova watch with the jeweled "J." Witnesses would identify this as the same watch that John and Lodema Hartman had purchased for Janice, the same watch that Janice had kept in the divorce settlement, and the same watch that John had told police that Janice was wearing when she vanished.

Hilland continued to reconstruct John's history after Janice disappeared, finding that in mid-1979, John had left Pullman-Standard to work for Copco Industries in South Bend, Indiana. He pulled away, too, from the Mintiers— no more dinners, no more tutoring Theresa—but he did keep in touch with Kathy by phone. At Copco, John was hired by Joseph Dabrowski, a friend of Scott Mintier's. While working at Copco, John also appeared to be making additional money on the side in real estate. Friends and co-workers got the impression that John owned or managed several apartment buildings in Ohio—in Seville and Cleveland. John had asked his old friend Dennis Evans to help him do maintenance on the buildings, because John was now living in Indiana and couldn't do it himself. Dennis held that job for about a year.

One Friday, John left work early—or early for him. Normally, he would stay late on Fridays, bringing the same work ethic to his new job at Copco as he had to others. He told Dabrowski he had to leave in a hurry; there was a problem with the Seville apartment building.

The following Monday, John wasn't at work. There was no phone call, no explanation—highly unusual. Then, on Tuesday, he showed up.

"John, where were you yesterday?" Dabrowski asked. "I didn't have a call, I didn't receive anything."

"Oh," John said, "I've got a long story to tell you."

Years later, Dabrowski would recall: "It was such a strange one that I have never forgotten it, because I like to repeat the story to other friends."

This is how the story went, according to Dabrowski: "He said he was driving from Seville at approximately two to three a.m. Sunday night or Monday morning, and he was high-balling it down Interstate 80 in his Corvette. And he said, 'I must have been going pretty fast, because apparently the cops were trying to catch me and they couldn't catch up to my car.' He said that they blocked off Interstate 80 with two semis because obviously they couldn't catch him.

"The next day, he said: 'I went to the judge,' and in front of the judge, the arresting officer told him that John Smith had been arrested for reckless driving—anything over a hundred miles per hour is considered reckless driving—and the judge looked down at the ticket and he says, 'Wait a minute, this only says seventy miles an hour. What's the problem?' And the arresting officer said, 'Judge, you're not reading the ticket right, we estimated his speed at one hundred and seventy miles an hour.'

"And I said, 'I have never heard anybody who got a ticket that high.' "

Smith told Dabrowski he was in jail overnight before appearing in court, and that's why he missed work on Monday.

Reviewing Dabrowksi's recollection, Hilland thought that this could have been a cover story. In reality, the agent thought, John may have been "high-balling" in his Corvette down to Seville, Ohio, to pick up the box containing Janice's remains.

Wrapping up the Indiana phase of the investigation, Hilland had more pieces of the puzzle that was John Smith's life. More important, he had Kathy Mintier, who not only provided yet another statement from John indicating that he knew his wife was dead, but also still had the watch. The investigation, which had started and stalled so many times, was building momentum again. The challenge was to keep it going—and not let this new information and these new witnesses go to waste. Somehow they had to use it to put more pressure on John. But how?

The answer would be Michael Smith.

CHAPTER 14

Although John's brother had at last purged his demons and told all to the FBI, his relationship with federal agents wasn't always a good one. They continued to question him, and one interview in particular, by an agent he wouldn't identify, was rough. "It was not a very good meeting," Michael recalled. "I no longer trusted them. I mean, the agent involved, we were talking and out of nowhere I had an agent [in] my face spitting in my face, screaming F-words at me . . . And that's when I decided I need something to protect me." While Michael felt confident he would not be charged with murder or aiding and abetting, he did worry about being hit with the rather unusual, but appropriate in this case, abuse-of-corpse charge. On June 11, 1999, about two weeks after giving the formal statement, he obtained from authorities a two-page non-prosecution agreement that protected him against criminal charges.

With this agreement in the bank, Michael Smith was ready to do one more chore for the FBI. "They wanted me to call my brother and ask him certain questions, and they wanted to judge his reaction to them," said Michael. "And I said OK."

Michael couldn't call John because he didn't have his

number, but John, unaware that Michael was working with the FBI, was calling him frequently to get updates on the investigation, with particular interest in the excavation of the Grace Lane Apartments, which had generated coverage in the local newspaper. The ABC news show *20/20* was also researching a story about the two missing Mrs. Smiths, and had tried to interview John in California. But the FBI wanted Michael to get more information out of his brother. "We had to establish a time when John thought it was safe to call me," said Michael. "I told him that my wife took piano lessons on a certain night of the week and that she was gone from a certain time period, so I started getting phone calls at that time period because he knew I was alone and I could talk to him."

One evening in June or early July, during the fake piano lesson, John called his brother. The tape machine began to record:

"Hi, how ya doing?" John asked.

"OK, how are you?"

"I'm excellent, thank you."

"Oh, that's good."

"Diana's doing a little better," John said, referring to his wife. "She hasn't had a flare-up with her problem lately, so that's good."

"What problem's she got?" Michael asked.

"She's got a kidney problem. Uh, she hates to use the big C-word."

"Hmm."

"Yeah," John said. "But, they've got her on medication. What they told her, though, is they want to put her on chemo, which doesn't exactly sound like anything good, but they said that it could either heal her or it doesn't heal her it will eventually take out the kidney and she'd eventually end up on dialysis, so she's not crazy about making that decision."

"No way."

"So she thinks as long as her condition is stable and she just stays on the medication, then as far as she's concerned she can just stay on it forever. I don't think the doctor's exactly thrilled with that viewpoint."

"Hum," Michael said.

"There's worse," John went on. "She's had a—jeeze—a whole bunch of good days now so that's real good."

"Yeah, yeah, that's good."

"She went through, for a while there she's had some bad times. What happens is, she retains fluid."

"Oh."

"Even though she's on diuretics, she'll just, like, blow up. One night it was strange, looked like something out of *Willy Wonka and the Candy Factory*."

"Yeah, Tanya"—Michael's wife—"swells up like that too."

"I was amazed at how fast it did this one time," John said. "It was like you could almost watch her getting bigger."

"Really? Tanya's not like that. Usually she eats pizza or something, you know."

"It'll trigger something?"

"I think it's the salt or something," Michael said. "She'll swell way up to where she can barely get her wedding rings off to go to bed or whatever. You know, 'cause usually she doesn't wear her diamond in the kitchen or whatever. It's hard to get off."

"Yeah."

"So, you know," Michael said, continuing to talk about health matters, even though the FBI wanted him to bring up murder, "she'll swell up like that, you know, all kinds of crazy stuff."

"Yeah."

"Hmm."

"That's—that's kinda weird, but—" John said.

"I mean you can actually see her swell up?" Michael asked.

"You know, I could, because over a period of an hour you can actually see where the buttons were pulling, you know, kinda getting tighter on her blouse. I notice that."

"No way."

"Yeah, that noticeable," John said.

"That's kinda weird," Michael said.

"Yeah, I thought so."

"Hmm."

"She's only done that once," John continued. "The, ah, onset of the attacks I guess, or whatever you want to call them, used to be more gentle and she'd get more warning. Now they're—now they occur rapid with a lot less fore-warning than they did. So I don't know if that's a good sign or whatever."

"That's pretty crazy," Michael said, now trying to change the subject. "Anyhow, Tanya's at a piano lesson."

"Oh, that's nice."

"Anyhow, I can't talk to you when Tanya's here," Michael said. "I can't really tell you what's going on or say anything about it when she's here. It's been driving me Goddamn crazy, John. I ain't kidding ya."

John responded with a non-sequitur. "Oh, I imagine they will be."

"I mean they are absolutely driving me nuts, you know," said Michael. "I'm serious."

"I can believe it," John said. "It's like I don't know what they think you know, but, you don't know anything."

"Absolutely nuts. I ain't kidding ya."

"Hum."

"Serious," Michael said, "you know, I believe that they are about ready to come back and start digging around Seville."

"I kinda heard that rumor," said John, "but I don't have any idea why. I don't know who's kickin' all this or who's trying to get themselves out of some kind of situation, you know, something."

"I don't know," Michael said.

"I think they're real receptive to listening—is part of the problem now—because anybody who invents any kind of story, you know, they are going to listen to, which is really bizarre," John said.

"You know, the whole thing's crazy," Michael said.

"Yeah," John said.

"Anyhow, that's just nuts. You know, I wanted you to know that that's going on, you know. I've taken a lot of shit here, John."

"I'm sure you have."

"Yeah, you know."

"I know Diane's taken a bunch of shit," said John. "It just doesn't make sense why people should get such shit."

"I don't know," Michael said. "But there is one thing I've got to ask you, and I never, ever want to discuss this again, John."

"OK."

"The box in Granddad's—"

"Yeah, the goat, yeah, what about it?" John said.

Goat? Michael knew there was no goat in the box.

"It's nowhere around Seville, is it?" he asked.

"No, no, the goat isn't anywhere near Seville."

"OK."

"That was a great practical joke by somebody," said John. "I've had a couple weird practical jokes like that, including the one in, ah, New Jersey where they did this big dagger thing and so on at a locker at the plant. You know, I don't know why people are sick like that and want to harass you like that."

"Hmm."

"I just think that harassment and those sick type of jokes like that are high on the list, it's just—"

"But that box is nowhere?"

"No," said John, "definitely not."

"OK, good."

"No, um . . ."

"I mean, sssssschwoo," Michael repeated.

"Yeah, I know, I know," John said. "It's like all the other practical jokes and everything can get construed into something, and I'm sure they will eventually, are or whatever."

"I don't want to discuss this again."

"Yeah, OK."

"That's cool. But anyhow," Michael said, steering to safer conversation territory—baseball—"so I guess a few of the Indians made it to the All Star team."

"Did they really?"

"Yeah," said Michael. "Like Manny; Manny made it. Thome made it. Let's see, I am trying to think who else. Oh, Robbie Alomar made it. You know, all that good, fun stuff like that. Let's see. They're looking for a third baseman. You know, Fryman's hurt again."

"Again?" said John.

"He probably won't be back until the end of August, I believe. They've got Enrique Wilson playing there now. So, you know, all that good stuff. But the Indians are doing pretty good. I don't even know who they're playing tonight. I think the Twins."

"Yeah."

"You know, I'm out there playing in my yard, and I've got corn that's coming on," Michael said, "and it's just, I don't know, maybe four, four inches long, and it's not even really an ear yet, and the coons got into it and ate it already."

"Aw, shit," said John—and this time, it was John who steered the conversation back to the murder case, still trying to get details out of Michael.

"When's the last time you've been harassed?"

"Probably about last week sometime," said Michael.

"Really."

"Oh, yeah, I just think they're coming back."

"Na, I don't get it," John said. "I mean what can they possibly think you know, or whatever?"

"I don't know," said Michael. "But anyhow, it's just a— I don't know what they think I know."

"Yeah, it's just, I don't know, the questions are bizarre and we keep going into these circles about so-and-so said this and so-and-so said that," John said. "And we checked— um, I had my lawyer chase down a whole list of this stuff.

And guess what, every single thing they said panned out to be a zero."

"Hmm."

"They weren't able to verify a single thing, you know," said John. "And of course when they are telling you that, they're: 'Oh, why would so-and-so have a, what, reason to lie?' or whatever. It's just amazing. It's getting so sick, sickening."

"Yeah, it's pretty tough here," Michael said.

"Yeah, I know," said John. "And we've got the famous ambush by *20/20*, and boy, that was tough."

"What?"

"Oh, yes, we got ambushed by, um, oh, jeeze, this was several weeks back, we got ambushed by *20/20* one morning," said John.

"Oh, really?" Michael said.

"Oh really, yeah."

Then there's a sound that John hears on the phone line. "Did you hit a button or something?" Michael asked.

"No, the phone cord acts up," Michael said.

"Oh, sorry. But, yeah, you know, that's . . ."

"You just don't know."

"Yeah, I don't want to talk about this no more."

"Yeah, OK."

"It just, um . . ."

"It's just terrible, but keep me informed what the heck is going on," said John.

"Yeah, yeah, but only when Tanya's not here," said Michael.

"Yeah."

"Other than that, I'm pretty sure that guy from New York is gonna come back to try to start digging some more," Michael said.

"I don't know," said John. "I can't figure out what somebody's telling him, so . . ."

"I don't know. Maybe it's Steven"—their step-brother, Steven Malz.

"It's gotta be Steven, I guess," said John. "I mean, I

don't know. Somebody's making something up. You'd think after they've made a fool of themselves several times and gave them bad information that they'd figure that out or something, you know."

"Yeah," said Michael—the real informant.

"Anyway . . ."

"Well, that's basically it, you know," Michael said. "Didn't want to talk to you about anything else, I guess. Just the Indians and the usual stuff. Yeah, but I was really, um, you know what I mean."

"Yeah, I know what you mean," John said.

"You know, I've taken a beating," Michael said.

"Who hasn't been taking a beating? And no one deserves a beating."

"No. And I didn't do anything, you know."

"Yeah, I mean, you know, it's like why— Who is so sick that they want to hurt a bunch of, you know, innocent people and so on, you know?" John said.

"Yeah, it's . . . it's . . . I don't know," Michael said. "Well, anyhow, what time is it? I want to make sure I'm not on the phone when they get home. I better get out of here pretty soon, 'cause Andy's supposed to be home sometime here. Well, he was supposed to be home earlier, but you know he's always late."

"Yeah."

"You know how that goes, they're always late," Michael said. "But I guess Marathon's gonna start digging tanks out." Authorities had arranged to have the Marathon gas company dig up the tanks at their grandparents' house to look for Janice's remains.

"Finally," John said.

"Yes, sometime here pretty soon," Michael said. "I don't know what Mother's doing with the estate." Their mother Grace was in charge of the family's estate, including their grandparents' home, since Sam Malz and their grandparents had died. "I couldn't tell ya."

"Yeah," John said.

"I have no idea," Michael said. "You know, it's just crazy."

"Oh, well," John said.

"OK, well, you know, it was nice talking to you again, John."

"Yeah, take care."

"All right, we'll see you later."

"Bye."

"Bye."

As they went back over the phone call, investigators knew that John Smith had not said anything incriminating enough to haul him in to jail. But once the brothers got through talking about their wives' medical problems, John did provide one more piece of damaging evidence: his admission that he was aware of the box, even if he did say there was a goat inside, and that it was a practical joke. Authorities had corroboration for the most important detail of Michael's statement.

Now, they wanted to tape-record another conversation in the hopes that John would say more. The plan was to bait him into incriminating statements by having Michael say he was being subpoenaed to appear before a grand jury and that he was going to take a polygraph test. The idea was to unnerve John—make him think the investigation was heating up more than it really was. Part of it was a ruse: Michael had received no such subpoena. He was, though, submitting to a polygraph. Investigators also wanted Michael to press John more on the box, challenging him on the claims that there was a goat, not Janice, inside.

The stakes were high: Michael had to keep his cool as he lied to his brother so as not to tip John off that Michael had become an FBI informant.

On the night of July 22, 1999, Michael received another call from John, who had just gotten off his usually long shift at LaForza in Escondido.

"Hey, how you doing tonight." John asked, the tape-recorder running.

"Hey, I've got some serious deep shit here, John."

"What?"

"Can you talk?" Michael asked.

"Yeah," John said.

"OK, listen, you know that mother-fucking FBI agent, that Bob Hilland son-of-a-bitch?"

"Yeah."

"Well, he brought me a grand jury subpoena. I gotta go to New York and testify in front of a grand jury."

"When?"

"On the fifth."

"Of September?"

"Yes. Or August, August fifth, like two weeks from to-day."

"Holy shit," John said.

"Yeah, I mean, like Goddamn, John, come on. You know, I'm scared to death here, you know."

"Hmm."

"Seriously, you know, I . . . I don't have any idea here. I'm telling you what I'm gonna do: I'm going there to New York and I'm gonna tell them the truth. That's exactly what I'm gonna do. I'm gonna tell them we seen you build a box, Granddad and I opened the box, we found Jan in it, you know. That's what I'm a doin'. I cannot see any other way out of this. I'm not gonna go to jail for you, John."

"No, I wouldn't expect you to, OK?"

"You know, there's just no way around it," Michael said.

"OK," John said.

"Unless you got some idea."

"No, I don't have any idea," John said.

"Unless there's . . . Unless there's some kind of some-thing," Michael said.

"No there isn't. I mean that wasn't. I don't know what else to tell you," John said. "You know, that was a joke or something that somebody dropped off in the box. That wasn't Jan in it. But if that's what you believe . . ."

"John, that was Jan in the box. We opened the box up, her fucking legs were cut off. Do you want me to con-tinue?"

"No," John said. "Anyway, all right, so you're going to New York on August fifth, huh?"

"Yeah, and here's the best part," Michael said.

"OK."

"I get to do a polygraph test the next day."

"You do?"

"Yes, I do."

"OK."

"So I'm not going to lie," Michael said.

"No, I don't expect you to," John said.

"Yeah, it's real simple."

"OK."

"You know, I don't know what else to say," Michael said.

"Well, I don't either," John said.

"I mean that wasn't no goat or no joke or nothing like that, John."

"OK."

"I can tell ya."

"All right."

"I mean, Jack and Granddad opened it up to begin with, and then Granddad and I opened it up later," Michael said. "I had nothing to do with this."

"OK," John said.

"You know," Michael said.

"All right," John said.

"I . . . I . . . I don't know what else to say," Michael said.

"No, no, don't say anything else," John said.

"You know."

"OK."

"I mean . . . I mean . . ." Michael stuttered.

"All right."

"What do you expect me to tell them?" Michael asked.

"I don't expect you to tell them anything but what you think," John said.

"What I think?"

"Or know or whatever. I mean . . ."

"You know, that's . . . I know what I know. I mean,

that's something that's stuck with me for years. I mean I've had nightmares over this," Michael said.

"OK," John replied.

"I mean, I've had nightmares where Jan chased me down the road and beat me with her legs, John."

"OK."

"You know?"

"OK."

"Well, I don't know what to say. I really don't, you know."

"Mmm-hmm," John said.

"But that's . . . That's what I'm gonna do, you know," Michael said. "And what will probably happen, I will probably wind up going to jail immediately. You know, I . . . I don't know. So I imagine they'll probably come pick you up, too."

"OK."

"We're talking two weeks from now, so just look for them."

"All right," John said.

"OK. I . . . I don't know."

"OK."

"I mean, I really don't know," Michael continued. "They've got me really upset here. I just don't know."

"OK, well, when did this all come about?" John asked.

"Pardon me?"

"When did this come about?"

"It came out last Friday," Michael said. "He showed— Bob Hilland showed up here at my door at about six at night and gave it to me. It's like, 'Holy shit, what a way to start a fucking weekend.' "

"Yeah, really."

"You know? But this is crazy."

"OK."

"You know, they're getting serious here, John. I don't know what to tell ya."

"OK, well, I appreciate it."

"All right. Well, at least you know," said Michael, then he sighed. "Man."

"Yeah."

"But I'm not going to jail," Michael said, "and I'm not gonna go up there and lie. I mean, I didn't do anything."

"No," John said.

"The only thing I'm guilty of doing is calling you to come get her," Michael said. "That's it, you know? If they wanted to do that . . ."

"Well, all right," John said. "Are you there?"

"Yeah."

"All right, well . . ."

"You know, what do you want me to tell them, you know? I . . . I don't . . . you know, I . . . I just don't know, John."

"OK. Well, that's . . . I love ya, you know," John said. "You just got to do what is right, Mike."

"All right," Michael said. "Well, I guess I will talk to you later. Good luck."

"All right, thanks," John said.

"All right," Michael said.

"Take care," John said.

"Bye."

"Bye."

With the exception of the profanity, John maintained his composure during the conversation, never agreeing with Michael's repeated claims that the legless Janice was in the box. But the call clearly unnerved John; he wouldn't have cursed otherwise.

After that phone call, John had dinner with Diane, who picked him up at LaForza and went to a restaurant in San Marcus ten minutes away. "He was very nervous, very agitated for some reason," recalled Diane. "He didn't eat, which was unlike him. He was just very nervous. I could tell that there was something going on, and prior to leaving the restaurant he gave me all of the money he had in his wallet, and then we left the restaurant and I took him back to LaForza, presumably to pick up his car to follow me." John was to go back to her home. Diane couldn't remember exactly when she dropped him off. She estimated she returned home at 8:30 or 9 p.m.

But John wasn't behind her.

He had disappeared.

When John didn't arrive at LaForza the next day, Friday, July 23, Diane called the FBI and went with her daughter Summer McGowin to the Escondido Police Department to file a missing persons report. The FBI office in California paged Hilland, who was still in Connecticut picking up the watch from Kathy. The printout on his pager read: "911." When he called back, he was told, "John is gone." The FBI had been keeping only a loose watch on him and had no idea where he was. Fearing that Michael may have pushed John too hard, the FBI quickly moved Michael and his family out of their home and Wadsworth, Ohio, and checked them into a hotel. The family then moved to another hotel the next night. Michael thought the FBI was over-reacting. He brought his family to a relative's house on Sunday before returning home Monday. As the weekend wore on, and there was no word from John, Hilland began to think he might have committed suicide. When Hilland returned to his New York office on Monday, a colleague ribbed him: "Congratulations, you're the first guy to start a case with two missing persons and end with three."

But John wasn't missing, and he hadn't killed himself. At noon Monday, John called Diane to ask her to pick him up at LaForza. "He was very skinny," said Summer, who accompanied her mother to get John. "He didn't look like he had eaten the whole time he was gone. He was very dirty, unshaven, and he was drinking an orange soda." The women brought him to Diane's home in Oceanside and asked him about his lost weekend. "He told me that the FBI had him in a hotel across the freeway [from LaForza in Escondido]," said Diane. "He told us that there were three or four FBI agents in the room with him and they—when he asked to leave or call his lawyer, they wouldn't let him use the phone, and that they stood in front of the doorway. They had suits on and dark glasses, and one of the women, the woman FBI agent that was there, roughed him up." Eventually they let him go.

John had apparently given the same account to his lawyer, because the attorney called Hilland and berated him and the FBI for subjecting John to a brutal weekend.

Hilland chuckled.

"What, may I ask, is so funny?" the lawyer asked.

"I find you and your client so funny," Hilland said.

The next day, Smith was back at work at LaForza, sporting a nasty cut on his forehead. "He said he'd hit his head on the door of the car," said co-worker Trevor Haywood. "He said he was trying to get in, he dropped his keys and he bent down and hit his head." But then he changed his story. "He said that he got that from the FBI," recalled Haywood, who didn't press the issue. "I just didn't want to get into it any longer. I'd had a long enough time with John living with me and . . . hearing these things that the FBI told [him]."

Diane was losing faith in John. The FBI and Fran's family had been in contact with her and her daughter Summer, passing on updates about the investigation. Diane now knew many of the details of Janice and Fran's disappearances, including John's inconsistent statements and seeming lack of concern, and Michael's claim that John may have stuffed Janice's body in a box. As Hilland had asked her to do back in May, Diane gave the matter serious thought, weighing what authorities and Fran's relatives had said about John against John's own stories.

One day, Diane said to John: "Tell Summer about the box."

Summer and Diane would have different recollections of what he said. Summer said John told them a box was dropped off on the front porch of his grandfather's house and that John's brother Michael claimed there was a dead girl inside. John said he never looked in the box. But he wanted to get rid of it, so he put the box in the back of a truck, drove out to a field and dumped it on the side of the road. Diane would recall that John told them the box was dropped off at his grandfather's house, but that it had a dead goat inside. He said he then dumped the box on the side of the road along a farm somewhere.

As much as Diane wanted to believe her husband, this was getting to be too much. Diane and her daughter confronted him again, several weeks later, at a restaurant on San Diego's Shelter Island.

"I asked him if he killed Jan," said Summer. "He never answered . . ."

CHAPTER 15

The idea originated with the FBI profilers in Quantico. Because he had such a common name, and because he traveled so much and had so many jobs, it was likely investigators still didn't have all the information about John Smith that they needed, including whether he'd had any other wives besides Janice, Fran and Diane. It was the profilers who had suggested taking the case to the national media. In the fall of 1999, ABC's news magazine *20/20* which had irritated John with what he called the "ambush" interview, reported on the two missing Mrs. Smiths. The show quoted Hilland as saying, "I'd have a better chance at winning the lottery than having two wives disappear on me."

As they had done six years earlier, Fran's daughter now remarried and going by Deanna Weiss, and sister Sherrie also revved up the publicity campaign, cooperating with the *20/20* reports and, this time, taking their cause to the Internet. An on-line chat the women and ABC newsman John Miller conducted would be the most extensive interview they would provide, as they led the cyberspace audience through the long, tortuous ordeal that had begun when Fran met John.

The women spoke of how little they'd known about John

at first. "He just told us that when he and Fran married that he was just so happy to have a family," Sherrie said. "He had said he came from a totally dysfunctional home. He had not had contact with his mother in eight years. The only member of his family that he shows any affection for at all was his maternal grandmother. He has two brothers— we never knew he had two brothers. He said he had a sister, then no sister. Take that type of background, and solicitation of prostitutes, and you know if he had a low opinion of women, or a low opinion of himself. Anyone with contact with John should realize that this man is a chameleon— he becomes whatever you want to see.

"We all referred to him as John Boy, as in John Boy Walton," said Sherrie, who described John as "very meek and mild." Except for the usual marital spats, the women never knew of any big problems until February 1991 when John abruptly filed for divorce, then just as abruptly withdrew the petition, leaving Fran's head spinning. The women said that they would later find out that John had a girlfriend in Connecticut. Still, in hindsight, they detected a controlling aspect to John. "John was a very generous person. He gave Fran anything she asked him for, but it had to come from him," said Sherrie. "To boost his ego, she did not even go to the grocery store without him, because it made him look like the super-provider if he whipped out the money to pay for the groceries."

Deanna recalled her final conversation with her mother, discussing Fran's broken hip and the sewing she was going to do. And the women told the cyber-audience of the mysterious—and highly suspicious—circumstances of Fran's disappearance. "This woman was recovering from a broken hip," said Sherrie. "She was eight weeks out from even getting a job. John had told us that he had given her money to travel. A woman in that condition, if she decides to leave, would at least take her toothbrush and toothpaste. If she has little money, she would take her belongings, because she had no means to replace them."

The women said that after the police investigation had

begun, John had failed a polygraph test. "Per his own words, he failed it miserably," said Deanna. "I said, 'What do you mean you failed, if you said you had nothing to hide?' He said, 'I guess I wasn't very good at it.' "

Sherrie added, "When I confronted John about it, he said he was physically and mentally exhausted."

Although the women said they had always thought of John as a mild-mannered guy, they theorized that he had killed both Janice and Fran out of anger because they became inconvenient. "I think it was a flash-temper thing," said Deanna. "And he just did it."

The women praised the three main investigators on the case, but expressed frustration that prosecutors had not filed charges against John. Deanna said, "As a family, we cannot say enough wonderful things about Mike Dansbury of New Jersey, Brian Potts of Ohio and Bob Hilland of the FBI. They have worked tirelessly on this. But it takes a prosecutor to carry it now." Sherrie added, "As a family, these guys have literally held us together. I don't know how we could have made it without them. We need help. We need someone to listen to these guys."

In a question-and-answer session, one cyberspace audience member asked the women: "If you could ask only one question of John Smith, what would it be?"

"The one question I would ask: Where did you put my sister?" said Sherrie. "If you want to get rid of me, the best way would be to give me my sister back, and then I don't care what happens to him."

Deanna said her question was: "Where did you bury her?"

The women said they held out hope that Betty Fran would be found. "We are very confident that at one point in time she will be found, because we will not give up until she is found," said Deanna.

Sherrie said she had no fear of John. "John knows that we know who he is. We see him coming. We know who he is. He preys on people who don't know who he is."

Miller told another audience member that the then-current Mrs. Smith "has been informed of everything by the authorities. We are told that she has discussed it with her husband and still has confidence in him."

And, in fact, Diane sent out that very message to the public, albeit anonymously. In an interview with KGTV in San Diego, Diane—speaking under condition that she not be identified—said that police had the "wrong man." Authorities were baffled: she pledged her support for John even as she and her daughter were grilling him.

John, meanwhile, fought back. His attorney, Michael J. McCabe, issued a fierce defense of his client and lashed out at what he called the overly aggressive tactics of the FBI.

In a letter to John Miller of ABC, McCabe wrote:

Dear Mr. Miller:

In response to your letter of October 6, 1999, concerning my client, Mr. John D. Smith, Mr. Smith has no information as to the current whereabouts of his former wives. Although Mr. Smith has cooperated fully with all of the investigators, both state and federal, who have looked into these matters over the years, he has never been provided with the results of their investigation. Whenever he or his attorney have inquired into the status of these investigations, they have been met with the same answer: "You're a suspect so we can't tell you what we have."

The most recent tactic of the FBI and the investigative agencies acting in concert with them appears to be to make Mr. Smith's life as difficult as possible. To that end, as you are probably aware, an investigative task force headed by FBI Agent Robert Hilland showed up unannounced on May 5, 1999, and subjected Mr. Smith to intense interrogation over two days in an effort to secure his confession. Failing that, the announced intention of the task force is threefold:

1) To convince Mr. Smith's wife, Diane, to leave him;
2) To cause him to lose his job;
3) To cause him to lose his friends.

As Agent Hilland announced at the commencement of the interrogation session, "Your life as you know it is over."

These tactics, and the attendant leaks to the press, will not have the desired result because Mr. Smith is innocent of any involvement in the unfortunate disappearance of his former wives.

Very truly yours,
Michael J. McCabe.

The publicity and the relentless efforts of authorities and the tag-team of Deanna and Sherrie were beginning to take their toll on John's marriage, in spite of what Diane was telling local TV. In late 1999, Deanna and Sherrie hired a private investigator to trail John in San Diego because, they said, they wanted to protect Diane. "I didn't know that she knew the animal that she was dealing with," recalled Deanna, who was shocked that John had remarried after all that had happened. "That's a tough thing to know that he's doing the same thing," Deanna said. "You know, he's got the opportunity to do the same thing and so we had the investigators just tracking him from work and back."

By now, Deanna and Diane were in daily contact, and Diane—growing leery of John—would help the women with their amateur detective work. Diane searched John's pockets and snooped into his computer files when he was at work. She also rummaged through a storage unit that John had rented. Deanna said John kept Merrill Lynch financial documents showing a highest balance of $98,000 in cash. This was in addition to the customized white 1990 Ferrari that he had given Diane. The women also found something even more disturbing in the storage unit: color photographs of two women. One picture showed a younger John standing next to a petite young woman in front of a small airplane. Several other pictures showed a woman with feathered 1980s hair posing in front of a jewelry store. The pictures were provided to authorities. Nobody knew the identities of these women. Investigators wondered if these were additional wives or girlfriends of John's. What had become of them? Investigators thought of the tooth fragments and feared the worst.

On December 17, 1999, Diane had reached her limit. She formally separated from John, filing an annulment with family court Judge Gerald Jessup of the Superior Court of San Diego County. She would later tell *The Daily Record* of Wooster, Ohio, that she'd changed her phone number and the locks, and that her daughter had moved in with her so she wouldn't be alone. "I was careful," Diane told the paper. "I was very, very careful."

Despite the precautions, there was a close call. After John was served with the papers, he drove to Diane's house, jumped out of his car, and bounded up the stairs, two and three at a time, his face as angry as Summer had ever seen it. John tried to break the front window, but couldn't. He broke open the front door instead and raced into the kitchen, where Diane was on the phone, calling the police.

Then John saw Summer. Suddenly, his anger subsided. His face softened. He was now the quiet, nice guy that he usually was.

The transformation was chilling.

A few days later, Diane and Summer were in their car at an intersection about two blocks away from their house when they saw John pull up next to them. They each rolled down their windows to talk to each other. John said of Diane's decision to file for separation: "This is what my last wife tried to do to me."

Frightened, the women drove away, and Diane would file a restraining order against John.

"Due to my intense fear of [John Smith], I have not dared to separate from him, or file the necessary documents to institute an annulment or divorce . . . until I could secure restraining orders preventing [Smith] from coming near me, my residence or place of employment," it read. "My fear is based on [his] explosive temper, the discovery of [his] two previous marriages and the fact that both of his previous wives have disappeared and are presumed dead." She added, "I am informed that the families of [Smith's] previous wives believe that they are dead and that [Smith] is responsible for their deaths. I believe that the FBI and other law enforcement agencies also believe this."

In the court papers, she said that she had married Smith on Sept. 5, 1998, after a "very brief dating relationship," and found that he was an "accomplished liar, and although he exhibits a gentle face, he has an explosive temper." Diane said that among the lies he told her was that he had been married to his previous wife, Betty Fran, for seven years, when in fact it was only seventeen months. "He told me very little facts regarding the marriage."

After seeking the protection order, Diane filed for divorce. In the December 17, 1999, papers she sought financial support and temporary use of their Ferrari. She also asked that John relinquish any guns he owned.

After the excavation of the Grace Lane Apartments had turned up no sign of Janice's remains—but perhaps those of another victim—the search turned to the home of John and Michael's grandparents. That's where the box had been stored for five years, according to Michael, and while he had seen John drive off with it, there was still the possibility that he'd returned to bury the box or other remains there. From late September through mid-October 1999, detectives conducted three searches of the little white Pleasant Street house, each time with the consent of John's mother, Grace Malz, who handled the Chaneys' estate. In two of the searches, on October 6 and October 17, authorities exca-vated the ground under the brick flooring of the garage and dug up the old gasoline storage tank from the now-closed Marathon station. Detective Potts crawled around inside the tank with a flashlight. He would find only disappointment. The searches of the grandparents' home produced nothing.

Meanwhile, Wayne County Assistant Prosecutor Jocelyn Stefancin was doing some digging of her own—in the law books. "We were looking at the possibility of prosecuting John Smith without a body," she said. She found some cases in Ohio, including one that was similar to the Smith case, with a wife missing and presumed dead but no body located. The wife had left behind her eyeglasses and car. She was close to her family, but had never gotten in touch with them after she disappeared. These facts fit closely with those in both the disappearances of which John was sus-pected with one major difference: "There was a little bit of blood found in a car," she said.

In the Janice Hartman case, authorities didn't have any-thing as incriminating as a bloodstain. Still, Stefancin thought she could prosecute a no-body homicide case, and was ready to present the evidence that had been collected so far to the grand jury for indictment. Though it was hard-ly a slam-dunk, she had tried—and won—weaker cases in her career. She had Michael Smith's damaging testimony, the suspicious circumstances of Janice's disappearance, and John Smith's different and outlandish explanations for her disappearance, not to mention his seeming lack of concern for her welfare. She also had his voice on tape in the phone calls to Michael and Sheila Sautter. And she had Hilland, who could recount John's emotional outburst from the 1999 interrogation that he didn't want to lie anymore.

By October 1999, Stefancin was so confident with the state of the case that she scheduled a grand jury presenta-tion. Then, at the last minute, her boss, elected prosecutor Martin Frantz, pulled the plug. He was concerned that they didn't have the legal goods. He implored Stefancin to be patient.

"Come on, Martin, it's been twenty-five years," she replied.

But he was certain they would get another break that would make the case that much stronger.

"And you know," recalled Stefancin, "he was right."

Potts had tried this before, with no success, but he was willing to give it another go. As he had in 1992, he drafted a letter seeking information about Jane Does who might turn out to be Janice or Fran. Only this time the letter wasn't just sent to coroners in Ohio, but—based on the lead provided by Michael Smith—to every law-enforcement agency in Indiana, from little rural sheriffs' offices to big-city police departments. Potts had some help in this endeavor: Sherrie Gladden-Davis collected all the addresses and printed labels for the letters. In the letter, dated February 17, 2000, Potts wrote:

Dear Sirs:

My name is Brian Potts and I am a detective sergeant with the Wayne County Sheriff's Office in Wooster, Ohio. I am investigating the disappearance of Janice Hartman Smith, who was reported missing from Wayne County on November 19, 1974. She was reported missing by her ex-husband and never seen again. They had been separated for several months and divorced for five days.

John David Smith reported another wife missing in October 1991 to the West Windsor Police Department in New Jersey.

Through a joint investigation with the New Jersey authorities and the FBI, credible informant information was developed that John Smith had possibly chemically preserved Janice Hartman Smith and placed her in a plywood box and stored her body in his grandfather's garage. In the early part of 1979, the grandfather discovered the box after it became damaged. John's brother was called to the garage by the grandfather and the brother took the box to his residence where he discovered the body of Janice. He described her as being gray and leather-like. The brother called John at his home in Hammond, Indiana, and told John the box and body was discovered. John arrived eight hours later and took the box, loaded it into his car, and left. Since then, John has told people that he dumped the box in a field to "let the animals take care of it."

We are sending these letters to every coroner's office and sheriff's office in Indiana, asking you to search your records for any Jane Does your office may have during the 1978, 1979, or 1980 time frames. Janice was described at the time of her disappearance as a white female, 5-4, 115, brown hair, blue eyes. Her DOB is 030251, making her 23-years-old at her disappearance.

We are enclosing a stamped envelope for your reply.

Thank you for your help.

Sincerely,
Brian Potts
Detective Sergeant

CHAPTER 16

As he was opening his mail one day in February 2000, Gerry Burman was thinking about retirement. He had spent twenty-three years with the Newton County Sheriff's Department, working his way up from deputy to detective. It might be time to hang it up. Going through the mail, he came across a letter from the Wayne County Sheriff's Office in Wooster, Ohio, a long way from his base in Kentland, Indiana. He opened the envelope and unfolded the letter. It was addressed, "Dear Sir," and asked for assistance in a missing persons case.

He read the letter carefully, the words leaping out at him: "body," "plywood box," "dumped," "field."

He read the letter again.

Then he read it a third time.

In his long law-enforcement career, Detective Burman had handled almost every kind of case possible. Some he remembered, some he didn't. One he did. It was nearly twenty years earlier, when he was a young deputy sheriff. On a clear, cool spring day he had responded to a call on Hopkins Park Road about the discovery of human remains by a road crew. Burman had helped protect the perimeter. Over the next two decades, he would occasionally think about what the locals had called The Lady in the Box. He would wonder who she was and how she had come to be dumped in a drainage ditch in rural northwest Indiana.

Staring at the letter, he thought: It has been so many years.

He called Detective Brian Potts.

"Hey," Burman told him, "I think I've got your girl."

CHAPTER 17

There was what Burman would later describe as a "poignant pause." Burman didn't know it, but Potts was shaking with excitement, which only built as Burman laid out the details of the case: a Jane Doe found in a plywood box on the side of the road in 1980; women's clothes stuffed inside; bones determined to be those of a young woman, petite and probably pretty; attempts at identifying her fruitless; eventually buried in a potter's field section of the cemetery in Morocco, Indiana.

And, Burman said, the woman's legs were cut off below the knee.

Potts regained his composure, thanked Burman and made arrangements to get up to Indiana as quickly as possible to get that body exhumed. Potts then called Stefancin, who at the time was in her office preparing for a trial in a separate case.

"Jocelyn, sit down," said Potts.

"What's the matter?" she asked.

"I think we found her," said Potts, and he repeated what Burman had told him just moments before.

A tingle went down Stefancin's spine. She asked him if he was sure.

Potts said, "I know it's her."

The next day, Larry Bartley got the same letter from Potts. He too knew immediately that it was the Lady in the Box case he had handled so many years before when he was a crime scene technician.

Bartley, now the elected coroner of Newton County, called his old friend Gerry Burman at the sheriff's department.

"Have you seen this letter?"

"Yeah," said Burman. "I got mine yesterday. I've already been in touch with the people in Ohio and told them we've got The Lady in the Box. Stand by, because you're going to get a phone call."

That same day Potts called Burman, who gave the Ohio detective the good news: all the paperwork and all the photographs from the case were still on file at the state police post. What's more, Burman could get his hands on some of the bones. The skull had been passed from coroner to coroner—it most recently was stored under a desk in a dentist's office—and bones were in storage in an evidence room. The rest of the remains were in the cemetery. And they still had the wooden box.

Burman hung up the phone. He couldn't believe that after all these years he would have a name to go with The Lady in the Box.

Janice Hartman.

He would soon get a photograph—a beautiful young woman, just like the forensic anthropologist had said she would be. And he just knew, now that the remains were identified, that it was only a matter of time before the killer would be caught, and the unsolved case that had nagged at him for twenty years would be closed.

As far as anybody could remember, there had never been an exhumation in Newton County, Indiana. Detective Burman read the state regulations and law books and made dozens of phone calls to various agencies to get the proper procedure. Papers had to be filed with the state health department. Probable cause had to be established before a judge. And if it turned out the remains were not those of Janice Hartman, then they would have to be reburied. On March 2, 2000, after a hearing before Newton Superior Court Judge Daniel J. Molter in Kentland, permission was granted to exhume the body.

It was a typical March day in northwest Indiana, sunny but cold, with temperatures in the high 20s and a stiff wind that made it feel much colder. The exhumation at Oakwood Cemetery, on US 41 on the edge of Morocco, Indiana, drew a crowd and created a party-like atmosphere. Nearly everyone involved in the John Smith case ventured to this corner of Indiana, including investigators from the FBI, Indiana state police, Ohio authorities, local politicians and the judge and his staff. The elected officials from Wayne County, Sheriff Thomas Mauer and Prosecutor Martin Frantz, also turned out. "It was a circus," recalled Burman. "I'm pretty sure P. T. Barnum was there, and I don't know who was running the concession stand."

Having handled the original case, Burman went about looking for the likely spot where The Lady in the Box was buried. All he had to go by was his memory, because the original Jane Doe marker had been removed, and somebody had replaced it with a New Age–looking marker that may or may not have been put in the right spot. Burman took his best guess and the backhoe operator from the county highway department—the same department whose employee had found the box—started to dig. The hole got deeper and larger, and, recalled Detective Potts, "We're thinking, 'Where the hell's the vault?' "

Then investigators noticed a small depression in the grass about three feet away from where they were digging. The backhoe was directed there and its first scoop, about a foot deep, ripped the top of a casket off with an unsettling crunch. Upon inspection, it was a small, child's-size white casket, made out of plastic: a pauper's coffin. "It looked like Tupperware to me," recalled Burman. With the lid torn off, everybody could see inside. There were three white plastic garbage bags and a pool of what forensic scientists call "glop": liquefied human remains.

There was some discussion among the various law enforcement people of what to do next—whether to look inside the bags to see if this was in fact The Lady in the Box, or whether the bones belonged to a child.

It was at last decided to take a quick peek inside the bags. Burman looked inside and could tell these were adult-size remains. The box was lifted out of the hole and placed in Potts' van. The show was over. The cemetery cleared out.

Potts drove north to Lowell, Indiana, to pick up the rest of the bones—the skull and leg bones that had been saved—along with the clothing that had been wrapped around the remains, and the original plywood box. From Lowell, Potts went to the Toledo, Ohio, laboratory of forensic anthropologist Frank Saul, for a detailed examination and hopefully a preliminary indication of whether these were the likely remains of Janice Hartman.

The sun was setting as Potts drove toward the Coroner's office, the bags of bones rattling around in the back of the van. It had been a long day, and a long night stretched ahead. His mind wandered, as minds do while driving. His thoughts drifted to all those ups and downs over the years in the John Smith case. He thought of Janice Hartman, whom he had begun to think of as a little sister—even though, had she lived, she'd have been older than Potts. To him, she was frozen in time, in 1974, young and beautiful. He wondered if, finally, with the discovery of the bones and the clothing and the box, that he had enough to close this case for good. Or would John Smith slip away again as he had so many times before?

He thought that only Janice knew for sure.

Then he did something he had never done before, or since. He spoke to a ghost.

"Tell me who did it," he said out loud as he drove. "Tell me how it happened."

The ghost didn't answer.

Potts focused on the road and the work that still had to be done, reviewing for the millionth time the facts of the case. He had been working it so long, the details were branded into his brain. Then another thought occurred to him. It was March 2.

They had dug up these bones on Janice Hartman's birthday.

It was late at night when Potts delivered the bones to the Lucas County Coroner's Office, located in a building near the Medical College of Ohio, in Toledo. The bones were placed on a stainless-steel gurney, which was wheeled into the examination room that Dr. Frank Saul used for special cases. It has a separate air-circulation system, so as not to introduce any contaminants, and a hood over a desk along one wall to suck up the fumes of particularly smelly body parts. Along the other wall was a standard autopsy-suite sink and counter. It was a tight squeeze in the 10-by-15–foot room. Not only were Potts and Saul there, but four other people came to witness the examination: Potts' boss, Sheriff Mauer, Frantz and two FBI agents.

Under these watchful eyes, Saul slowly went through the bags in the little white plastic coffin, pulling out bone after bone—the shoulder bones, the shoulder blades, the vertebral column, the ribs (there was an extra one, which occurs in about 1 percent of the population), the pelvis and the leg bones. He placed them on a sheet in roughly the same location they would have been in the body. He added the skull and the leg bones that had been stored by Indiana authorities since 1980. By comparing the base of the skull with the top vertebra, he determined that this skull fit this body. The leg bones from storage also fit in with the bones from the box.

Standing back, the men in the room saw the skeleton—a skeleton with the legs cut off just below the knees.

Saul easily determined these bones were from a human and that they appeared to be relatively recent, as opposed to ancient Indian bones that are often found in the Midwest. He also determined that the bones came from a female, both by the smaller size of the frame and by the shape of the pelvis. "Female pelvic bones have been designed for success in child-bearing," he would explain. "A normal pelvis will have contours and size relationships that will enable it to pass our large-headed offspring through that bony birth canal as fast as possible."

Saul believed this woman was probably in her twenties, based on clues found in the joints. When people are young, the joint ends of their bones have not completely fused with the shafts; there's still some cartilage in between. In this skeleton, the cartilage was gone, but an X-ray of the joint found that it had disappeared only recently before death, as evidenced by the scarring. Therefore, the woman was just out of her teens. Characteristics of the ribs, hipbones and collarbones also strongly suggested a woman in her twenties.

This woman was also probably Caucasian, based on the shape of the bridge of the nose and the shape of the jaw, and probably petite, no taller than 5-foot-6, based on a height formula using the length of the right thighbone.

But beyond that, Saul could say little more about her identity. His visitors placed the skull next to a picture of Janice Hartman and "tried to get me to say: That's her. That's her smile," recalled Saul. "Of course, I told them there's no way you can make a positive identification that way." As there were no dental records available for Janice, investigators were going to have to wait for DNA tests. Saul cut out a part of a rib, part of the femur and two molars, which were packaged and sent to FBI scientist Isenberg in Washington for mitochondrial DNA analysis.

One of the last questions to be addressed was cause of death. While the woman could have bled to death from having her legs cut off, there were no other obvious signs of trauma—not unusual in cases where authorities find only bones, and none of the soft tissues of skin, muscle and organs, which are more helpful in determining cause of death. The bones revealed no signs of gunshot, stabbing or beating severe enough to break bone.

Saul was able to come up with a theory of how she lost her legs. Based on the smooth, uniform nature of the cut marks, the legs appeared to have been cut off with a saw rather than chopped off with a hatchet. But Saul couldn't be 100 percent certain. The interpretation of cut marks on bones was outside his expertise as a forensic anthropologist. But he knew somebody who might know.

The world of forensic science, like so many other areas, is so specialized that it's not enough just to be an expert in bones. Steven A. Symes, a forensic anthropologist and an assistant professor at the department of pathology at the University of Tennessee Medical Center in Memphis, is an expert in the trauma to bones—more specifically, sharp trauma, any incision or shaving wound to a bone. He has published about twenty papers on the subject.

Referred to the John Smith case by Frank and Julia Saul, Symes examined the four cut leg bones: the two tibias, or shinbones, and the two fibulas, or calfbones. Each bone was only about three inches long, from the joint at the knee to the cut. The bones were a brownish color, which told Symes they had not been left out in the sun where they would have been bleached white. Also, the bones were discolored in the area of the cuts, which meant that the bones decomposed at the same rate as the cut marks. This meant the legs were cut just before or after death, and not months or years later.

As to how the legs were cut, the original 1980 Indiana State Police report theorized that a power tool was used. A power tool, like a circular saw or radial arm saw, creates smooth, uniform-patterned cuts like the ones that, at first glance, seemed to have been made on these bones. But examining the cuts through a microscope, Symes found a number of marks going in different directions, which meant that the blade of the tool had moved during the cutting. There also were what he called "false starts." Whoever cut off these legs had tried to make a small cut, or kerf, as a guide, then cut somewhere else on the bone. Symes concluded that the marks weren't uniform enough for a power tool, and that a hand tool had been used.

The kerfs gave a clue as to the kind of tool. Handsaws, for instance, leave a telltale mark when a kerf is made. Handsaws are designed with little cutting points, or teeth, that are slightly bent, one blade to the left, one to the right, in an alternating pattern down the saw, so that the saw doesn't bind up when it goes through material. These are called set teeth. This alternating blade pattern creates a square kerf, two straight sides and a straight base. But these kerfs on the bones were V-shaped, meaning that a standard handsaw was not used. "It fits the definition of a saw mark, but it's not a saw that has set teeth. There is no set," Symes would later say. "So this just had a row of teeth but no set teeth essentially, so it actually is not a tool designed to cut hard materials or efficiently."

Looking at the false-start kerfs under a microscope, the cuts were not only V-shaped, but one side of the V differed from the other. One side was smooth and polished while the other was rough. This meant the cutting tool had one kind of surface on one side, and a different cutting surface on the other: a serrated knife. "A serrated knife has teeth manufactured into it," Symes said. "These teeth are machined out on one side of the blade . . . and are pretty much smooth-cut on the other side."

Looking at the spurs left when the bone was severed, Symes could determine the direction of the stroke. The right leg was cut from the front—the tibia—through to the fibula behind it. But the left leg was cut from the back—the fibula first—then through the tibia. It was a gruesome image: the woman was lying on her back when the right leg was cut off with the serrated knife, then she was flipped over, and the left leg was cut off. What's more, it's very difficult to cut a bone with a serrated knife, he said. "Without that set, the blade is going to bind," he said. "It would have to take a lot of power, a lot of strength, persistence."

CHAPTER 18

It was cool and damp on March 9, 2000, perfect weather for finding a scent. Since the excavation at the Grace Lane Apartments ten months earlier, Sandra Anderson hadn't thought about the John Smith case much. She and Eagle had moved on to other cases, other smells, and for all she knew, there was nothing left for them to do in Ohio. So when she got the call to return there to have Eagle search a residential property in Seville, she had little knowledge about the dramatic developments. As usual, she intended to work as blindly as possible, letting Eagle do what Eagle does best.

They were called out to Seville to find evidence to bolster Michael's statement that the box had been stored for years in the garage of his grandparents' house. The only witnesses who could back him up, besides John, were now dead: the Chaneys and Chaney friend Jack Bistor, who had recently been killed in a freak accident at an auto repair garage when a car slipped off a lift and crushed him. The grandparents' home had been searched three times and excavated extensively with no physical evidence visible. Investigators hoped Eagle would have better luck.

After pulling up to the house at Pleasant Street, Sandra

let Eagle out of the truck and pointed him toward the garage. The dog sniffed around the perimeter, but detected no odor of human remains. Anderson opened the door to the garage, leading Eagle into the cluttered, musty area, with boxes, cans and stacks of wood surrounding an old car. Immediately, Eagle perked up, pacing back and forth, wagging his tail, barking, jumping—a more enthusiastic reaction than usual. That meant there was a strong scent of human remains. Eagle caught the scent where a cinderblock wall met the floor, next to old, stained pieces of plywood— boards that looked like those that had made the box—and near an old weight-lifting bench, right where Michael Smith had said the box was stored. The plywood was taken out of the garage to see if the smell was coming from the wood or from inside the garage. The dog smelled nothing on the wood, but continued to hop around in the garage. The odor was coming from the floor and the brick wall.

Investigators would search anew over this area, probing and digging, but would never find what they were looking for: the lower part of Janice's legs and her feet. Detectives theorized that what Eagle smelled was the lingering residue of death. As the body had decomposed, the fluids had seeped out of the box and onto the floor and part of the brick wall, then dried up so as to be undetectable to anything but a dog's sensitive nose. It would be argued that this was strong, if invisible, evidence that Janice's body had been stored in the garage.

The same day that Eagle was searching the Chaney garage, Alice Isenberg at the FBI's lab received a package in the mail containing parts of a femur, rib and tooth—samples of the remains from the box dug up in Morocco, Indiana— to test for DNA. These were not ideal samples for the extraction of DNA, even mitochondrial DNA. The bones had been in the box for more than twenty-five years, subjected to environmental assaults, from heat and cold to bacteria.

And Isenberg was not, in fact, able to extract sufficient

DNA from the rib or the tooth. But the femur did have enough.

On April 24, 2000, FBI Agent Roy Speer in the Akron, Ohio, office called Jocelyn Stefancin to give her the results of the lab report: the DNA extracted from the femur had the same DNA sequence as Betty Lippincott's.

The Lady in the Box was Betty's daughter Janice.

CHAPTER 19

In July of 2000, Jocelyn Stefancin called a meeting in Wooster with members of the sheriff's office and the FBI to go over the final evidence she felt was needed before she could present the John Smith case to the grand jury. Stefancin, once willing to seek an indictment without a body, now wanted everything in order before making the big move. Timing was critical. Under Ohio law, prosecutors must bring a person to trial within 270 days of an indictment—just 90 if the person is in custody. John would almost certainly be held in jail without bond awaiting trial, which meant that, unless he waived time, prosecutors would have to be ready to go to trial in three months from the moment John was charged. That didn't give prosecutors a lot of time. This was a complicated case that had unfolded over years and across thousands of miles. It meant tracking down witnesses from around the country, organizing the physical evidence and coordinating with law enforcement agencies in California, New Jersey, Ohio, New York and Connecticut. "With everyone being out of state, that's really pushing it for a case of this magnitude," said Stefancin of the ninety-day requirement. "I wanted all the loose ends tied up before I presented it before a grand jury."

Some loose ends seemed destined never to be tied up. One was finding an explanation for John's statement that he had been able to recognize Janice's face when he opened the box. Although the Armstrong Funeral Home was next door, authorities found no evidence that John had swiped embalming fluids or had any knowledge of how to use them. Richard Armstrong said that John Smith used to play in the field behind the funeral home but was never allowed in the embalming room. Dr. Saul would say that after five years in the box, the body could have retained some of the skin—enough to at least make Michael *think* he recognized Janice. Also, detectives couldn't explain Michael's recollection that Janice's head had multi-colored hair. The best theory they could come up with was that the dyes from the clothing stuffed in the box had seeped onto the head.

Authorities also needed to corroborate Michael's statement that the box had fit in the cramped interior of John's black Corvette. Stefancin didn't want to get all the way to trial only to find out that Michael's recollection was physically impossible. At the very least, investigators wanted to measure the interior of a Corvette like the one that John had driven and compare it with the dimensions of the box. At best, they would find John's old souped up Corvette.

It was found in New Jersey, tracked down by motor vehicle records, in the garage of a man who had purchased it in 1982 and kept it protected and in pristine condition, hardly ever driving it. That made for ideal circumstances when FBI Agent Thomas Cottone inspected the inside of the car, measuring distances from the back window to the front windshield. He folded down the passenger seat, and determined that a box of about four feet long, one foot wide and eighteen inches deep would in fact fit. What's more, Cottone found scratches on the doorframe and by the right passenger seat, and damage to the defroster foil strips on the back window. The damage was all located in places the box would have touched.

The discovery of the Corvette was one of the last pieces of unfinished police business before Stefancin presented the case before a grand jury.

Janice's family also had some unfinished personal business. On August 21, 2000, Larry Bartley—who as a young crime scene analyst had examined the remains back in 1980—signed the Certificate of Death Registration, in his capacity as the elected Newton County Coroner, and stamped the document with the country seal. Twenty-six years after she disappeared, Janice Hartman was declared legally dead.

CHAPTER 20

As in other states, grand jury proceedings are closed in Ohio to everybody but prosecutors and investigators. Suspects, defense lawyers and the public are not allowed in the room—or even entitled to know that the proceeding is going on. And so this grand jury proceeding in August 2000 was stacked against John David Smith. An indictment from the nine members of the grand jury was a foregone conclusion. The only question was how tightly authorities could keep this under wraps. Through news reports, and friends and relatives, John appeared to know quite a bit about the investigation. He was even one of the first to find out that a box that may have contained Janice's remains was exhumed in Indiana; a reporter called him in California and told him. But as far as authorities knew, the word had not gotten to John that a grand jury was about to hear evidence against him. Stefancin wanted to keep it that way. A grand jury proceeding meant that John's arrest was imminent, and authorities didn't want him blowing town.

To maintain as much secrecy as possible, the grand jurors were assembled in a conference room in the juvenile court section of the courthouse rather than in the grand jury room. "It was very large, quiet and secure," said Stefancin.

The grand jurors sat around a conference table as Stefancin presented evidence over two days. They were shown photos of the wooden box, of the bones taken from the box and the clothing; Janice's watch that the FBI had gotten from Kathy McDonald; blown-up pages from the original missing persons reports; and a chart to help them keep track of who everybody was and when certain events had occurred. Testimony came from Detective Brian Potts, FBI Agent Bob Hilland, New Jersey Detective Michael Dansbury, FBI Agent Roy Speer, Janice's friend Kathy Paridon, and the most important witness of all, Michael Smith.

The witnesses went over the basics, from the day Janice disappeared, to the DNA identification of the bones. After presenting her case, Stefancin left the conference room so the grand jurors could take a vote in private.

As expected, the vote came down against John. Delivered on August 25, 2000, the indictment read:

> *The jurors of the grand jury of the state of Ohio and for the body of Wayne County, on their oaths, in the name and by the authority of the state of Ohio, do find and present that:*
>
> *Count 1: On or about Nov. 17, 1974, in Wayne County, Ohio, JOHN DAVID SMITH with prior calculation and design, purposely caused the death of Janice Elaine Hartman Smith, said act being AGGRAVATED MURDER, in violation of Revised Code Section 2903.01.*
>
> *Contrary to the form of the statute in such case made and provided, and against the peace and dignity of the state of Ohio.*

It was signed by the grand jury foreman and Stefancin. If convicted, John faced twenty years to life in prison. The death penalty wasn't an option; Ohio didn't have capital punishment in 1974 when the crime was allegedly committed.

The clock started ticking. It was time to arrest John David Smith for murder.

CHAPTER 21

The setup was the same as before when John was interrogated, only the motel was different. This time the FBI had reserved two suites at the Comfort Inn in Escondido, not far from LaForza Motors. One suite was set up as an interrogation room, where two FBI profilers, rather than agents, hoped to question John. The other suite was a monitoring room, where Detective Brian Potts and others would watch the interrogation.

It was the morning of Tuesday, October 3, 2000. Down the street from the motel, John Smith arrived at work at 8 a.m. He was met by Escondido Police Officer Christopher K. Wynn, who handcuffed him and placed him in a squad car. John put up no resistance. But while the arrest was easy enough, John made it clear he wasn't going to a motel suite for a date with FBI interrogators this time. "He had attorneyed up," said Potts. John invoked his right to remain silent and his right to counsel. The suites at the Comfort Inn would go unused.

John was taken to the San Diego County Central Jail, where he was to wait—without bond—for an appearance in Superior Court in Vista and what authorities hoped would be a one-way trip back to Wooster to face trial in the murder of his first wife. Officials publicly announced for the first time that they had found the remains of Janice Hartman. "Justice never forgets," Wayne County Prosecutor Martin Frantz told reporters. "We have a case, and we will prosecute." Sheriff Tomas Maurer told the media: "We can finally put Janice Hartman to rest and give her family some closure to this tragic event."

As the elected officials spoke to the press, Jocelyn Stefancin, who had flown out to California for the arrest, went to the Escondido Police Department's jail and got the first close look at the man she was about to try for murder. Sitting with his hands cuffed, John was still very much the geeky 19-year-old from the wedding portrait with Janice. "To look at him, I could see how he got away with things for so long," Stefancin recalled. "He's still got this John Boy Walton–type of look. He's just a little heavier. As he was leaving the jail to be transported, he just sort of looked at me. It was his eyes. He sort of had an evilness to his eyes. His eyes looked very dark."

Detective Brian Potts was assigned to bring John back to Ohio. The Wayne County Sheriff's Office had authorized one other person to accompany him. He chose Doug Hunter, head of the SWAT team. "I wanted somebody to kick ass if he got out of line," said Potts.

John had waived extradition—there would be no fight in court against shipping him to Wooster—and so on Saturday, Potts and Hunter arrived at the San Diego lockup at about 5 a.m. It was still dark. When John was led out, Potts was unimpressed. "He looked scared, just frail and sickly," he said. Jail guards had found some old ill-fitting street clothes for him. He was also put in a leg brace and had his hands shackled.

From the jail, the officers drove John to Lindbergh Field, the airport in San Diego. Walking through the terminal toward their gate, clothes were draped over John's shackles so few people noticed that he was a prisoner. As arranged,

Potts and Hunter—and their concealed Glock .40-caliber handguns—were whisked through the security checkpoint. But when they got to the America West gate, the airline officials told them they had to take John's arm and hand shackles off for air safety purposes. The only restraint he would be wearing during the four-hour flight was the leg brace, which irritated Potts and Hunter. They led John down the jetway toward the plane, paused and took off his shackles. "I want you to know," Hunter told John in his best special-tactics voice, "that any action taken by you will be met with a swift and violent reaction." Smith was shaking as they led him onto the plane.

They sat in the back-row seats reserved for them, Smith in the window seat, Potts in the middle seat, Hunter on the aisle. Before picking up John at the jail, Potts had purchased a mini–cassette recorder to get down anything John said during the journey, but John never spoke during the flight, not even when he was served a meal by the flight attendant. He took his food and silently ate.

The flight was uneventful, Hunter's SWAT skills unneeded. John was as docile as he was quiet. They got off the plane in Columbus and stepped into a whirlwind of TV crews, police officers, curious bystanders. Deanna Weiss's father was running around with a camcorder. Under guard of Columbus PD, they got John through the airport and to a waiting Wayne County van, black with gold stripes and a star on the side. Potts sat shotgun; Hunter stayed in the back with Smith. It was 5:55 p.m. when they got to the Justice Center in Wooster. John was booked into custody, fingerprinted, photographed, then put in a small jail cell, no bars, just a door with a window, to await his first court date in Ohio.

That night, Potts made a phone call.

"We've got him," he told Betty Lippincott.

"Keep him," Janice's mother replied.

CHAPTER 22

The entrance to the historic courthouse on Liberty Street in downtown Wooster is flanked by large statues of Atlas, his muscular arms holding up the overhang bearing the year of construction—1878—his eyes downcast and blank. Inside, Court of Common Pleas Judge Robert J. Brown presided over the Wednesday, October 11, 2000, arraignment of John David Smith on aggravated murder charges. It was a day that many had waited so long for, including Sherrie Gladden-Davis, sister of Betty Fran Gladden Smith, whose life, disappearance and presumed death were not—and may never be—an issue in this court or any other. But this could be as close as Fran's family would ever get to justice, so Sherrie was there, sitting in the front row and giving what two local papers described as a "cold stare" at John, who had been led into the courtroom in shackles and wearing a jail jumpsuit. Sherrie would not get the satisfaction of even the slightest acknowledgment by John.

Except for the spectacle of hauling John before a court of law, the session was perfunctory and unexceptional. Under questioning by the judge, John acknowledged receiving a copy of the indictment and waived the reading of it in open court. Flanked by his new attorney, Kirk Migdal of

Akron—a former clerk of John's San Diego lawyer Michael McCabe—John entered the standard arraignment plea of not guilty. The judge did note that while this was not a capital case, the state could still hold John without bail, under the terms of a newly revised law. The defense and prosecution would have to argue over whether to grant bail at a separate hearing, the following Monday, before another judge, Mark K. Wiest, who would also be the trial judge.

After court, in what would become a routine event, Sherrie Gladden-Davis held a court of her own for the media, telling reporters how much she had looked forward to seeing John Smith answer to his alleged crime. "I wanted him to see me sitting there when he walked into court," she said, according to the *Beacon Journal*. "I wanted him to know I'm not going anyplace until I know where my sister is." Sherrie spoke of her family's long, expensive struggle to reach this day—and how their efforts wouldn't end until John was held accountable for her sister's disappearance. "I'm just glad a body was found to at least get this far," she said. "One down, one to go." And she didn't care what John thought of her. "He has let it be known that he despises me . . . more than anyone else in the world," she told a *Daily Record* reporter, "because of everything my family has done to make his life miserable for the last nine years."

Migdal's was the lone voice on John's behalf. "This has been a trying time for him emotionally," the lawyer said, according to the *Beacon Journal*. "It's been going on for a long time."

As scheduled, the case moved to the court of Judge Mark K. Wiest for the bail hearing. This time another family member, Janice's brother Garry Hartman, spoke to the media. "It took a long time to capture and get him here," Garry said, "and now that he's here, I am very pleased." Seeking to have bail denied, prosecutors had to prove a great presumption that Smith had murdered his ex-wife and that he was a risk of harm to the community. To do so they called two witnesses, Detective Potts and FBI Agent Roy Speer, to go over the basics of the investigation.

But the news from the hearing was Speers giving the public the first hint of what the key break in the case had been. Without providing the name, the agent said that after the May 1999 sweep of interviews a "source" came forward with eyewitness testimony linking Smith with The Lady in the Box. This source saw Smith building a box, then later saw the body in the box and watched Smith take off with the box toward Indiana. The information was so damaging, Speer said, that "the source is frightened for the source's life and the life of the source's family." He added: "The source's unique knowledge would make the source a threat to Mr. Smith. And the source has recognized Mr. Smith's temper in the past." Migdal broke the suspense about the source, saying, "Obviously it was his brother."

Ruling three days later, the judge found that the state had proven by "clear and convincing evidence" that bail should be denied. Trial was set for January, which, though just two months away, was too long for Garry Hartman, whose nerves were frayed. "I was hoping for a speedy trial. January is not speedy," he said, according to the *Beacon Journal*. Asked if he was angry, he said, "I've got anger toward everyone," and walked away.

CHAPTER 23

Even though John Smith was in custody and awaiting trial, the investigation continued. Acting on information found by Sherrie Gladden-Davis and Deanna Weiss, investigators went to search a storage unit on Greenwich Road in Norton, north of Wooster. One of the units had once been used by John Smith or his mother for the family apartment business. John and his mother no longer used the unit, and the new tenant gave authorities consent to search it. Once again, Sandra Anderson and Eagle were brought in to look for human remains. Fran's body had still not been found; the teeth fragments found the year before had raised the possibility that at least one more body was out there.

It was a bitterly cold afternoon with a sharp wind, and snow and ice on the ground. Despite being bundled up, Anderson had to keep moving just to stay warm. The big door to the storage unit was opened and Eagle was led in. The unit was stuffed with junk, from boxes to old magazines to luggage, dishes and old model trains. Eagle sniffed around but picked up on no scent. Anderson led Eagle out of the facility and, it being so cold, the two of them wandered around to keep their blood flowing.

"And dang if he doesn't run over to this door and do

his I-want-in-here thing," recalled Anderson. It was another storage unit nearby. The tenant was contacted and the door unlocked. Eagle darted toward a sofa and got excited. The sofa was moved. Eagle picked up a scent where the wall met the floor, and lay down. A crime scene analyst poked around in the crack between the floor and wall and retrieved some small dark fragments.

It was bone, three pieces, two of them charred, the third larger, with what looked like skin still attached. The bone pieces were sent to Dr. Frank Saul, who could tell by their shape and the density that these were pieces of a human skull.

Authorities knew right away that this bone didn't come from Janice Hartman—her skull was intact. DNA testing was conducted to see if the skull fragments had come from Fran. The test was negative. Just to rule out some other reason for the bones being there, Detective Potts obtained a list of everybody who had rented that unit, and contacted them all to see if they'd ever stored cremated remains there. None had.

First the tooth, then the skull shards. Authorities wondered if they had found evidence of yet another victim of John Smith.

CHAPTER 24

Kirk Migdal was a graduate of Ohio State University, the same school John Smith had attended in the 1970s before he dropped out as his marriage to Janice crumbled. Migdal had spent much of his legal career in California, studying law at the California Western School of Law and, after passing the California Bar, working for the public defenders' offices in San Luis Obispo and San Diego. Before returning to his home state to set up a private practice in Akron, he had also worked for John Smith's California lawyer Michael McCabe. When John was arrested on murder charges, McCabe called Migdal, who was immediately drawn to the case. The connection wasn't Migdal's shared educational past at Ohio State with John. And it certainly wasn't for the money. Although Fran's relatives thought they had found evidence of wealth, John claimed to be broke and unable to pay Migdal. The best Migdal could hope for was some money from Wayne County, and even then he'd likely take a loss when other expenses and lost work were factored in. But it was worth it. "How often do you get twenty-seven-year-old murder case?"

Migdal wasn't going to be alone on this. He was paired with Beverly Wire, an experienced and highly respected public defender in Wayne County, who was appointed to the case by the judge. Although this was a circumstantial case, with no murder weapon and no witnesses to the killing, Migdal knew the defense had serious problems. The biggest, as Migdal saw it, wasn't the testimony of Michael Smith or the dark bones dug up in Indiana. It was Betty Fran Gladden. "From day one, we knew we had to keep the second wife out," Migdal recalled. "If the second wife came in, we had no chance. We can't imagine the jury would say, 'That was a hell of a coincidence, but we'll still acquit.' "

And it was for this very reason that the prosecution was so eager to persuade Judge Wiest to let the jury hear details of Fran's disappearance in New Jersey. In legal terms, the prosecution wanted the judge to allow "other-acts" evidence.

Going into the admissibility hearing, neither side was confident of victory. Legally, it was a toss-up. On the one hand, the law tends to frown upon allowing evidence that is not linked directly to the crime at issue, the theory being that other-acts evidence is too prejudicial to be of any value. There are exceptions. If a prosecutor could prove enough similarities between the murder of Janice Hartman and the disappearance of Betty Fran Gladden Smith, then the New Jersey evidence would be considered helpful and relevant: its probative value would outweigh its prejudicial nature. And that worried the defense. "Under the evidence code, if you show a common plan or scheme, the other-acts gets in," Migdal said. "We were concerned about that. If it was in, we were dead in the water. We had no chance. It would just be a question of aggravated murder vs. murder."

That was the cold legal analysis. Ohio judges, who are elected, had been known to make rulings with at least a passing thought to the polls. But Judge Wiest had a reputation as a jurist unaffected by politics and possessing a strong grasp of the law. This gave the defense lawyers hope. They knew the playing field would be level.

By now, late spring of 2001, the January trial date had long since been delayed to allow for pre-trial matters. The hearing was set for Tuesday, May 29, 2001. Right off the bat, the prosecution ran into trouble, what Stefancin called a "horrible chain of events," that had nothing to do with either the law or politics. Her 7-year-old daughter Tricia became extremely sick that morning. Stefancin called her boss, Martin Frantz, and told him to ask the judge for a continuance.

"I can handle it," Frantz said.

Stefancin wasn't so sure. Reluctantly, she faxed him the questions for the witnesses, and Frantz went in cold. The arguments had already been stated in detail in court papers, showing what the prosecution saw as the many similarities between the disappearances of Janice and Fran. In both cases John had initially told family members that the women had packed suitcases and headed for family in Florida, both women had been married to John and either had left or were about to leave his life, both women had left clothing behind and both women had disappeared without a trace. Although coming in at the last minute, Frantz hit all the key points in his opening statements to the judge, contending, "Case law suggests that this evidence is admissible if two deaths occur under identical circumstances or nearly identical circumstances."

In the defense's opening remarks, Migdal argued that there weren't enough similarities—the biggest difference being that Janice Hartman was found dead, but that there was no evidence Betty Fran was even killed. She was still only missing.

With that, two witnesses were called, Detectives Brian Potts and Michael Dansbury, who had come in from New Jersey. In the cross-examination of Dansbury, Beverly Wire honed in on the biggest difference between the two cases— and the biggest aggravation for New Jersey police and family members.

"Officer, you have no idea where Fran Smith is, do you?"

"No, I don't."

"You don't even know if Fran Smith is dead, do you?"

"I believe—"

"Do you know if Fran Smith is dead? Not what you believe. What do you know?"

"I don't know that she's dead, but I believe she's dead."

After the testimony, prosecutor Frantz argued in more detail why the disappearance of Betty should be introduced in the trial, listing all of what he called the similarities and citing what he saw as the relevant case law. He did admit "there are some differences," but that this was "for the jury to decide."

"Based on the evidence and based on the law and the briefs that the parties have filed, we urge you to rule that the common features surrounding the disappearance of the defendant's first wife, Janice Hartman, and the defendant's second wife, Betty Fran Smith, establish a behavioral fingerprint which warrants admissibility of the evidence from New Jersey," said Frantz.

Migdal argued that the law requires *great* similarities, not just similarities, and those just didn't exist. The two cases are so dissimilar, he said, "There's absolutely no evidence whatsoever" that John was involved in Fran's disappearance. "There's no evidence . . . of what has happened to Betty Fran Smith to show that there was foul play at all," he said. "There's certainly innuendo, and, Your Honor, we're aware of the coincidental nature of all this, but that doesn't make that legally admissible." The law's requirements, he said, were just too strict. "They are basically arguing to you coincidence, coincidence, coincidence."

In a victory for John Smith, the judge agreed. "We don't know the circumstances under which Fran Smith's death occurred," Wiest said. "There are certainly some similar circumstances surrounding the disappearances of the defendant's first two wives. But the court finds lacking the substantial proof required before it can admit this evidence."

With that, the prosecution would have to convict John

David Smith on the merits of the Janice Hartman evidence alone. Stefancin tried to put the best face on it. "I don't think it was a serious blow," Stefancin recalled later. "But it's always nice if you could get in that extra bit." She had reason not to worry too much. There was a good chance that even with the judge's ruling, potential jurors would already know about the New Jersey case from media reports, and that even if they were told to ignore it, it would be in the backs of their minds. Still, Stefancin said, "I had some difficult hurdles to overcome. It was a strong circumstantial case and I felt very strongly about it, but if they didn't believe Michael Smith—that was reasonable doubt."

Michael Smith was on the minds of the defense attorneys, too. With the other-acts evidence barred, Michael was now the next big problem for the defense. The options for dealing with him were limited. The defense couldn't claim that Michael was lying about the box because of the taped conversation between Michael and John. "I didn't think we'd have any credibility with the jury if we said Michael was lying. The tape speaks for itself," said Migdal. "John acknowledges the box. That's the problem. We didn't think the jury was going to not believe that at some point he had knowledge of the box." The defense would have to think up another way to lessen the impact of Michael's testimony.

In California, Diane Smith had shed both her anonymity and her support for John. "I never loved him," she told *The San Diego Union-Tribune*, claiming she married him for financial reasons and that she had known nothing about the missing women in his past. "The marriage was a farce. I would never have married him had I known."

The strength of the relationship, as she described it, seemed to have fluctuated with her money needs. She had filed a restraining order against him, then rescinded it months later when her Ferrari broke down. "I called up John and he said, 'Don't worry about it, honey. No problem. I'll take care of it.' " She added, "Since I didn't have his income anymore, I was destitute again. I was going to sell [the Ferrari] and subsist on it."

Even after she'd filed for divorce, they would continue to talk, by phone, in the evenings, but she had trouble believing the things he said. As his trial neared, she said his struggles with the truth would make it impossible for him to take the stand in his own defense. "He tells these stories, but he can never tell the same story twice," Diane told *The Daily Record*. "They'd be stupid to put him on the stand. He'd never get through the cross-examination."

On July 5, 2001, John's last marriage became no more. A family law judge in San Diego approved the annulment Diane had filed in December 1999. But this would not stop Diane from communicating with John, who wrote her almost daily and occasionally called from jail, as they maintained this perplexing relationship. "I think I'm the only one that communicates with John," she told *The Daily Record*. "It's always the same thing with him. Everybody's out to get him. He's been wronged by everyone." And that, she said, is part of the problem. "I hope to God he doesn't get out," she said. "He should be locked up for the rest of his life."

CHAPTER 25

Murder doesn't come very often to the courthouse in Wooster, Ohio. In her ten years as an assistant Wayne County Prosecutor, Jocelyn Stefancin had handled ten murder cases; seven of them had pleaded out, three went to trial. That alone made the case of *People* vs. *John David Smith* unique. That this trial followed by twenty-seven years the alleged crime made the case all the more special, and for opening statements on Friday, July 6, 2001, the local and national media descended on the college town, including reporters from the major Ohio newspapers, the TV stations from Cleveland and Columbus and a crew from ABC, which had brought the case to the national TV audience on *20/20*. About 100 people squeezed into Judge Wiest's courtroom, so many that some sat in folding chairs set up along the back wall. The judge allowed limited use of cameras in the courtroom. No jurors would be photographed, and any witnesses who didn't want to be photographed could refuse.

It had only taken two days to select the jury of nine women and three men from a pool of 150 people to consider John's fate, the most important questions focusing on defense concerns that panelists could set aside what they had heard in the media, and that they appreciated and understood the concept of reasonable doubt. The defense tested one of its theories on panelists, asking if they could convict John of murder if all they knew about him was that he had had knowledge of the box holding his dead wife. Jurors said they would not. They would need more evidence than just possession of a dead body. Migdal hoped the jurors meant it.

For the first day of trial, John was dressed neatly in a shirt and tie—gone were the tight jeans and loud shirts he once fancied. He had on no leg irons or handcuffs, but under his clothes an electronic shock belt would zap him if he tried to escape. What struck most who saw John, in some cases for the first time in years, was not his conservative dress or the fact that the now-50-year-old John had put on a few pounds, but the total absence of any expression. This man who allegedly possessed the rage to kill one, two and maybe three or four people, had a blank face with eyes that never seemed to focus on anybody. The most animated he would get was when he sometimes leaned over to whisper to one of his attorneys, who sat on either side of him. Even the legal pad on the table in front of him would remain blank throughout the trial.

The speedy jury selection would set the pace for what would be a relatively quick trial, considering how long it had taken for the case to get to court. Judge Wiest made it clear from the start that he would allow no wasting of time. As spectators settled into their seats in the packed courtroom, jurors took their chairs to hear the judge's introductory remarks. He explained that the attorneys were about to give opening statements, which would be a road map of each side's case, but that these statements were not actual evidence. That had to come from the witness stand or from the items introduced into evidence. The judge said that jurors could take notes, but that they shouldn't be impressed by somebody taking more notes than somebody else. With that, the trial was to begin.

• • •

The night before, Jocelyn Stefancin had put her daughter to sleep and practiced her opening statement in private, pacing around the kitchen, addressing an invisible jury, as she summoned her inner actress (She had played Anne in *The Diary of Anne Frank* in junior high school back home in Uniontown, Pennsylvania). This may have been the biggest case of her career, but Stefancin was hardly in Perry Mason condition. She was tired, having just come off trials for manslaughter, arson and sexual battery that left her sick and weak of voice. Her body burned with fever.

As Stefancin had thought about the opening, and how she would begin, there was one image from the case that she couldn't shake: Janice Hartman's skeleton with the severed legs. Why, Stefancin wondered, had the legs been cut below the knee? Why didn't John just kill her and stuff her in the box and be done with it? The legs were cut off with such exertion, with that serrated knife, one leg cut away, the body flipped over, then the other leg cut away. This took effort, power. Then it hit Stefancin. It was a symbolic gesture.

"She'll never walk away from him again."

The line became Stefancin's mantra during the opening statement, portraying John as a control freak who wouldn't loosen his grip on Janice even after death.

In outlining what would be a streamlined case against John, Stefancin began, as many prosecutors do, by introducing the jury to the victim, highlighting her good points, dodging the dicier areas. "Janice Hartman was a fun-loving individual. She was easy-going, she was a free spirit," Stefancin said. "And on June thirtieth, 1970, she married John David Smith."

The prosecutor went over their lives together, their home on Hubbard Street in Columbus, before "the marriage began to take a turn" and Janice moved to Wayne County to live with her father on Portage Street in the village of Doylestown. The couple entered into a separation agreement in September 1974, and on November 14, 1974, the marriage was over, officially and legally, if not psychologically for John. Three days later, Stefancin told jurors, Janice was at the Sun Valley Lounge in Doylestown with her friend Kathy Paridon. John Smith was there, too. Janice took Kathy home, dropped her off, and pulled away in her Mustang. "It was the last time Janice Hartman was seen alive," the prosecutor said.

On November 19, 1974, jurors were told, now ex-husband John Smith filed a missing persons report from the home of Kathy Paridon, telling the officer what Janice was wearing, down to the jeweled watch, and giving a contact name of Paridon's mother—not himself and not anyone in Janice's family. When an officer came by Smith's house, it was clear why John didn't want the police around: Janice's Mustang was parked out front, but no Janice could be found. "There was no leads, there was no indication of where Janice Hartman was. She never contacted her family again, and the case lay dormant for a number of years," Stefancin said.

It wasn't until 1992, she told jurors, that Detective Potts of the Wayne County Sheriff's Office started looking into it again. The prosecutor didn't tell jurors why the case was reopened—no mention of the disappearance of Fran in New Jersey and the efforts by her daughter and sister to prosecute Smith. This was evidence barred by the judge. All the prosecutor said to explain this was: "New information that the office had gathered indicated that John David Smith was now a suspect in the disappearance of Janice Hartman."

Stefancin said the FBI got involved, interviews were conducted, and finally on May 14, 1999, investigators got the big break. John Smith's brother Michael decided to offer damaging information—information about a box that John was building. The prosecutor painted the macabre picture of the box sitting in the garage of John and Michael's grandparents for years until the grandfather decided to clean out the garage so he could rent the space. And she told jurors about the day that Michael looked inside that box.

"Michael Smith saw what he believed to be kneecaps, and he saw that the bone had been cut just below the knee," she said. "He moved up to the other end of the box, and he moved the items around with the stick that he had and he saw hair. He will tell you it was multi-colored hair. It looked like it was red and it was blue and it was yellow and it was green. And he saw Janice Hartman."

She told jurors how the family decided not to say anything for the sake of the grandmother's health, how John Smith picked up the box and drove off with it in a Corvette, leaving his brother with an odd explanation for what had happened to Janice. She told them about how Janice's watch, which Smith said she was wearing when she disappeared, showed up on Smith's own wrist—and how he gave it to a teen-aged girl as a gift, saying that it once belonged to his former wife, who was dead.

The prosecutors told jurors about the letter that Detective Potts sent seeking information about any unidentified bodies that may have been found—and how Indiana authorities responded with their own lady in a box. DNA tests proved that those remains were a descendant of Betty Lippincott. "Now, Betty Lippincott had four children, two sons, two daughters," Stefancin said, "and only one of them was missing."

Finishing her statement, Stefancin said: "If you listen closely to the evidence that is presented to you throughout this case, you will see that the state will show you that the defendant purposely took the life of Janice Hartman. He purposely caused her death, and he did so with prior calculation and design. The evidence will show that he is responsible for the death of Janice Hartman Smith in November of 1974. She would never walk away from him again."

Like Jocelyn Stefancin, defense attorney Beverly Wire had worked on the case in the solitude of her home. Her husband and children knew to leave Beverly alone when she was gearing up for trial. The children had gone off to Orrville, northeast of Wooster, for a parade and games at the annual festival. Her husband just stayed out of the way. It was July 4, two days before trial, and as Wire sat among the mountains of paper the modern legal system generates, she needed a break. She turned on the television and there was the 1939 classic *The Wizard of Oz*, with Dorothy opening the door to Munchkinland and becoming overwhelmed by the colorful sights and sounds—and the realization that she had killed a witch.

"Now I can relate to that," Wire told jurors in her opening statements. "I felt overwhelmed sitting there in that paper, and I know that now and throughout this trial you're going to feel overwhelmed by not only the amount of information we throw at you, but by the very nature of this case and the accusation." First Stefancin and now Wire engaged in a common courtroom tactic: The prosecution tries to make a case look simple, the defense tries to make it look complex. Complexity, defense attorneys believe, breeds reasonable doubt. "I wish I could promise you that when you reach deliberations that you had some wizard who could guide you through those, some wonderful person who could help you make your decision," Wire continued. "I wouldn't mind having a person like that help me through this trial myself. But we don't have that person. We just have ourselves. And so we must do what Glinda says and we must start at the beginning and we work our way through."

Like Stefancin, Wire defined the beginning as 1970, when Janice and John eloped in Detroit, and the lawyer went over some of the same marital ground as the prosecutor, only painting a slightly darker picture of the victim. "Janice had a different crowd of friends," said Wire. "She was a dancer in a bar"—a detail the prosecutor happened not to mention. "She worked night hours, she was a night owl. John worked in manufacturing, had to get up early the next morning and go to work." Conflicting schedules, not abuse and obsession, ended this marriage, but, Wire said, "The relationship did not."

"She'll never walk away from him again?" Wire said. "Janice Hartman was abused and hurt in November 1974, but not at the hands of John Smith." And thus came the heart of the defense case—the possible link between Janice's attack by several men and her disappearance. Janice was bruised, inside and out, and had to be given phenobarbital to get through it. Janice at this time told people she was a narc, wanting people to believe that she was "helping local law enforcement bringing down drug dealers."

"How terrifying it must have been for her during that attack when she was threatened with a shotgun and told that narcs have an easy way out," said Wire. "She prophesied: If something happens to me or if I disappear, it will be because of this [narc] work."

Far from being a creepy controller, John was there for her. "She freely went to John's home," Wire said. "She walked right in."

Going through the last night that Janice was seen, Wire offered a key detail that had been left out of the prosecution's scenario. "In the missing persons report that was made at Kathy [Paridon]'s house, Kathy indicates to the police that there was a man in the car, a man of whom she gives a detailed description down to his bad case of acne." John Smith filed the report at Kathy's home "because, knowing that Kathy Paridon was Janice's good friend and had stayed there occasionally, she might be there."

Returning to the attack on Janice, Wire said that whether there was in fact a link between the attempted rape and Janice's disappearance may never be known, because the matter was so mangled by poor investigation by police. "Neither of them were adequately investigated, singly or together," Wire said.

With these questions left unanswered, the most the prosecution will be able to prove against John was not murder, but that he "was in possession of some of Janice Hartman's possessions"—the box in the grandfather's house. The defense would concede that nearly everything that Michael Smith had said was true: the construction of the box, the fact that it was Janice in the box, that John moved the box about. But, said Wire, "Even if you believe that, even if it's true, questions still remain: How did Janice Hartman die? When did Janice Hartman die? Where did Janice Hartman die? And who killed her? Because the state will not be able to provide evidence to answer those questions. And those questions are the questions that need to be answered here."

Wrapping up her presentation, Wire asked jurors to imagine a gorge—with one side being the year 1974, the other 1979. "What the state must do throughout this trial is provide evidence that will build a bridge from 1979 to November 1974," she said. "And they cannot build it on speculation. They cannot build it on conjecture. They cannot build it on assumption. They must provide solid evidence that will establish each and every element of this crime beyond a reasonable doubt. The state will not be able to do this. The state cannot build that bridge."

The prosecution called its first witness, Janice's mother, Betty Lippincott. The plan for the first day of trial was to give the case emotional punch and to establish John's temper. Lippincott had an important role in the trial as the first witness, and she performed it without having been prepared or even interviewed by Stefancin. "I went in cold turkey," Betty recalled. Her appearance in court gave her a chance to look at John Smith, the man she had been convinced from the beginning had killed her daughter, for the first time in decades. He was older and heavier than the skinny young man of her memory, but still looked about the same, still gave her the creeps. And, she recalled, "He wouldn't look at me."

Betty took the oath and fought some early jitters as she was questioned by Stefancin. After explaining that her surname is due to her second marriage, of twenty-seven years, to Edgar Lippincott, following her twenty-seven years with Neal Hartman, Betty went over the basic facts about Janice:

the year she was born, her high school. She fumbled on the year of graduation.

"Nineteen-fifty-one. No, Nineteen-seventy-nine," she said.

"Seventy-nine?" asked Stefancin.

"Sixty-nine. Sorry."

"OK. I understand you're nervous."

"Yes."

Betty spoke of her daughter's graduation and the plan to send her off to become a stewardess. Instead Janice "ran off with John and got married," she said. Betty described where her daughter had resided, with and without John, and how Janice had preferred living with her father because of the strict rules in Betty's house.

"Do you remember," Stefancin asked, "when you last saw Janice?"

Betty lost her composure. Her voice wavered. "Yes," she stammered. "Excuse me."

"That's OK, Mrs. Lippincott, I know this is difficult. If you need some tissues or some water?"

"Please."

"OK, we can get—the bailiff will get you a glass of water in just a moment."

"Thank you."

"Mrs. Lippincott, I know how hard this is for you, but do you remember the date when you last saw Janice?"

"It was just before Thanksgiving," she said. "We were discussing the meal, her and John were going out, and she just told me she'll see me Thanksgiving. But she never did."

Describing what she said were John's flashes of anger and callousness, she testified about the day that John and Jan came by her house, and how John got angry over the lack of food in the house—how he "flared up like a firecracker and pounded my cupboard, stomped his foot." And she concluded by saying that after Jan's disappearance, John never came by or spoke to her.

"Have you had any contact with the defendant since November of 1974?"

"No."

"He never came around?"

"No."

"Never called and asked if Jan was around?"

"No."

"He knew that she was missing?"

"Yes."

"And he never checked in with you to see if she was found?"

"No."

Taking on the thankless chore of cross-examining the grieving mother, Wire gently poked holes in this picture of a close, loving family that Betty had described.

"Going back to when Janice first came back to this area after leaving Columbus, I get the sense from your testimony that you weren't, you aren't real certain as to where she was living at that time?"

"Not really. I thought she was with her father."

In redirect, Stefancin hammered at the theme that John Smith didn't follow up on Janice's disappearance, implying that John knew full well where she was—dead.

"He never stopped by to see if she had been found?"

"Never."

As courtroom theater, this was perfect for the prosecution: the tears, the shaky voice, the tissue, the bailiff summoned to get water. Betty was excused from the witness stand, and Janice's brother, Garry Hartman, took her place. The jury would never hear about Garry's pivotal role in the case. It was Garry who had been contacted ten years earlier by Sherrie Gladden-Davis in her search for other wives of John, only to find out about Janice. That phone call had set in motion the Ohio investigation.

Instead, operating under the no-mention-of-Fran rule, Stefancin went for the emotional angle.

She asked him if he had a sister named Lodema.

He said yes.

"Did you have another sister?" asked Stefancin.

"I used to have another sister. Janice."

To bolster the prosecution's "She'll never walk away from him again" theme, Garry recounted how he and a friend had visited Jan and John one day when John was at work—and how the atmosphere suddenly turned tense when John came home, the mood changing to a "domineering kind of situation." He spoke of the chess game that had enraged John.

And he spoke of Jan's life after she'd moved out and moved from Columbus, how even though she was working as a go-go dancer with high white boots and a frilly top that shook when she danced, she was no slut.

"So it was a clothed dancer?" the prosecutor asked.

"Yes. Yes," said Garry, and he recalled how he and his wife visited the bar where Jan was dancing "to see exactly what was involved here because, you know, [I was] a little skeptical."

"But we were surprised," he said, describing Jan's routine as three minutes of dancing, followed by a thirty-minute break. "She was pretty good."

The atmosphere was so family-friendly that he and Jan could discuss plans to get together at their mother's house for Thanksgiving.

And, setting up the testimony about the suspicious circumstances surrounding Janice's disappearance, with her leaving behind the kinds of things she never would have left behind, he described her beloved Mustang. "That was her property. Nobody was gonna take it from her," he said.

The defense had no questions of Garry Hartman.

Following Garry to the witness stand was his father Neal Hartman, who added little to either the prosecution or defense case. He was confused over times and dates and events. Shown pictures of some of Jan's clothing and asked if he recognized them, Neal said, "No, I didn't, not really."

• • •

After the testimony from family members, prosecutors turned back the clock twenty-seven years and tried to reconstruct the original missing persons investigation, calling Thomas Gasser, who in 1974 was a young Wayne County sheriff's road deputy rookie, seven months out of the Mansfield Police Academy. It was Gasser who had been sent to Kathy Paridon's house in Doylestown on November 19, 1974, to take a report about the missing Janice Hartman Smith.

The report had to stand on its own because Gasser, now a lieutenant with the sheriff's office, said he had no memory of that day. All he could do was interpret the report for the jury, and in some cases he couldn't do that. It appeared the information on the report came from both John and Kathy, but Gasser could only guess. "I believe Mr. Smith would have provided a large portion of that," he said under questioning by prosecutor Martin Frantz. "To say specifically how much he gave versus Kathy Paridon, I don't recall specifically."

Under cross-examination, defense attorney Kirk Migdal sought to use Gasser to bolster the theory that Janice had worked as a "narc," ratting out drug dealers, and that this could have gotten her killed. Gasser agreed that the word *narc* does at times refer to a police informant.

"And the idea is to keep, obviously, their name away from the drug dealers, because that's the danger, if the drug dealer finds out, they're then in danger. Is that true?" asked Migdal.

"That could be."

"Because drug dealers are dangerous and they can bring harm to people who want to bring them down? Would you agree with me?"

"That's possible."

Suggesting the investigation was slipshod, Migdal elicited from Gasser that he had made no follow-up investigation on the missing persons case, though he said somebody else in the department had.

Migdal went through the report with Gasser to make a few more defense points: that Janice's hair was blond, not multi-colored as Michael had described her corpse; that Janice had bruises on her face and arms when she disappeared (a reference to the attempted rape); and that when Kathy Paridon was dropped off, Janice was in the car with a man, described as "stocky, with a mustache." The report also says the man had a bad case of acne and dark hair. Gasser speculated that Kathy provided some of the description, John the rest. John also had a name: John Richardson.

Under redirect, Gasser was asked by prosecutor Frantz whether the Richardson lead had been followed. "I don't recall if I went there or called there," he said. "Contact was made with someone with a similar name. We were not able to locate anyone with the name that was provided to us."

Next up to the stand was the man who did do that follow-up investigation, Timothy J. McGuire. A detective at the time, with just about a year on the job, McGuire was now retired from the department, working as a business manager at a company in Orrville. In direct testimony, he described how he had gone to John Smith's trailer and found Janice's Mustang parked there—and how a check of the plates returned an address in Columbus, Ohio. Answering questions by Frantz, McGuire told jurors he'd tried to talk to John, but couldn't find him, and had spoken instead with John's grandfather, Mr. Chaney, though he couldn't remember what had led him to Chaney's gas station. "All I know is it was a message that I had to go up and interview him. Why I went up there, I can't say," he said.

It was this air of uncertainty that made McGuire a witness as important to the defense as to the prosecution. Migdal used his questioning of the retired investigator to support the defense claim that nearly everything about this investigation was uncertain, including John Smith's possible culpability. Under pointed questioning that had Mc-

Guire bristling, the former lawman was asked to what extent he had investigated the attempted gang-rape of Janice as being a factor in her disappearance just days later. McGuire said he'd never even seen the attempted-rape report.

Migdal pounced.

"This is something you should have looked at, isn't that right?" he asked.

"If I was assigned to that, yeah."

"Well, you were assigned to follow up on the missing persons report."

"There was other officers with this case."

"You read the missing persons report?"

"Right."

"Somebody should have followed up on it, is that what you are telling me?"

"I am saying I did not make those decisions."

"Somebody should have done it, would you agree?"

"Yeah."

Migdal then led McGuire word-for-word through the assault report, and asked again, "Somebody, either you or your boss, should have followed up on this, this important lead?"

"Yes, sir."

"And not one person did it that you know of?"

"That I know of, yes, sir."

Frantz did his best to rehabilitate McGuire under redirect questioning, trying to give the jury some reason why investigators didn't link the assault on Janice with her disappearance. The prosecutor first elicited from McGuire that he was only taking orders from superiors—superiors who would never be in the courtroom. Frantz also had McGuire note that injuries described on Janice in the assault report were considerably different from those in the missing persons report. The addresses given for Janice were also different in the reports, McGuire said.

"Is it possible that somebody didn't connect these two

as the same person because of the different addresses?"
Frantz asked.

"Anything's possible," he said.

That first long day of trial was capped off by the testimony
of West Windsor Police Detective Michael Dansbury, who,
like Garry Hartman, was barred from talking about the disappearance of Betty Fran Gladden. Dansbury recounted his
interview with John Smith on October 16, 1991, but didn't
say that this interview had nothing to do with Janice Hartman. Still, Dansbury's very presence as an investigator
from New Jersey—and even the nuances of some of his
answers—would subtly remind any juror who had been following the news in recent months of the missing second
wife.

During that interview with John, Dansbury said: "I asked
if he was married and who his first wife was"—a subtle
hint that there was a subsequent wife. "He advised me it
was Janice E. Hartman, that he had met her, he eloped and
got married in City Hall in Detroit, Michigan, in 1969 or
1970. Shortly after he continued that he got a no-fault divorce and he last saw her heading towards Florida to a
commune."

Dansbury described the second time he talked to John,
on April 9, 1992, when John had told him that Janice was
heavily into the drug scene, that her brother Ross had come
back from Vietnam and was also heavily into drugs, and
that he'd divorced Janice because of her drug problems. He
also recalled how Smith had said that the last time he saw
Janice was in a bar where she was with a boyfriend. He'd
first denied having anything to do with reporting her missing, then confirmed that he had after being told police had
the original report.

After the direct testimony, John's lawyers had no questions of Dansbury: the defense wanted to get him and
Fran's ghost out of the courtroom.

Dansbury would be the last prosecution witness of the day,
though that's not how Stefancin had planned it. One more

witness was supposed to have taken the stand between McGuire and Dansbury. But right before she was to testify, Kathy Paridon fell apart.

"I can't do it. I'm scared. This is so hard," she told Stefancin in tears.

There was no point in pushing her. She was too upset to coherently testify. It was a setback for the prosecution. Kathy was going to change her story from 1974, Stefancin said, and now say that she didn't recall a second man in the car the night Janice disappeared—that the man with bad acne simply didn't exist. She was also going to testify about once seeing Smith slap Janice across the face.

Her testimony wasn't going to be all positive for the prosecution. She had also heard Janice talk about being an informant in a drug case. Migdal recalled: "If we could have gotten in all the statements, Kathy has Janice saying, 'If you never see me again, I'm with the FBI,' and 'I'm going to leave for a while, I'm working for the FBI.' It was probably hearsay and tough to get in, but it was great stuff. We would have loved to have had that from Kathy." And she'd surely have to answer to what would no doubt be sharp cross-examination questions about why she had changed her account of that night at the Sun Valley Inn.

The subject was moot. The prosecution scratched her from the list. She'd never appear in court.

Reviewing the long day, Stefancin could only be pleased. The family witnesses provided an emotional wallop, the investigators highlighted some of John's suspicious statements and actions surrounding Janice's disappearance and the New Jersey case crept into the trial, if only by inference.

The defense team was feeling good, too. "The family helped us," Migdal concluded, noting that the worst anyone could say about Smith's supposed controlling and possessive nature was that he hadn't liked Janice's smoking, and he'd once gotten mad during a chess game. Hardly homicidal behavior. "There was an amicable divorce. They never showed that John ever hit her," said Migdal. The witnesses also pointed to the problems with the original police investigation of Janice's disappearance, opening the door for the defense to argue that the original investigators botched things up. It was impossible to say whether the attempted gang-rape was linked or not. "I can't imagine anything dumber," said Migdal. "When somebody comes up missing, you think they would retrace her steps. . . . I think they didn't care. She was a dancer. And I thought it was incompetence. I think it was a combination of both: incompetence and not caring enough." Still, the defense could only suggest that Janice's disappearance could have been linked to some sort of upcoming testimony in a drug case. The defense's private investigator searched far and wide for any written record of that testimony, but could never find it.

There was little time for the defense to feel relieved. After the weekend, Monday's session would bring what promised to be the most damaging witness of the trial: Michael Smith.

CHAPTER 26

The night before Michael was to take the stand, his mother Grace had called and tried to talk him out of it, according to Potts and Stefancin. (Grace Malz declined to comment.) But Michael had made his decision. He was going to testify against his brother.

Michael Smith, with immunity from prosecution and an inner peace that had eluded him for so many years, took the oath and sat in the witness chair. The strain of the moment showed. The prosecution's case depended on Michael to be thorough, clear, sympathetic and calm. If he did everything right, his brother would never leave his cell. "It was difficult to watch Mike," recalled Michael's former neighbor, Richard Armstrong of the Armstrong Funeral Home. "He didn't want to be there. He didn't want to do it. But he knew he was doing the right thing. He spoke very soft, kind of staggered through his words. He had a difficult time."

Under gentle questioning from Stefancin, Michael methodically went through all that he knew about his brother's relationship with Janice, from the early days of marriage to the fateful night that John had asked him to drive him to the Sun Valley Inn—the last place Janice had been seen before she disappeared. Michael recounted John's explanation for Janice's disappearance—that she was in a witness relocation program—and he testified about the days after her disappearance when he and John had loaded up bags of her clothing from a trailer in Wooster.

Michael then got to the critical part of his testimony: that day in 1974—he thought it was Thanksgiving weekend because the Ohio State–Michigan game was on TV—that he had seen John building a wooden box and putting Janice's clothing inside. He then recalled that horrible day five years later, in 1979, when he'd pried open the box and seen Janice's face with the multi-colored hair and the legs cut off below the knees. He testified about the telephone call to John, the discussions about what to do with the body—how he feared this awful event would kill their grandmother. And he recalled how he'd seen John drive off in the Corvette, with Janice's corpse in the box.

Listening to the testimony, the jury was rapt. They nodded, made eye contact, took notes; not a word seemed to miss their attention. Michael told the jury about the nightmares that had haunted him for years. That, he said, was why he'd decided, finally, to turn on his brother and talk to police and the FBI, spilling the entire sordid story in 1999, then becoming a government informant who'd allowed his phone calls to John to be tape-recorded.

The prosecution then played tapes of those calls. By the time John Smith said, "Holy shit," on the tape, the jury was transfixed, the profanity slicing through the air of the hushed courtroom.

After she finished her questioning on direct, Stefancin felt pleased and relieved. She watched the jury and she liked what she saw. They didn't just seem to listen to him, they seemed to accept him. Her only concern, of course, was cross-examination, and her sense that Kirk Migdal would try to rile Michael, tapping into years of anger and frustration and resentment. This was, Stefancin knew, a family that could get upset easily. If Michael lost his cool, all that acceptance would fly out the courtroom door.

As he stood to begin his questioning, Migdal knew that Michael had made a good impression on the jury. He knew that he couldn't—and shouldn't—try to destroy him, because jurors would resent the attack and hold it against John. The lawyer felt he needed to chip away at the edges of the testimony, building a little pile of uncertainty. The idea wasn't so much to show that Michael was lying or outright wrong about the facts, but that he may have gotten a few—an important, reasonable-doubt–worthy few—of the details mixed up.

Migdal dispensed with a greeting, and launched right into his questioning.

"Mr. Smith, when you talked to the FBI May fourteenth of 1999, that was in New York?"

"I'm not sure of the date, but I talked to the FBI in New York."

"They first talked to you on May fifth. That's when you lied to them. Then you contacted your lawyers. Then, as you said, you threw everything away and told the truth. And that was sometime after May fifth, 1999?"

"That is correct."

And on the questioning went, as Migdal brought Michael through his statement to the FBI—a statement that, the lawyer suggested, had some flaws.

"You testified on direct examination that you first saw John building the box the Saturday after Thanksgiving because the Ohio State–Michigan State game was on?" Migdal asked.

"That's correct."

"You're sure of that?" the lawyer said.

"Ohio State–Michigan was on, yes," replied Michael.

"And it was after Thanksgiving?"

"I believe it was."

"You are sure about that as anything else you have testified to?"

"I am sure that the Ohio State–Michigan game was on."

"And you testified on direct that was after Thanksgiving?"

"I believe it was after Thanksgiving."

Stefancin knew what was coming and she was ready for it. The judge then told the jury that both sides had agreed that "after extensive research," the game actually was played on the Saturday before Thanksgiving.

Michael, even the prosecution conceded, had given the wrong weekend for when the box was built.

It wasn't the only wrong information Michael would give, the defense attorney suggested. Migdal took Michael through the day he was questioned by Detective Mansue and Agent Drew at the Medina police station.

"I assume you were pretty scared?" the lawyer asked.

"Yes."

"And you lied to them?"

"Yes."

When Michael decided finally to tell what was the truth, he did so only with the help of a lawyer, Migdal elicited, suggesting that Michael feared prosecution, possibly tainting his revised statements.

"Did you pay him?" Migdal asked, referring to the lawyer.

"We paid him some money, yes."

"OK, what do you do for a living?"

"Right now I work at Falcon Industries."

"And how much do you make?"

"About ten dollars an hour."

"How much did you pay the lawyer?"

"I believe we took about twenty-three hundred dollars out of savings."

"Twenty-three hundred dollars. A large sum of money for somebody who makes ten dollars an hour?"

It was a cheap shot, one that Migdal would later regret.

Michael, striving to regain some dignity, answered, "I made more than that previous to that."

The lawyer then challenged Michael's suggestion that he really didn't need legal protection—and that his statements to the FBI in New York weren't shaded by any hopes of getting a non-prosecution deal—because the statute of limitations had run out on any crime with which he could have been charged.

"You paid [the lawyer] twenty-three hundred dollars, you paid for his plane ticket, you paid him for a hotel room to protect you from what he told you was basically nothing, because the statute of limitation has run? Is that correct?"

"That is it. But I wasn't listening to him."

"You were paying money to your lawyer and you didn't listen to him?"

"No, because I still believed I was in trouble, I was in big trouble."

And so was the defense at this point, as Migdal continued to pound on this sympathetic witness, a nice-enough, blue-collar guy who had been faced with an extraordinarily difficult situation and was doing the best he could with what he had.

Still, the defense lawyer pressed on. He turned to other inconsistencies in Michael's statements to law enforcement. Michael acknowledged that in at least one police interview he'd said he believed he saw the box being built by John one month after Jan's disappearance, which would have been into December. In another interview, he said it was one to three months after Jan disappeared.

Migdal elicited from Michael that he had also given different explanations for why the family agreed not to tell anybody about the box.

"Didn't you tell the FBI: 'We decided we weren't going to call the police. Grandpa was concerned it was going to hurt his business'?"

"That is the statement I gave them," Michael said, "but I was ashamed and embarrassed that I had anything at all to do with this."

"This was given in New York after you promised to tell the complete truth? You are telling us on the witness stand today it was because your grandmother is gonna die if she hears this, but you told the FBI on five–twenty-nine it is because your grandfather's gas station business was gonna be hurt?"

"There was still a little bit of a—I can't remember all of the exact details. That was quite a long time off."

Michael was becoming flustered.

"Did you lie to us in court when you said you told the entire truth to the FBI?" Migdal asked.

"Yes, that would be a lie," said Michael.

"So you lied in court?"

"No, because I—What it was is, I told them to take all their stuff, throw it out the window. I told them I'd try to tell the truth the best that I could."

"Well—"

"I was ashamed. I was ashamed and embarrassed that I had anything at all to do with this."

Again, Migdal pointed out that Michael had given different explanations for why the family kept the box a secret. This time, Stefancin objected.

"We have been through this. He has asked the same question to this witness a number of times," she said.

"I haven't got an answer yet," Migdal snapped.

"He has gotten an answer. He just doesn't like the answer he got."

The judge allowed Migdal to go over the subject one more time, then move on. Migdal did go over it, a few more times actually, before turning to another subject, pressing Michael on whether he had ever told an investigator the story of John's explanation for his missing ex-wife: that the FBI and sheriff's deputies had been in on a kidnapping of Janice and John. The defense lawyer suggested that it was only at this trial, more than twenty years later, that Michael seemed to recall this.

"Does it say in any of your four or five statements that John ever told you that?"

"I don't know."

"Would it help to refresh your recollection if you reviewed all those statements?"

"No."

The lawyers, at Stefancin's request, then approached the bench and spoke to the judge off the record. They emerged from the sidebar with Migdal announcing that both sides had stipulated that none of the FBI reports contained any reference to John telling his brother that the FBI and sheriff's deputies had kidnapped Janice.

"I have no other questions, Your Honor," Migdal said.

There wasn't much need to rehabilitate Michael—he'd endured cross—so Stefancin used her redirect questioning to underscore the most damaging information.

"Michael, Mr. Migdal asked you about what you didn't tell the FBI. I'm going to ask you about what you did tell them. You told them about the box?"

"That's correct."

"And you told them about how you found the box?"

"That's correct."

"How you saw your brother building the box in 1974?"

"That's correct."

Migdal objected on the grounds that the questions were leading, which they clearly were, but the point was made.

"Are the facts about the box the same?" Stefancin asked.

"The facts about the box are the same. They have been the same the whole time."

"And how are you so sure?"

"It burnt," he said. "It's like having a branding iron burn at your brain. It is something you don't forget. It is something I wish to God I could forget now. If there's something I could do to change it, I would change it. But I can't. I can't forget it. I can't get rid of it. It's there. It's horrible."

On re-cross, Migdal returned to the theme that Michael had changed aspects of his story about the box over the years, including the reasons why the police weren't called. But the questioning backfired, badly, as Michael ended his testimony with a heart-wrenching statement.

"The reason I didn't call the police—I was scared to death. I thought I was part of a murder that I had nothing to do with," he said. "I was there. I seen the box. I found the box. And I opened the box. I called my brother, he came and got it. Now, unfortunately when you are guilty of something, you don't think about the statute of limitations or whatever. I mean, it happened. I mean, it is nothing that you want to think about, you know? I was hoping to bury this, but this thing just don't bury. It don't go away. You don't have the nightmares. I do."

The courtroom fell into a stunned silence.

Stefancin couldn't have gotten a better answer if she had scripted it herself.

Migdal immediately felt regret. He thought he had been too aggressive with Michael, that the jury sensed the real love Michael had for his brother, and how hard all of this was on him. "It was a bad day," recalled Migdal, "But we knew it was going to be a bad day."

As the next witness, FBI Agent Robert Hilland, took the stand, it was clear the day wasn't going to get any better for the defense. It wasn't just Hilland's testimony. He brought into the courtroom the plywood box.

The highlight of his testimony, from the prosecution's standpoint, would be his dramatic account of the interrogation of John in the California motel room on May 5, 1999—John's apparent emotional breakdown, his statement to the effect that "I don't want to lie anymore," the curling up in the fetal position and asking to lie on the couch forever, and the 911 call because John had said he thought he was having a heart attack.

Cross-examination by Beverly Wire did little to mitigate the harm. Wire elicited that Smith was fully cooperative for the interview. She also suggested through her questioning that Smith's behavior could have been the result of nerves, put on edge when he was read his Miranda rights even though he wasn't under arrest.

"While lying on the couch, or even before, he indicated to you that he was scared?" asked Wire.

"Concerning the question of his involvement in Janice Hartman's disappearance, he said he was scared to talk about it," said Hilland. "He didn't know how to begin talking about it."

"He was scared, that's what he said?"

"In the contention of he was tired of lying. He was scared. He didn't know how to begin to talk about it, he said."

Wire noted that John's brother also expressed fear during his FBI interview, even though authorities ultimately decided he had done nothing wrong. "Had you ever questioned other people in the course of your career, prior FBI, where they were nervous and scared when you were questioning them?"

"Yes, ma'am."

"OK. So it's the emotion that you've seen before, that you are used to seeing?"

"At times, yes, ma'am."

She also made it clear to the jury that this was Hilland's version of the questioning.

"Was that tape-recorded?"

"No, ma'am, it was not."

"Is that not unusual, sir, considering that this was a person who is being considered as the major suspect in a murder case, taken into a hotel room, and it is not taped?"

"It's not our standard practice to tape interviews, ma'am."

"The only reason I ask is that testifying here today you must have said at least three or four times: 'I am doing this from my memory.'"

"Absolutely, yes, ma'am."

The prosecution had no follow-up questions for redirect, and Day 2 of the trial—the mountainous day that Stefancin had so carefully prepared for—had gone as well as she could have expected.

For the first two days of the trial, the jury only heard about what John was alleged to have done to Janice. Now they were going to see it. Beginning on July 10, and then later with Symes, jurors were re-introduced to Janice Hartman

Smith—piece by piece. As the trial went from the gripping to the grisly, Dr. Frank Saul took the stand to talk about his examination of the Jane Doe skeleton exhumed from the potter's field section of the cemetery in Morocco, Indiana, on March 2, 2000. Going over his examination procedure, he told jurors how he'd determined the bones to belong to a female of white ancestry, about 20 to 30 years old, with both legs cut off below the knee. Then, to the horror of Janice's mother, who was in the courtroom, Saul opened a bag of bones—Janice's bones—describing them for the jury, beginning with what was now called Exhibit Number 12.

"What I have wrapped up here are two pieces of a femur or thighbone, upper and lower pieces," he said, opening the bag. "What I'm holding up now is the upper portion of a left femur or thighbone." He took out another bone. "What I'm holding up now is the lower portion of a left femur or thighbone."

Later, Stefancin said, "I'm going to show you what's been marked for purposes of identification as State's Exhibit Thirteen. Do you recognize what that is?"

"Yes," said Saul. "This is the right third rib." The rib that had been sent out for DNA testing.

"I've placed on the rail before you a small bottle that's been marked Exhibit Fourteen," the prosecutor said. "Do you happen to know just by recognizing the vial what's inside?"

"I assume it's the left lower second molar."

Janice, a once vibrant young woman, was reduced to a collection of numbered parts.

"I nearly had a fit," Janice's mother would recall, but she insisted on sitting in the courtroom through the gruesome ordeal. "Stubborn Irish: I just stayed." That night, in the motel, Betty saw the bones again, this time in a TV report on the testimony. "I broke down again," she said. "I never want to see that again."

Under cross-examination by Migdal, Saul spoke of the limits of his efforts. He said he could not determine a cause of death, or even injury, having determined that the legs were cut off after death. The defense seized on this point, in its efforts to show the jury that the prosecution had no idea how Janice Smith had died, much less who might have killed her.

"Now, you could not identify any signs of trauma in the skeletal remains, is that correct?" asked Migdal.

"That is correct," Saul said.

The jury and family members were given a respite after Saul's testimony, as FBI Agent Thomas Cottone testified about tracking down John Smith's old Corvette and determining that a box the size of the one holding the remains could have fit inside it. He also testified about scratch marks found on one of the seats. This corroborated the testimony of Michael Smith, although Wire tried to suggest that the scratches could have come from anywhere, the car having been owned for the last nine years by somebody else. But Cottone said the car was rarely used. "It was a collectible. He didn't hardly drive it at all," he said, adding that it was stored in the man's garage. There was only one small point scored for the defense: Cottone acknowledged that no trace evidence of any value was found in the car.

After Cottone left the stand, the judge excused the jury so the lawyers could engage in an important hearing focusing on whether the prosecution could introduce more evidence to back up Michael's testimony—the evidence that couldn't be seen by human eyes. At issue was whether dog trainer Sandra Anderson could testify about Eagle sniffing out signs of human remains in the Chaney family garage where Michael said the box was kept for five years. The prosecution wanted her presented as an expert witness, akin to a witness testifying about fingerprints or fibers. The defense wanted Anderson barred from trial because the science of dogs' sniffing out remains didn't meet legal standards. The judge wanted to hear more about Eagle and his nose, so Anderson was called to the stand outside the jury's presence.

Under questioning by Stefancin, Anderson spelled out her credentials, the training techniques used with the dog, and Eagle's extraordinary track record. Anderson then told the judge about the search of the Chaney garage and how Eagle had quickly picked up on the scent of human remains. Under cross-examination by Migdal, Anderson said the dog's nose was so good it can differentiate between human and non-human blood. But she acknowledged that when Eagle found remains, there was no way to tell how long they'd been there.

After her testimony in the hearing, Migdal lodged his objection to allowing Anderson to appear before the jury.

"I don't know that she's qualified, Your Honor, because the testimony comes from a dog, not her," said Migdal. "She's basically testifying, and this dog is the only one who doesn't say stuff, so I don't believe it can be verified by other people."

It was a weak argument and Stefancin easily refuted it, noting that similar testimony from trainers of drug-sniffing dogs has been allowed. "She's been accepted as an expert in twenty other states," said the prosecutor. "This particular type of human residual odor was accepted in the state of Wisconsin just last year with this dog. I believe she meets the qualifications of an expert."

The judge said simply, "The court would agree," and the jury was brought back into the courtroom to hear in detail about Eagle's findings.

Anderson repeated her testimony from the hearing, giving her credentials and those of Eagle and going over the search at the Chaneys' garage. To illustrate her testimony, the jury was shown a videotape of an excited Eagle bounding into the garage and lying down next to a cinderblock wall, emphatic that he had found something. "He barked and he barks and he's trying to tell me there's a lot of odor there," said Anderson, narrating the video, "and that's what he's doing right now. He's preserving that area and—There, he's jumping up. He's barking. He's very excited. The tail's wagging."

Migdal, in his cross-examination, tried to show through a hypothetical question that Eagle's nose may have found something—but not necessarily the death scent of Janice Hartman. Migdal suggested that if that were so, and if the box were moved as Michael Smith had said it was, then Eagle should have hit two scents, not just one. Anderson said she didn't know what to say, since all she knows is where the dog found odor. Also, she said, it would depend on whether the body had decomposed in the new spot as to whether a scent was left.

After trying the hypothetical three times without success, the prosecution objected, the judge sustained the objection, and Migdal gave up.

Next up were John Smith's co-workers and friends, who spoke of his sometimes-strange behavior at work. Scott Mintier, Smith's boss at Pullman-Standard, talked about how in about 1978 the guys made fun of Smith for wearing a women's watch to work. Richard Anthony Gromlovits, another supervisor at Pullman-Standard, spoke of how Smith had followed Mintier's stepdaughter Kathy McDonald around "like a puppy dog." Then McDonald herself testified that Smith had given her a silver ladies Bulova watch with a jewel beveled "J" and diamonds. And she told the jury of her shock at hearing Smith say it was from his wife who had died. Shown a watch in court, she identified it as the same one.

Under cross-examination, the witnesses acknowledged some minor inconsistencies between their courtroom testimony and written statements taken by the FBI, but otherwise the defense made no headway. The fact remained: John Smith possessed the watch of his dead wife, a watch he had said she was wearing when she disappeared. Joseph

Dabrowski, Smith's boss at Copco, then told the jury of that Friday in 1979 when Smith had had to leave work early for some business in Seville, then came back the following Tuesday with an incredible story of being arrested for driving 170 mph in his souped-up Corvette. The implication, to be argued by the prosecutor later, was that this was the same time that John would have gone to Seville, Ohio, to pick up the box holding Janice's remains.

The third day of trial ended with the testimony of Janice's sister, Lodema "Dee" Hartman, who in a shaky voice described her older sister as "my best friend," and how she would perform little skits with her. She recalled how she'd gone with John Smith to buy Janice that jeweled watch that John would later give Kathy McDonald after Janice's disappearance. And she talked about that last time she ever saw her sister, before Thanksgiving, when they'd swapped clothes.

As sympathetic as Dee Hartman was, the defense was able to use her to make one of its few important points of the day. In cross-examination, Dee said that her sister had told her she was a drug informant and that on that last day they saw each other, Janice said she would see her "after graduation"—years away.

But it was the prosecution that would get in the last question.

"Did she ever show up for Thanksgiving dinner?" Stefancin asked during redirect questioning.

"No," Dee said.

It was a bittersweet note on which to end the day—another good day for the prosecution—but the defense team remained confident. "As a defense attorney, you want no surprises, and nothing came in that we didn't think would come in," Migdal recalled. "Our defense theory—that at some point John possessed the remains, but nothing more—is still there. Nothing came in that could show anything different from what we told the jury. I was feeling good."

More than twenty-one years after he'd responded to the call about The Lady in the Box discovered on the Indiana roadside, Gerry Burman finally came to court to testify in the case that would bracket his career. It was Day 4 of the trial, July 11, as the prosecution wanted to lead the jury back to that lonely road in Indiana twenty years ago. Burman spoke of being a young patrolman in 1980, protecting the crime scene while investigators questioned the men who'd found the bones that later were identified as those of Janice Hartman. And he recounted that day in 2000 when, as a detective near retirement, he received the letter from an Ohio detective asking whether his department had a dead Jane Doe in a box. There was no cross-examination from the defense.

Though Burman was only on the stand for a few minutes, his testimony gave him a chance to look into the eyes of a man he had long thought would never be caught. "I've seen some hard-shelled defendants. This guy would make you into cold ice cream. Totally unemotional," he said. "The entire time I testified, he may have glanced at his attorney, but that was it. He just had absolutely no facial features. He was attentive, but he didn't smile, made no gestures. I can't explain it. I guess God makes us all differently."

Memories of the discovery of The Lady in the Box continued, as Sam Kennedy, the road crew foreman, recalled the grim discovery when he'd pried open with a crowbar a box he had found on the side of the road. "A skull fell out, rolled out, and I just dropped everything. I left," he said. The remains had then been put into the care of crime scene analyst Larry Bartley, who told the jury how he and the now-deceased coroner had examined the remains in the funeral home, finding the skeleton's legs severed just below the knee. Bartley also recounted how the remains were finally buried in a Jane Doe grave.

While Bartley was on the stand, he identified all the clothing taken from the box—the little 70s dresses, the shirts, the underwear—leading up to one of the final items. "That was the crucifix that was found in the bottom of the box," he said, holding the cross in a small clear package.

Like Burman before him, Bartley had to look at John.

"It was nice to see the expression on his face—or the lack of expression on his face—as I was testifying," Bartley recalled. "It was obvious that he could not believe that twenty-one years later, we still had all this evidence. The evidence had a chain of custody so airtight that his attorney couldn't break it. Through all the years and all the coroners, nothing was lost, everything was still there."

The next day, Thursday, July 12, brought just one witness, Dr. Steven Symes, the expert in cut marks on bones, who explained how he'd determined that one of Janice Smith's legs was cut off with a serrated knife before the body was flipped over and the other leg was cut off with the same knife.

"It would have to take a lot of power, a lot of strength, persistence for something like this," he told the jury.

It was a powerful image, and jurors seemed to take notice. But it was not, as defense attorney Migdal would point out, an incriminating image.

He asked Symes: "You have no instrument in your possession or ever given to you by the prosecutor that made these cuts, is that correct?"

"I have no instrument that matches," said the doctor.

It was a key defense point. Symes could not say, could not even imply, that John Smith had cut off Janice's legs. The murder case lacked a murder weapon.

Still, the strength of Symes' appearance before the jury, from the prosecution's perspective, was not so much what he said, but what he showed. Prior to the cross-examination, more of Janice Hartman's bones were shown to the jury, the dispassionate, technical testimony contrasting starkly with the creepy sight of the old dark bones.

"I'm handing to you, sir, what has been marked for identification purposes as State's Exhibit Eighteen-A," Stefancin said, giving a clear package to Symes. "Do you recognize that item?"

"Yes," he said, "this is the proximal end of the left tibia." Janice's shinbone, carved in half by a serrated knife wielded by somebody hell-bent on cutting off her legs.

"And handing you now, sir, what has been marked for identification purposes as State's Exhibit Eighteen-B, do you recognize that item?"

"This is the left fibula joint"—the top of the calfbone.

Symes would also show the jury the rest of the chopped-off leg bones. Wearing gloves, he took them out of the packages and displayed them for jurors, describing exactly where the cut marks were made. He spoke of Janice's bones as if they were pieces of two-by-fours he had found on the shop floor. "There's nothing here that suggests a mechanical-powered saw," he said. "It's all hand-powered tool." The blade wasn't offset, so as to avoid binding on the bone. There were "false starts," and the cut was in a "V" pattern. The cutter used a lot of muscle. "The blade is going to bind," he said. "It's going to take power."

The trial week ended with a stipulation: both sides agreed that DNA tests showed that the remains had a similar DNA sequence to that of Betty Lippincott. The defense conceded that the bones in the box were those of Janice.

As the trial sped toward its conclusion, with just two days of testimony left, the prosecution on Monday, July 16, called a string of women whose lives had intersected with John's, beginning with Sandi Norwood, who described herself to the jury as John's "very close" friend. Sandi told the jury that her relationship with John could have advanced to marriage—that John had even spoken of getting married, though it wasn't for love. He was an up-and-comer at work, she said, and he wanted his bosses to see him as stable, dependable, marriageable. It wasn't to be, however, and for the duration of her relationship with John, the only talk of marriage concerned his first one, to Janice, which John had told Sandi was loving and wonderful until Janice had started hanging out with tough people and using drugs. Career-minded John didn't like this sort of thing around him.

Sandi also recounted for the jury the incredible explanation that John had given for the end of his marriage to Janice. He'd told Sandi that Janice had been murdered in what might have been a kinky-sex killing, her anus filled with semen. He'd retrieved her wedding bands from her lifeless body, and later showed them to Sandi. But he'd never told police about what happened.

During cross-examination, defense attorney Wire suggested there was a reason why John never went to authorities.

"You had an interview with a Sergeant Potts and an Agent McQuillen. Do you remember meeting them together?"

"Yes," Sandi said.

"And at that time, in your statement to those officers, after you recounted the story that you just told us, you indicated that you asked John why he didn't call the police, and he told you that he thought that they would kill him if he did?"

"Yes."

"OK. That is an accurate statement?"

"That is an accurate statement."

The defense had no more questions.

Next up was Janice Miller, who, unknown to jurors, had been summoned to court from the York Correctional Institute in Niantic, Connecticut, where she was serving time for violating the terms of the probation for a prostitution beef. Both sides had stipulated before trial that there would be no evidence presented that John had used prostitutes, though from her testimony it was obvious what Janice Miller's relationship with John was. She told jurors how Smith had picked her up in Washington Park in Bridgeport, Connecticut, and that she had begun a relationship of sorts with him, but that she'd refused to travel to Atlanta with him. He had creeped her out with the story about the death of his first wife with the same name by drug-dealer–hired hit men.

Stefancin then suggested that Janice Miller had more in common with Janice Hartman than the first name.

"Janice, in 1992, the summer of 1992, how much did you weigh?" asked Stefancin.

"About one-twenty"—roughly the same as Janice Hartman.

"And how tall are you?"

"About five-five"—a few inches taller.

"And was your hair color about the same then as it is today?"—light brown, the same as Janice Hartman.

"Yes."

"Were you wearing it along the same lines?"

"Yes."

Janice Miller also told the jury about the trip she'd taken to Ohio for a family gathering—John bringing her to the family home for Labor Day weekend 1992. And she told how the relationship ended with her throwing a pumpkin at him.

In the defense's sharpest cross-examination of the trial, Wire elicited that at the time Janice Miller knew John, she was using heroin and cocaine three or four times a day, that John was buying it for her, and that she had a boyfriend, Robert, on the side while living with John.

"Isn't the incident that basically brought your relationship with Mr. Smith to an end was that he thought that Robert had come into the house and stolen money from him?"

"Yeah, well, part of it, yeah."

"In fact, the relationship sort of fell apart when the money ran out and there wasn't any more for you and Robert?"

"Right."

"So basically during this period of time you used Mr. Smith?"

"Right."

The defense had no further questions, and the prosecution didn't either.

The next of John's women to take the stand was Sheila Sautter, a reluctant witness to say the least. Over the years, she had tried to put the whole relationship behind her, and wasn't interested in testifying. Not that she had a choice— she was subpoenaed. Sheila told the jury about the seven-and-a-half–year, off-and-on relationship with John, and how, after five years together, she'd found the old résumé that listed him as once having been married. She said that John at first denied it, then admitted he was married and that the separation had been amicable.

But it wasn't Sheila's testimony that struck hardest at the defense case; it was her voice, and that of John's, from a decade earlier, in the secretly recorded phone conversation, a portion of which was played for the jury. With all references to John's second wife, Fran, edited out, jurors could hear Sheila confronting John about first-wife Janice. Jurors heard John telling Sheila that Janice "headed her way and I headed my way" after the split. "I didn't know she was dead until today," he says on the tape. "You're lying to everyone around you," Sheila is heard saying, and Smith replies, "That's correct."

The defense had no questions.

John's alleged problems with telling the truth dominated the testimony of the next two women. Summer McGowin, the daughter of Smith's most recent wife, Diane, recalled the day that John spoke of a dead girl in a box that had been dropped off on the front porch of his grandparents' house. She told the jury about the Shelter Island meeting in which she and her mother had confronted John about whether he'd killed Janice—and John's failure to provide an answer.

"He never answered your questions?" asked Stefancin.

"No."

"Did he ever deny it?"

"No."

Summer's mother Diane then took the stand, describing her marriage to John, which had ended in divorce. Still using the surname Smith, Diane spoke of how John had disappeared for a couple of days in July 1999 when the FBI was closing in. She also repeated John's story about a box showing up on his grandparents' porch, with his brother or another relative telling him there was a dead goat inside. Then, like her daughter, she told the jury that John had never denied killing Janice.

"There wasn't a response," she said. "There was no response."

"No denial?"

"No nothing."

Another silence in the courtroom.

The defense had no questions.

The final day of testimony began Tuesday, July 17, with Diane being re-called to the stand to make a small correction in her testimony from the previous day: she had said she was married to John on September 5, 1999, when in fact they were married on September 5, 1998. Given the night to strategize, the defense used her brief reappearance to take some of the sting out her claim that John had refused to deny murder allegations.

"The statement you gave us here that took place at Shelter Island, that was in about August of '99?" asked Migdal.

"I think so, around then."

"When John was arrested in October of 2000, he was living with you, wasn't he?"

"He was."

The prosecution didn't seek an explanation.

• • •

And with that, the prosecution case was finished. All those years and all those times investigators had thought they had John, only to have him get away, culminated with a prosecution case of just seven days. But the prosecution had made the points it had to, the only weakness being in proving motive, something the defense would no doubt stress to the jury. The family members had put a face on the victim, Michael had linked John with the box, and John had done nothing but sit there, blank, expressionless, revealing no sign of simple human emotion. The prosecution couldn't have coached him better.

After the prosecution rested, the defense made the routine motion at this point, asking the judge for an acquittal on the grounds that there wasn't enough evidence to even send the case to the jury. Normally a motion made with little effort by the defense, and quickly denied by the judge, John's lawyers put some emphasis on the issue in this case. It was a highly circumstantial case, without a murder weapon or eyewitness to the killing. It seemed worth a shot.

The defense cited a number of legal grounds, beginning with a contention that the prosecution had simply failed to prove that Janice was murdered. Her chopped-off legs notwithstanding, Janice's remains showed no evidence that she had been killed at the hands of John Smith or anybody else, the defense said. Migdal said that one could reasonably argue, "There is no crime." Wire then joined the argument, telling the judge that there also was no evidence of premeditation—no evidence that anybody had calculated and planned the murder of Janice Hartman. If anything, Wire argued, some of the evidence showed that John and Janice had been getting along fine in the days leading up to her disappearance. The defense's final argument was technical: there wasn't enough evidence to support trying the case in Wayne County, because the prosecution had failed to prove that the crime, if there was one, had occurred in the county. All that the prosecution had shown, Wire argued, was that Janice and John had lived in Wayne County and that she was last seen in Wayne County.

The prosecution countered that there was plenty of evidence to rebut all three of the defense contentions. As for whether there had been a crime committed, everything from the missing persons report to the fact that Janice's body had shown up in a box, without her legs, in her ex-husband's grandfather's garage was more than sufficient cause to prove a murder, Stefancin argued. In terms of whether the killing was calculated, Stefancin pointed to Michael's testimony about John going to the Sun Valley Inn the night Janice had disappeared, the fact that Janice's Mustang had turned up at John's trailer, John's building of the box, the putting of her belongings in the box. "I believe that there has been sufficient credible evidence to prove elements of prior calculation and design," the prosecutor said. As for the trial being held in Wayne County, all of the critical events in the case had occurred in the county, and her body was found in the county.

The judge agreed with the prosecution. He said, "I don't think there's any question" that Janice Hartman had died as a result of a crime and "the inference certainly can be drawn" that John did it. He also said the state had met its legal burden on the question of the trial venue. "So the motion will be overruled," he said. "Is the defense ready to proceed?"

"Yes, sir," Wire said.

"You may proceed."

"We would call Leonard Bennett," she said.

It had been more than twenty-five years since Bennett had gone through what must have been the worst night of his life: being in the same house—and taking part in—the attempted rape of his friend Janice Hartman. The defense actually hadn't planned on calling him. Migdal traditionally hesitated to put on any case at all, opting instead to make his points during the prosecution's case by raising reasonable doubts through cross-examination, then tying it all up in summation. And while the prosecution in this case had put on plenty of damaging witnesses, who either seemed to endure cross-examination well or who weren't crossed at all, Migdal's inclination again was to call no witnesses of his own. Bennett had actually been on the prosecution's list, but Stefancin never called him.

Under questioning by Wire, Leonard described his relationship with Janice as "just friends, friendship," and that he had probably seen her once every two days, usually to go dancing at the Far West Lounge and another bar in Doylestown whose name he couldn't remember. Wire tried to get Leonard to support the defense contention that Janice was at risk from other people besides John.

"Did she ever express to you fear of certain people in the Doylestown area?"

"Yes."

"Do you remember their names?"

To this, Stefancin jumped in with an objection, which the judge sustained on the grounds of hearsay. A witness can't testify about what somebody else has said to them, even if that somebody else is the victim. The only hearsay statements that usually can be presented to the jury are what the accused has said.

Wire pressed on.

"Did she tell you why she was afraid of them?"

"No."

"Did she ever tell you that she might disappear?"

Stefancin objected again, but not fast enough, as Leonard answered, "Yes."

Bennett then was led through the night of the attack on Janice, from Janice dancing to Janice being dragged into a bedroom, to Bennett himself going into that bedroom and taking off his clothes, though he said he did so because of "threats" and because he was frightened.

"The threats came again: If you don't do it, don't get on top of her, we'll get rid of both of you."

"Go ahead," Wire said.

"So I did, but nothing happened."

Later, Wire asked, "Did you ever hear the statement, 'Bitches like you don't deserve to live'?"

It was clearly an objectionable hearsay question and a lawyer of Wire's caliber knew it. Stefancin objected and the judge sustained the objection, but Wire got to at least get that statement into the jurors' heads.

After the direct testimony, Stefancin made Leonard her own witness, as if she had gone ahead with the original plan to call him. Under cross-examination, he was shown a photograph of the broken crucifix that had been taken out of the pine box containing Janice's bones.

"Does it look familiar to you?" asked Stefancin.

"Yes, it does."

"And who wore a crucifix like this?"

"I gave it to her."

"You gave it to Jan?"

"Yes."

"This looks like the crucifix you gave to Jan?"

"Missing a few parts."

If the prosecution case was fast, the defense case was but a blip. Having no more of its own questions for Leonard, the defense rested, its entire case amounting to a few minutes with one witness who was on the prosecution's list. The prosecution offered no rebuttal to the defense presentation, and just like that, the presentation of evidence was over. The judge told the jury that closing arguments would be given the next day. Then, deliberations.

CHAPTER 27

Most lawyers, by trial's end, are worn out, physically and mentally. On Wednesday, July 18, Jocelyn Stefancin was actually in better shape for her summation, her voice strong and clear, her body all but recovered from the illness that had hobbled her during opening statements. "Janice Elaine Hartman Smith disappeared November 17, 1974, and although she was close to her family and her friends, she was never heard from again," Stefancin began in her closing arguments. "What happened to Jan? That is a question, a mystery that plagued her family and law enforcement for over twenty-five years." The Smith case, she said, was like a mystery novel, and, "Throughout this trial, you have had twenty-seven chapters given to you. Each witness who took the stand was a chapter in the mystery novel of what happened to Jan."

"Ladies and gentlemen," she continued, "every chapter in this book, every word, every piece of evidence, points to the defendant in this case."

Simple, clear and bereft of doubt—that was the John Smith case, she argued in prosecutorial fashion. That's how she'd described it in opening statements. That's how it was now after jurors had heard all the evidence.

She then led the jury through the story of John and Jan—their marriage, which ended November 14, 1974, the separation agreement, the disappearance after Jan was last seen in the early morning hours of that Sunday in 1974. Stefancin went over the filing of the missing persons report at the Doylestown home of Kathy Paridon—a report that had given Jan's address as that of her ex-husband's trailer, even though she was living somewhere else. She went over John's behavior after Jan had disappeared—how he'd claimed they were still married when they were not, and how the report didn't list one of Jan's relatives as a person to contact.

"The first thing that points to the defendant is in fact, that missing persons report, because that report tells a lot about what the defendant was thinking at the time," Stefancin said. "If you want the police to be able to contact family members of Jan, a wife that you love, who fixes you breakfast every morning, if you want her located and everyone to know that she's safe, you list as a contact person either yourself or her family. You don't list somebody who's not part of that circle." That report also listed the jewelry that Jan had been wearing at the time—a diamond watch that John himself was seen wearing years later, and which he had given to another woman.

Moving to the testimony of John's brother Michael, who had seen John building the wooden "shit box," Stefancin reminded jurors how John had yelled at Michael when he asked about it. That box was being built on November 23, 1974, the same day as the Ohio State–Michigan game. "Now, why? Why would the defendant need to build a box to store Jan's belongings only four days after he reported her missing?" asked Stefancin. "That's not even time enough for her to be found, unless you know she's never coming back." The prosecutor recounted Michael's other testimony—about how he and his brother John had retrieved Jan's clothing from the mobile home, and how that clothing had ended up in the box.

She recalled how Jan's Ford Mustang, her pride and joy,

which she wouldn't let anybody else drive, had turned up at John Smith's mobile home—and that Smith would drive it after her disappearance.

Then there were the lies, and what those lies said about John. She spoke of how John had told his friend Sandi that Janice was dead. "Now, Jan's body hasn't been recovered," Stefancin said. "The police don't know Jan's dead, nor does her brother or her sister or her father, but the defendant knows in the summer of 1975 that Jan's dead."

John also told Kathy McDonald, the woman who got Janice's watch, that Jan was dead, Stefancin noted.

"And then time caught up with him," said Stefancin, recalling how in 1979 John's grandfather had decided to clean out the garage. "And what do they find?" she said. "They find that box, where it had sat for years out in the open with other bags and boxes on top of it." Michael Smith opened the box, the prosecutor said, and "he saw what he believed, what he knew was Jan's face." The prosecutor noted the testimony about John picking up the box and driving off with it in his fancy Corvette. But not before telling brother Michael the story of the FBI and the sheriff's deputies and the warehouse, the story that Michael desperately wanted to believe.

Nineteen-seventy-nine would turn to 1980, and the prosecutor went over how the road crew found the box in Indiana, and how a skeleton with the bottoms of its legs missing was found inside, and how the remains could not be identified. Stefancin spoke of how Michael Dansbury, his initial work in the case not explained, heard John tell him in 1991 that the last time John saw Jan, she was heading off to a Florida commune. Dansbury would say had the story changed a year later, with John then claiming that Jan had been into the drug scene and they had gotten a divorce. Then Stefancin reminded jurors of the taped phone calls between John Smith and his longtime love Sheila Sautter, and how the FBI had gotten involved, conducting a sweep of interviews in May 1999, including one between Agent Hilland and John, in which John cried and said he was living a nightmare. "You see, ladies and gentlemen, between 1974 and May of 1999, the defendant continues to give conflicting stories about Jan, conflicting stories of what happened to Jan, how she disappeared. Some, he says she's dead," Stefancin said. "To some, to law enforcement, he says sorry, said she was going to Florida, never heard anything."

It wasn't until Michael Smith came forward that investigators got the "huge, huge break," the prosecutor said. That provided the leads about the body with legs missing, leading to the letters that were sent out, leading to the identification of the Jane Doe in Indiana as Janice Hartman Smith. Jurors then heard the taped phone conversation between Michael and John, the conversation that culminated with Michael telling John that he was about to testify before the grand jury—and how that elicited from John a "Holy shit."

Turning to the defense case, and its suggestion that drug dealers may have killed Jan, Stefancin said that it was flawed logically. "Because the defendant built the box and he put Jan in the box," she said. "This is not a woman who was killed by drug dealers. It is not a woman who was killed by the FBI. This is not a woman who was killed by representatives from the sheriff's department. This is not a woman who was killed by the men who attacked her on November 10, 1974. This is a woman who was killed by the man in this courtroom. She was killed by the man who took the box and built it and then dumped it along the road in Indiana . . . He wanted to keep her with him. He kept her watch and he kept her body." He had cut her legs off, hidden her body and hidden the truth, she said.

Stefancin summed it up this way: "The evidence in this case does show that the only reasonable person to have committed this crime is the defendant. All evidence points to him, from the missing persons report to the watch to the conflicting stories to the days he disappears. All evidence points to the defendant."

. . .

In the high-stakes world of litigation, everything that goes on in the courtroom has been studied, tested, examined and evaluated to the point of excess, to find that tiny little edge that could mean the difference between success and failure. In some big-money civil cases, one side or the other—or both—will conduct entire mock trials, with mock juries and mock adversaries before a mock judge, to get an idea of what the outcome of the real trial might be—and whether the risks of going to court rather than settling are too high. So, it stands to reason that somebody would sit down and make a study of what lawyers wear in court, finding that, with some juries, the clothes do make the lawyer. That's why Migdal wore his blue suit for closing arguments, because, he said, "a study shows that blue is sincere."

But studies don't try cases, lawyers do, and it was up to Migdal to convince the jury that John David Smith should be acquitted of murdering his first wife. Since the defense had put on only one witness and had to make all of its points in cross-examination, much rested on this summation.

"I don't envy the job you do," Migdal told the jurors.

It was an echo of Wire's theme from opening statements: this was not the simple case the prosecution wanted jurors to think it was. It was a case fraught with problems, with holes in the logic, with shortcomings in the evidence, with reasonable doubt at every turn. It was a case, Migdal said, that the prosecution had simply failed to prove. Add up all the evidence, no matter how grisly, and evaluate all the testimony, no matter how emotional, and there was not enough there to convict John Smith of murder. "This is an uncomfortable case with some very disturbing facts," he said, "but the fact that at some point in time John Smith possessed her remains does not prove that he killed her."

Carefully, he shifted some of the burden in this trial

from the prosecution to the jury. The attorney asked jurors to remember his remarks during the jury selection process. "I said, 'You have the remains here in a box and you have the murder over here,' and we talked about that, and I asked you: 'Is that enough for you?' And each one of you on this jury raised your hand and said no. It's a disturbing fact. It's something that causes you great concern. But that is not enough." At jury selection they told him it wasn't enough, he argued, because they wanted proof of murder, "not that he possessed her remains, not that over a period of twenty-seven years he told various statements to people. You wanted proof that he killed her and you wanted proof beyond a reasonable doubt."

Migdal said that the case hadn't started on November 17, 1974, as prosecutors claimed, with Janice's disappearance, but on November 10, 1974, when Janice was attacked in that Doylestown house. "Five men held her down. Five men tried to rape her," he said, noting that one blond-haired man toting a shotgun told Janice that narcs like her "have an easy way out," a strong suggestion that Janice was ratting out drug dealers, Migdal argued. "Ladies and gentlemen, this is seven days before she disappears," he said.

The details of the attack on Janice were just some of the evidence that ran counter to the prosecution's claim that John had murdered her. He asked jurors to consider Janice's relationship with her family. "Janice didn't live at home because her mom had rules," he said. "Janice was twenty-two. Recently her marriage was dissolved. The rules were—what?—be home by eleven, no strangers, no smoking. Janice didn't want to live at home. I'm sure they were in some respects a very close family, but Janice didn't have constant contact with her family."

It was one of those family members who offered "very, very important" testimony, the lawyer said. Janice's sister, Lodema, recalled that before Thanksgiving, Janice and John had come to Janice's mother's house, and as Janice was leaving she told her younger sister that she was a drug informant and that she'd see Lodema again after graduation. "She was fourteen years old," Migdal said of Lodema. "She wasn't going to graduate for four-and-a-half years. Why would you tell your sister that? Why would you say, 'I will not see you for four and a half years'?"

The attorney didn't answer his own question. He said he didn't have to. "Don't forget, we don't have to prove anything," he said. "The state of Ohio has to prove each element beyond a reasonable doubt. We have to prove nothing. They need to eliminate all the doubt from you, and that doubt exists because of this: because Lodema Hartman told you what her sister told her, that she was a drug informant and that she was going to be gone."

What's more, Janice's mother testified that she had received a call from police saying that Janice was supposed to testify in court against drug dealers. "Isn't that quite a coincidence; a week, ten days before all this happened, the day after she is to testify in court?" he said.

The biggest source of reasonable doubt, Migdal argued, came courtesy of the Wayne County Sheriff's Office. "Not one person from Wayne County Sheriff's Office did a damn thing in this case," he said. "That's why there's a reasonable doubt. They didn't even go to Janice Hartman's trailer. Who knows what evidence may have been in there? The car, the Mustang that prosecutors think is such an important piece of evidence, was never analyzed." He noted that, according to the missing persons report, Janice was last seen with Kathy Paridon and another man—a man with bad acne. "The Wayne County Sheriff's Office didn't do anything," he said. He noted that none of the men involved in the attempted rape were interviewed. "Maybe it's because [of]—and this was 1974—Janice's line of work" as a go-go dancer. "I don't know why, but what they did was inexcusable."

Migdal then returned to the defense's central theory. "At some point in time [prosecutors] proved John Smith possessed her remains, and over a period of twenty-seven years, he told different statements about that," he said. "And that is their case. That is their case. . . . You've got a murder here. Well, give me the how, the when, the where, the why, because before you get to the who, you at least need some of those questions answered, and not one of them has been answered. They can't prove beyond a reasonable doubt that John Smith killed her."

He said they couldn't even prove the catchy line in Stefancin's opening statements: "She'll never walk away from him again." Migdal argued that there was no evidence that Janice had tried to leave John and he couldn't deal with it. The best the prosecution could come up with was that John was a bad sport at chess and that he got mad at his wife for smoking, the lawyer argued. "Is there one witness who came in here and said Janice was afraid of John? Didn't you expect to hear some 911 calls? Didn't you expect to see a police report with some domestic violence? Didn't you expect to see some evidence that Janice wanted to be separate from him and John would show up at work, John would show up outside her house, John would do this and John would do that? Nothing."

As for the prosecution's scientific evidence, he said it proved nothing. Migdal argued that Dr. Symes, the bone expert, could only give a description of the kind of knife somebody likely used to chop off Janice's legs, but not who that somebody was. "I expected someone to come in and say, 'We found an instrument, a cutting instrument somewhere in John's possession, and that's the evidence beyond a reasonable doubt,' " said Migdal. "They never found one. They can't connect the box to murder."

Nor, argued Migdal, could they connect John to murder, as defined in the Ohio law books. He said that jury instructions will include directive asking jurors to decide whether John had killed Janice and whether he did so with "prior calculation and design." "There is no evidence beyond a reasonable doubt that he killed her and, more importantly, there's no evidence of prior calculation and design," he said.

The lawyer concluded by making reference to the attention the case had gotten, a subtle effort to make the jury think—really think—about the case, because they may be asked about it later by the media. "The cameras have been here every day. The courtroom's filled. You guys know it's not usually like that," he said. "There's a lot of pressure on you. I understand that. It may be easy for you to go into the jury room and say—and I know this is going to happen—that there's some evidence he probably did this." But "probably" is not enough, Migdal told the panel. It has to be guilt beyond a reasonable doubt. That's what the jury took an oath to do. "When you go to the jury room and you talk to each other, be stubborn in that fact," he said. "Be stalwart in that fact, and when you come out and you've found reasonable doubt and you acquit him, you be proud of the fact that you took an oath and you lived up to it."

It's the bane of every defense attorney, but it's the practice in every court in the land. The prosecution has the burden of proof, so the prosecution gets the last word. Stefancin was determined to make the most of this opportunity, to the point of going out on a legal limb. She wanted to show the jury something that she herself hadn't seen until recently.

But first, she brought jurors back to November 17, 1974, the last night Janice was seen alive. "There were only two people in the trailer that night in Doylestown," she said. "Only two people know exactly what happened to Jan. And Jan is dead." The prosecutor rejected the defense suggestion that Janice could have been killed by some of the same people who'd tried to rape her. "Jan was a fighter. She fought off an attack by five men, five of them," said Stefancin. "She fought them off and she left that home and she left it alive. No, the person who killed Jan was a person so close to her that he would have access to her clothing and her jewelry. It was a man so close to her that she could be in *this*."

Now it was time for the big finish. "This" was what Hilland had seen. Stefancin went to a pile of decaying garments and pulled out a long, colorful nightgown and said, "You see, this was pulled over Jan's face. Look what you see." Stefancin pointed to markings near the hem. "You see the eyes." She pointed to another marking. "You see the mouth."

The image was haunting. It looked like a face, like the Shroud of Turin. Nobody had seen it before, because it was hard to make out when the dress was viewed right-side-up. But when the dress is looked at upside-down, the scary image was clearly visible.

Migdal was beside himself. "Your Honor, I'm going to object. There's no evidence that this was anywhere in this case."

But the judge overruled the objection. The Shroud of Janice was before the jury.

Stefancin pointed again to the image on the dress—the image surrounded by a rainbow of color, the result, she said, of the dye from plaid pants seeping into the garment. "The multi-colored hair that Michael saw," she said. "You see, this was over Jan's head, and somebody very, very close to her had to put it over her. You see, ladies and gentlemen, she fought off five men who tried to attack her, but she wouldn't suspect the man that she was married to."

From these theatrics, Stefancin proceeded along a more traditional rebuttal route, answering the defense's contentions about the shortcomings of the prosecution's case.

As for Migdal's suggestion that the prosecution never proved that John Smith had the rage to kill his ex-wife, she said, "The family described John's temper, his 'hissy fits,' as the defense calls them. But think about what that tells you about this man. This is a man with a temper, a man who hates to lose, even at a chess game. He would throw the chessboard across the room when he lost. This was a man who was domineering over his wife." She called him, "domineering, possessive, controlling, and she left him. She moved back to Wayne County and he followed."

She said that Michael Smith had driven his brother to the Sun Valley Inn and dropped him off there—on November 16, 1974. "His domineering self went to Jan," said Stefancin. The attack on Janice five days earlier had offered John Smith a convenient cover story. "What a perfect opportunity," said the prosecutor, "because then he could make sure that his wife didn't walk away from him again and he could blame it on somebody else—the five guys who assaulted her."

She urged jurors to look at the heinousness of the crime—and what it said about the killer. "The instrument used to dismember Jan was a serrated knife, a knife that took a lot of persistence to cut through that bone, that soft tissue and that bone—persistence, controlling, possessive, domineering," she said.

The defense's concession that John Smith possessed her body "should not alleviate his guilt," the prosecutor said. "He went to her home and he killed her and then he dismembered her, and then you can infer from the evidence that he built that box and he hid her," she said. "He thought it all out, and waited and waited for a proper time."

"Somebody close to her killed her and the person who was close to her at that time, at that night, was none other than that man," said Stefancin, pointing at John, who showed no reaction. "He was close enough to her to see her in that trailer, to see her in that nightgown. And that man dismembered her. That man built the box that she was ultimately found in, a box that she laid in for almost five years in a garage in Seville, a box where she decomposed, and then he took that box, this man took this box and he threw it in a field in Indiana.

"And now this man wants to hide behind the fact that he concealed the body for twenty-six years and we can't tell you exactly how Jan died," the prosecutor continued. "Well, she didn't die by accident, ladies and gentlemen. She didn't kill herself and cut her legs off. She was killed by the hands of another human being, by the hands of the man who built that box. Jan was killed that night by the defendant and he cut off her legs. She would never walk away from him again."

• • •

With the prosecution's rebuttal completed, the judge instructed the jury in the law, and, at 1 p.m., deliberations began, as did the tension. Stefancin went across the street to a restaurant called The Old Jail and had a Caesar salad. She returned to the courthouse and waited in her office. She couldn't do any work; it was too hard to concentrate. She felt relieved that the case was finally over, but nervous about what the jury would do. Though confident in the evidence, she had learned early on that juries could be unpredictable, that even the strongest case can be lost. By dinnertime her boss, Martin Frantz, brought her a chicken sandwich and fries from Wendy's. After she ate, she spoke on the phone with daughter Tricia, who had just returned home from her grandmother's house where she had been staying near the end of the trial. By now it was 9 p.m.—the jury had been deliberating for eight long hours. The judge had wanted to send jurors home, but they told him they still wanted to work.

While Stefancin was on the phone with her daughter, the other line lit up. Putting her daughter on hold, Stefancin pushed the button, and spoke briefly with Judge Wiest's bailiff, Chris Findley. Stefancin got back on the phone with Tricia to give her the big news: there was a verdict in mommy's case.

While Stefancin was eating her Wendy's sandwich, Kirk Migdal and Beverly Wire were holed up in Wire's office downstairs from Stefancin's with food from the bagel shop next door. They didn't want to talk about the case—it might jinx them—but they couldn't help it. It was getting late; the jury had been out past the dinner hour. There would be no snap verdict, which they thought was good news for the defense because it meant the jury was at least considering all the arguments and the evidence on both sides. Maybe jurors had found some reasonable doubt. Migdal looked at his watch: 8:30 p.m. He had tickets for a Neville Brothers concert later that night in Cleveland, an hour's drive north, where he was to meet friends. He wondered if he would make it. In half an hour, word came to Wire's office. The jury had reached a verdict.

As she walked to the courtroom, Stefancin felt the butter-flies in her stomach. She had thought deliberations would have lasted longer. Unlike Migdal, she believed that a long deliberation would be good for the prosecution. But she told herself that eight hours was enough—enough time to go over the evidence, but not enough time to get involved in discussions about reasonable doubt. As Migdal went into the courtroom, he felt mostly relief; there was nothing left he could do. But there was some anxiety; the second-guessing had already begun.

At 9:15 p.m., the judge took the bench. Smith was brought in from a secure alcove over the courtroom and seated at the defense table between Wire and Migdal. Stefancin sat next to FBI Agent Bob Hilland at the prosecution table. In the packed audience section were Janice's brother, Garry, and his wife, and Fran's sister Sherrie and daughter Deanna, Detective Potts and FBI Agent Roy Speer.

Jurors walked in from the deliberation room and sat in the box.

"It's my understanding that the jury has reached a ver-dict," the judge said.

The bailiff collected the jury forms and gave them to the judge. Wiest warned the audience, "I know there's a lot of pent-up emotion and feelings about this case, but I would ask that the decorum of the courtroom be maintained and that there be no outbursts or anything of that nature."

He looked over the jury forms. He turned to John Smith. "Would the defendant please stand?"

Smith stood, expressionless as usual.

"As to the charge of aggravated murder, the verdict of the jury is not guilty," said the judge. That meant the jury had rejected the most serious charge. Smith didn't flinch.

"As to the charge of the lesser offense of murder," the judge said, "the verdict is guilty."

Smith didn't react, stone-faced, empty-eyed, like the statues outside at the courthouse.

Everybody else showed no such restraint. Stefancin reached up and hugged Hilland, who lifted her off the ground. A friend of Stefancin's, Tammy Cruise, leaned over the railing, hugged Stefancin and said, "I'm very proud of you." In the audience, Garry Hartman embraced his wife and daughter. Sherrie Davis and Deanna Weiss hugged. Kirk Migdal lowered his head and felt the inevitable disappointment, but he wasn't crushed; he had known this was going to be a tough case to win. Then his lawyer's mind kicked into gear, thinking ahead to the appeal.

As the outpouring of emotion died down, Smith was led away back to the jail and the audience was cleared out, with relatives of Janice and Fran expressing joy and relief. "He's not going to kill anybody tonight," Sherrie said. "He's not going to kill anybody else for a long time." Her husband, Navelle Davis, said: "Now we have to find her sister." Garry Hartman called his mother in Florida and said, "Mom, we did it. He's guilty." Betty Lippincott replied, "Amen, thank God."

Back in the quiet of the courtroom, Stefancin, Hilland, Potts, Speer and the sheriff, Mauer, congratulated each other. Then Stefancin cried, for the first time in her career.

That night, Stefancin went home. Her daughter Tricia was waiting up for her with a babysitter. She ran up and hugged Stefancin. She knew that mommy had won the trial, that the bad man was found guilty. Stefancin was glad to see her.

Migdal didn't go home. He didn't have any hard work to do the next day because the sentence, fifteen years to life, was mandated by statute. There was nothing to file, nothing to argue. He ended up going to the Neville Brothers concert after all. He wasn't sure why he went. After other losses, he'd go out and have a beer, or stomp home angry. This time, a night of friends and music just seemed like the right thing to do.

CHAPTER 28

John had had five jurors willing to acquit him at the beginning of deliberations. That was the word from jury forewoman Dione Jones, 31, an assistant consumer loan clerk with a bank in Wooster, who, on Thursday, July 19, offered a peek inside the jury room. She told a newspaper the most compelling evidence in the trial had been Michael Smith's testimony—unchallenged by defense—that John had possessed the box with Janice's body inside. But the prosecution case wasn't airtight. The jury quickly rejected the most serious charge, aggravated murder, because the prosecution didn't adequately prove that John was violent toward Janice or that she was afraid of him. The panel then split 7–5 on the lesser charge of murder, with Jones initially among those voting not guilty. "At first, some of us really did have a little doubt," she told the Akron *Beacon Journal*. "But when you consider all the facts and evidence [that] were presented, I don't see how anyone could say the man was innocent . . . Eventually, everyone came to the same conclusion." Guilty of murder.

Jones was among those who had returned to the courtroom. Also there were lawyers for both sides, family members of Janice and Fran and some investigators. John was brought in from the jail. Gone was the shirt and tie. He wore a bright orange jail jumpsuit and sandals.

"The jury in this case, last evening, returned a verdict of guilty of the offense of murder," said Judge Wiest, "and we are back here today for sentencing. Is there anything from either counsel before we begin, any previous unresolved matters or motions?"

Both Stefancin and Migdal said no.

"All right," the judge continued. "Will the defendant please rise? Mr. Smith, is there anything you want to say to the court at this time?"

In a flat voice, Smith said, "No, Your Honor."

After Smith's attorney told the judge that Smith had been informed of his rights to appeal—and wished to be represented by a public defender during that appeal—the judge told Smith to sit down.

"The penalty for murder which existed in 1974 was an indefinite term of fifteen years to life in prison. The court has no discretion to change that one way or the other," Wiest said. "Even though it won't affect the actual sentence that's imposed, I think it would be appropriate if someone from the Hartman family wishes to make a statement or read a statement, or the prosecutor read a statement."

Then the judge, who had been so careful during the trial to limit things to only the absolute legal necessities, offered a small surprise.

"Also, I think at this time, although the court didn't allow the evidence in the trial, it would also be appropriate to hear something from the relative of Betty Fran Smith," said the judge.

But first, it was a word from Janice's family. The judge asked Garry Hartman to come up to the podium.

"I don't have a whole lot to say to John," said Garry. "The prosecution's done an excellent job. But my mother, even my father, may forgive John for what he's done, but my brother, my sister, and I will never forgive you for what you've done. You kill women in your life that you loved, and that's very hard to understand.

"Your past is just now starting to catch up with you, and believe me, it will continue. Sooner or later, you will be tried for others. Your sentence for killing Janice is just the first step. My family is not alone when we say you never—we hope you never have another free day the rest of your life.

"I'll say one other thing about Michael's testimony. The family will forgive Michael. We hope that his nightmares go away—and that you receive them."

Then Sherrie Davis, whose work along with her niece had started the series of events that led to the conviction of John Smith in one killing—but not that of her loved one—went to the podium.

"Your Honor, I would like to thank you for allowing our family to speak," she said. "Not knowing how this worked, my notes are addressed to John, and I would like to just read them if I may."

She then read.

"John, you came into our lives by way of my sister's love. Because of her love, we trusted you, we trusted you to put her welfare above your own. You have violated that trust. By your hand, my sister's children have lost their mother, her grandchildren have lost their granny. I have lost my sister, my best friend.

"As a family, we have proved to be a force to be reckoned with. For the past two-and-a-half weeks, Janice has spoken in this courtroom, and through these proceedings, Janice has found justice for herself and her family. Fran has not spoken yet, but we as a family will continue our efforts to give Fran's memory the justice it deserves. With the help of authorities, this family has tracked you for nine years, nine months, eighteen days to get to this day. But this is not over for our family. We are not going away until you tell us what you did with my sister's body after you killed her.

"I promised my mother on her deathbed that I would find my sister. I will to my last dollar, my last breath, [work] to fulfill that promise.

"And guess what, John? When I'm gone, there will be some other member of my family to step forward and continue this investigation. It is our intention to work as hard as possible to see that you are never released to prey on another woman who makes the mistake of loving you.

"It is my firm belief that if you are ever released, you will kill again. DeeDee and I hated you for so long that one day we just came to the realization that hate would eat us up, and it was certainly counterproductive to the job we had to do—that being to find Fran. So we put that hate aside. We only feel sorry that your life, a life that should and could have been so productive, is a waste, ruined by your lies, your obsession for control, and your temper.

"John, just for one minute, I would ask you just to look at me in the eye for one minute, because I have only one other thing to say to you. I can live with my last memory of my sister. Can you?

"Thank you, Your Honor."

John didn't look her in the eye. He stared forward.

Finally, there was a statement from Janice's mother, Betty Lippincott, who had returned to Florida. It was read by Stefancin. "She wants you to know," the prosecutor said, "that her family feels that you are guilty of Jan's death. You have taken joy and love from her family. The family will never forget Jan, as she is always in their hearts and in their prayers.

"She loved life and she did not deserve to die. They tell me that I have to forgive you as I want to be a good Christian. [I] will do that, but [I] hate you for what you have done to her daughter. If you love someone, you give them a proper burial. You do not throw them in a ditch like a bag of garbage. You had no right to play God. I hope you feel His wrath a million times before you die.

"If you have any decency in you at all, you will tell Fran's family where she is at. They need the closure as well as we do. We waited too long for that closure. Don't let them wait that long. That's all I have to tell you except I never want to see you again.

"Thank you, Your Honor."

With that, the judge said, "Will the defendant please stand?" Smith did. "Mr. Smith, now that you've had the opportunity to hear what those folks have to say, is there anything you wanted to say in response?"

"No, Your Honor." Again, no emotion.

"Well, as you understand, you are sentenced to a fifteen-year-to-life term. I can't speak for the parole board, but I'm confident that you will serve the rest of your life in an Ohio prison.

"And it's not going to happen today, but maybe some day, you will do the right thing and respond to the questions of these people. You can't overcome, you can't change the bad that you've done. But since you are going to be living, albeit in prison, you do have the opportunity to do good and to answer their questions, and I would hope that you would take that to heart.

"So, at this point, the court sentences you to serve a term of fifteen-years-to-life in prison, and the sheriff is directed to take you to the Lorain Correctional Facility to begin serving that sentence.

"Is there anything further from the defense?"

Migdal said, "No, Your Honor."

"From the state?"

"No, Your Honor, thank you," said Stefancin.

"That'll be all."

CHAPTER 29

Throughout the trial, the judge had been careful to keep any mention of Betty Fran Gladden's disappearance away from jurors. After ruling that this "other act" was barred from the trial, attorneys made sure that the name never passed from anybody's lips, not from FBI Agent Bob Hilland who'd spent so many months investigating it, not from West Windsor Detective Michael Dansbury who'd testified about everything except the case he was originally assigned to investigate. The tape-recorded conversation between John Smith and Sheila Sautter had been edited to delete John's references to his missing wife. But despite the judge's best efforts, it got out. After reaching their verdict, members of the jury, while debriefed by the prosecutor and defense lawyers, revealed that evidence of Fran's disappearance did enter the jury deliberation room.

It came in the form of State's Exhibit Number 48: the written statement that Michael Smith had given to Agent Hilland. Nearly all the statement deals with Janice. But in the question-and-answer section, Michael Smith was asked, "Did you ever know or meet Betty Fran Smith?" and he answered, "No." Then he was asked, "Did John ever discuss Betty Fran's disappearance?" and Michael answered, yes, that his brother had mentioned she'd left a note and had never come back.

It was an oversight by John's lawyers that these questions and answers made it into the jury room. Had they objected to the material, the judge surely would have redacted the document. But John's attorneys didn't object and the judge didn't redact. So now the defense attorneys had to deal with the matter.

On the day after sentencing, they appeared before Wiest to argue that John's rights to a fair trial were violated because the jury was infected by improper information. It was a fight that would unfold over weeks, as both sides filed papers. John's trial lawyers, Wire and Migdal, would bow out of the case, leaving it for the newly appointed appellate attorney, Pamela A. Conger-Cox of the Ohio Public Defender's Office in Columbus. "The evidence was highly inflammatory other-acts evidence that was admitted apparently by accident and without any cautionary instruction," the defense wrote in court papers. "This clearly violated Mr. Smith's right to due process and a fair trial and created an unacceptable risk that the jury convicted him in part due to the prior wife's death." The defense concluded, "The jury's unguided review of that evidence was egregious, prejudicial error. This court should grant Mr. Smith a new trial."

Facing the daunting prospect that the case that took so long to reach a jury may have to be retried, prosecutors countered that the defense didn't object at the time the document was introduced, and that the jury foreperson later told the judge that jurors had decided to disregard the references to Fran. That the jury could and should disregard any details of the New Jersey case had already been a settled issue, the prosecution said. The media was full of accounts of the New Jersey case, and jurors were ordered to set that aside. The prosecution argued that the Exhibit 48 matter was harmless error—that the jury would have voted to convict even if it hadn't seen the document.

In his ruling, on September 18, 2001, Judge Wiest said,

"It could be argued that [defense] counsel was ineffective by not objecting to Exhibit Forty-eight," but he believed the real question was whether John was harmed by the mistake. Looking over the questions and answers, the judge said, "It should be noted that the statement contains none of the evidence concerning the disappearance of Betty Fran that the state sought to introduce into evidence. It simply establishes that he had a second wife and she disappeared." Wiest said that this was no news flash: some jurors already knew this. "The evidence in this case clearly and compellingly pointed to the defendant as the person responsible for the death of Janice Hartman Smith," the judge wrote. "The court believes that the defendant received a fair trial. Motion overruled."

CHAPTER 30

Before John Smith had been put on trial in Ohio, Betty Fran Gladden Smith's daughter Deanna and sister Sherrie had filed a civil wrongful death lawsuit against him in Mercer County, New Jersey. The suit sought monetary damages for the loss of Fran, though money wasn't the motivation. Justice was. Deanna and Sherrie wanted *their* day in court, and they weren't going to wait for a criminal trial that they suspected would likely never happen. They wanted an official finding, in a court of law—even if it was a civil court—that John had murdered Fran.

After being put on hold during the Ohio trial, the case of *Deanna W. Weiss, et al* vs. *John D. Smith* was heard on October 18, 2001, before Judge Maria Marinari Sypek without a jury. Deanna and Sherrie wouldn't have the satisfaction of hauling John into court and facing him. He didn't fight the civil case, remaining in prison and sending no lawyer to represent him. A default was entered against him and the trial went on without John.

"This is a damages hearing," plaintiff lawyer Donald Veix said in an opening statement, which, being delivered in front of a judge and not a jury, lacked oratorical flourishes. "The purpose of the hearing is to enter a default judgment against the defendant John Smith . . . It is a survivorship action, wrongful death action and intentional infliction of emotional distress, three counts in the complaint." Veix told the judge that this trial wouldn't compromise the police investigation, which was going nowhere anyway. "And that was part of the reason that I believe the family wanted to pursue the civil side, to bring some closure to this, to seek justice and to go after Mr. Smith and bring him to task for what they believe are his criminal acts." Even though all he needed to present in a civil action like this was a *prima facie* case, rather than the strict proof beyond a reasonable doubt required in a criminal trial, Veix promised: "The evidence will show that without a doubt Mr. Smith murdered Betty Fran Smith and disposed of her body."

As his first witness, Veix called Detective Dansbury, who would now be allowed to say in this New Jersey court what he was barred from saying in Ohio. After giving his background, Dansbury recounted the details of the investigation into the disappearance of Fran, from the original filing of the report by John, through the interviews and interrogations with him, to John's arrest in California for Janice Hartman's murder. Dansbury said he had suspected John early on. "There was a lack of emotion," he said. "He was never, never upset. It's not your normal case, and during the years of my police work, seeing if you have somebody that has a missing family member, they're constantly on [the] phone—'What are you doing to find my wife or my missing son or daughter?' We never got these calls from John. He never once called me to volunteer or help to further this investigation." He said this contrasted sharply with the reaction of Sherrie and Deanna. "They were just trying to move heaven and earth to find their sister and mother." Meanwhile every time the detective talked to John, all he got were lies.

"Did you ever count how many lies John had given you during the course of this ten-year investigation?" Veix asked.

"Hundreds. And if I'd confront him with a lie, it's just, he would make up another lie for the lie that I would confront him with."

As he wrapped up his questioning, Veix asked: "Do you have an opinion, as a police officer for some twenty-six years, as to whether John Smith was involved in the murder of Betty Fran Smith?"

"I strongly believe if he's not involved, he has personal knowledge of some involvement for being responsible for the disappearance or missing status of his wife."

"Do you have an opinion as to his involvement in the concealment or disposal of Betty Fran Smith's body?"

"During these ten years there's never been anything that I could glean or learn that would point to somebody else that could have been responsible."

Since John had not taken part in the trial, there would be no cross-examination of Dansbury, leading Veix to call his second witness: Deanna Weiss.

In the decade since her mother had disappeared, Deanna had spoken to virtually anybody who would listen, from the local *Trentonian* newspaper to ABC's *20/20*. Never, however, had she spoken in a courtroom. With no defense attorney to object, and no jury to worry about, Deanna was allowed by Judge Sypek to let out a decade's worth of fear, frustration, anger and depression, her testimony often tumbling out in long statements. She spoke warmly of her mother—"really bubbly," "really good spirit"—and how she had sewed for her grandchildren and spoken every other day on the phone with her loved ones. She spoke of how her mother had tried to make the best of things—of moving to New Jersey, of recovering from the broken hip, of living with John Smith.

"My mother was really good at being a mother," she said. "If you have a good relationship with your mother, there's no one that can replace that. You know, there's no one that knows that when you pick up the phone, and say, 'Hey, Mom, everything's great,' that it's not. And, cares when you're really sick. She cares if you're sick and it doesn't matter if you are two or twenty-six. You know, [she says] Did you do this, did you do that? That's being a mom, and no one can replace that. A mom doesn't have any other agenda but being a mom to her children. That's it."

And that's why, Deanna testified, she never believed her mom abandoned her husband and family that fall day in 1991—and why Deanna was, and is, convinced that her mother was killed. "She would have never done this to me. Never in a million years would she have done this to me," she said. "She wouldn't have done this to anybody in my family." They didn't give up trying to locate her—or at least find out what happened. "Everything humanly possible," Weiss testified. "We had great employers. We spent probably five hours out of an eight-hour day, calling everybody we knew, trying to get John to do something. He wouldn't. He said he was. But he never really did."

John—the man they never really knew, the Mennonite bachelor who turned out to have been married at least once before and had girlfriends all over the country, the John Boy Walton–type with the potential for rage, the husband who never really seemed to care when his wife disappeared one day. Deanna recalled how she'd once asked Smith for telephone directories so she could call local pawn shops to see if any of her mother's jewelry had turned up, but Smith waited months to send them, and only then provided ten-year-old phone books from his factory that weren't even from the West Windsor area. "I mean, he continued to lie about who he was, what he was. He never picked up the phone to call the police. He'd just get the information from them through me," she said, noting that he obviously was interested—if from afar—in the police's progress, "which is why he was calling me every morning, to find out what I had found out from the police." John continued to act taken aback by the women's efforts. "He was like, 'I can't believe she's putting me through this.' That was the kind of comments that he would make," said Deanna. The lies, she said, flowed from him constantly: the sister in Connecticut who never existed, and the longtime girlfriend who did; the suicide note from Fran that looked like something he'd pulled from an old journal; the suitcases that Fran supposedly took with her that had shown up in a closet. About the only thing she'd believed was when he said he'd failed a polygraph test; he could only tell the truth about his lying.

Although convinced that her mother was dead, Deanna said that she and her Aunt Sherrie had embarked on a campaign to solve the case—and to hold John accountable for what they believed he had done. The effort had taken its toll. Weiss estimated she had spent at least $51,000 over ten years, from $78 for posters—a big expense in 1991 for a single parent with two kids in daycare—to $300 for airline tickets and the costs of postage, court documents and private eyes. This didn't include the $2,500 in expenses to attend the criminal trial in Ohio. The women also spent money on a memorial service and a marker that has not been placed in a cemetery yet. But they said they had to do it, to protect other women, to keep them from John. "I don't trust people like I used to," said Deanna. "I trust, but verify. There really are monsters out there. People really do vanish off the face of the earth. You really do have to tell people every day that you love them, because you may not get [another] chance. I'm very glad to say that out of all of the torturous things that you think about—How did he do it? What did he do? Did she suffer?—I can't do anything about that. But I remember I told my mom when I hung up the phone that I loved her. That, I remember."

"Before he was convicted and sentenced and incarcerated," Veix asked, his questioning of Deanna coming to a close, "did you have concern for other women?"

"Oh, that's why we did this," she said. "I mean, we know the beast. It's hard when you know that someone is a beast and they're walking around."

"Is it your opinion that John Smith murdered your mother?"

"Absolutely."

"Is it your opinion that, based on your investigation, that

he has disposed of and purposely concealed your mother's body from you and your family?"

"Yes, I believe that he made a few mistakes with Janice Hartman and he did not repeat that with my mother."

"You have any opinion as to why he engaged in all these lies?"

"Some of them obviously were to cover him. Some of them—he'd have been better to tell the truth."

"So what was the point of him telling all these lies?"

"I think he just likes to mess with people," Deanna said. "I think he likes being this chess master and moving these parts all around and seeing how vicious he can be and how hurtful he can be."

"Now, there came a point in time when you took legal action to declare your mom dead?"

"I did. I thought it would give us some finality."

"And did it?"

"No."

That finality would probably never come, according to the third and final witness, Dr. Richard D. Rubin, a Trenton psychiatrist who had examined Deanna to render an expert opinion on the emotional impact of the last decade. Rubin found that this was a woman who up until 1991 had never suffered any emotional problems. But now, he said, she had sunk into a "major depression" of the sort the psychiatric texts had no name for. He diagnosed her with a mental malady that was a combination of depression and post-traumatic stress disorder of the sort troops returning from war suffer. Weiss had sought counseling a few times over the years, but felt that talking about it only made her feel worse. "I concluded that, in view of the fact that ten years has transpired since the disappearance of her mother, that I don't think any psychiatric treatment is going to remedy the problem at this point," said Rubin, a prognosis particularly bleak even for a plaintiff-hired expert. "So I concluded that she has this permanent problem, and that declaring her mother dead, or even having Mr. Smith convicted of it, is not going to cure anything."

"Is it your opinion," Veix asked, "that this condition is approximately related and caused by the murder and the disposal and concealment of her mother's body?"

"Yes it is. Indubitably."

"Thank you, doctor," Veix said, and the last witness was released.

A good defense lawyer would have mocked that last "indubitably" and pounced all over Rubin's lost-cause scenario for Deanna, based as it was on just one meeting with the woman, but there was no defense lawyer and no cross-examination, because John had conceded this battle. And so the plaintiff rested, its case strong, but unchallenged.

"This case involves and focuses on the murder of Betty Fran Smith," Veix said in his closing arguments. "Clearly, no one knows where Betty Fran Smith is. And that's part of the damages here. That is the suffering beyond the murder, beyond the disappearance. It's the fact that there are no answers as to where she is. Was she buried properly? Was she disposed of in a wooden box, a small wooden box, just like Janice Hartman Smith? Was her body dropped off on the side of a rural road off an interstate? Or is her mother's body currently in a pauper's grave somewhere, unidentified as a Jane Doe, as Janice Hartman Smith's body was for many years?"

Fran provided love and caring for her family members— love and caring that would have continued for the rest of her natural life. "A forty-nine-year-old woman," Veix said. "I know our court rules are somewhat cruel and cold when they have a [chart] that lists life expectancy, much like insurance companies do, but I believe in my last review of the most recent rules, Betty Fran Smith had a life expectancy of 29.65 additional years. And I don't know and I don't think anyone could say how many of those years she would continue to be the vibrant, bubbly, energetic, compassionate mother and grandmother that she was, but I would say a substantial portion of that 29.65 years was taken away from them by John Smith."

And just as surely as she had loved, in her final moments she must have suffered—a pain for which John should pay, the lawyer said. "We don't know how she met her demise. We don't know how violent it was, how sudden it was," said Veix. "What we can say is, and what I would argue to the court is, murder is the absolute and ultimate violent act. If you look at pain and suffering, I can't think of any other act that would qualify at that extreme. Maybe it was seconds. Maybe it was hours. If it was just seconds, those seconds were extreme. To know that, in those few seconds, you were being taken away from your family, from your life and from this earth—that has tremendous value, and the damages are significant." And then, after she disappeared, there were other costs, financial expenses incurred by her relatives to search for her killer, and to bury her, and to "really bring finality to this part of their life, this significant part of their life." Then there are punitive damages deserved of the first order. "There's nothing beyond murder which would qualify or require punitive damages," he said. Noting that John had once lived the high life in San Diego—and that there was still a chance he could get out of prison, "The message should be sent by this court through this action that punitive damage will be entered in an amount that will take all of that California lifestyle away from him, and it will not be there for whenever he gets out of jail."

Finally, Veix said, there was the pain and suffering extended to Fran's family, to Deanna, who is "suffering a major depression" caused by John. "What I would ask the court to do is take into account . . . his rather lavish California lifestyle, the heinous nature of his acts, the evil-minded personality and the fact that he was convicted of murder of the first wife," said Veix, summing up his case. "And there's also indications that he didn't stop at just these two women. There were the jawbones that were found in the Ohio storage unit that have yet to be identified. So there could be at least three murders that he is responsible for. So a punitive damage award sends the message to him that society will not tolerate him moving from one murder scene to the next and improving his life as he moves through this cycle of violence."

The judge considered the case for two months, and rendered her decision on December 21, 2001. In her ruling, Sypek noted that no criminal charges had been brought against Smith in the disappearance of Fran. "It was represented that there was nothing actively being done by the West Windsor or the Mercer County prosecutor's office at this point," she said. She noted that this proceeding was not a substitute for a criminal trial: it would be much easier to go after Smith in civil court. Neither he nor a lawyer ever showed up, so a default was entered, and no defense was offered. What's more, the burden of proof in a civil case was much lighter than in a criminal one. The plaintiffs needed to show that it was only more likely than not that Smith had killed Betty Fran.

That being said, the judge then covered what evidence there was and concluded: "The court finds that, by a preponderance of the evidence, that it is more likely true than not true that John D. Smith had caused the death of Betty Fran."

Deanna Weiss and Sherrie Gladden-Smith finally got their official validation of what they had been saying for years.

All that was left now was to figure out the money. The damages, the judge said, would have to cover any money the family members would have gotten from Betty Fran had she lived out her life. It would also cover the value of any services, assistance, training, guidance, counsel and care that they would have received from Betty Fran. The judge noted that at the time of her disappearance, Betty Fran was 49 years old, in good health, other than the hip problem, and was making about $20,000 a year as an administrative assistant. "Since 1991, Deanna and her family have not had her guidance, love, support with respect to their careers and their relationship and the upbringing," the judge said. "As a result, the court notes . . . the losses to the family including Deanna and her two children, who had spent a significant time with their grandmother." The rest of the damages related to funeral expenses, punishment and pain and suffering, of which there was much, the judge said, finding that Deanna is suffering a "major depressive condition that is permanent in nature."

All told, John was ordered to pay $1 million for killing Fran.

Deanna and Sherrie got their court victory, but they will likely never see a penny of it. After the hearing Deanna said she hoped the verdict would turn up the pressure on police and prosecutors to solve the case, and find her mother's body. She said she wanted to bring her mother to the little town of Niceville, where Deanna grew up with her grandparents, where everybody was happy, and where it was home.

At age 50, a fifteen-year minimum sentence in prison means that there's still a chance, though a slim one, that John David Smith will one day be a free man. Most people involved in the case believed that the state of Ohio would ensure that John spends more than fifteen years behind bars—much more. And while he's serving his time, investigators will wonder whether John has killed anybody else, those tooth fragments found under the apartment garage and the skull fragments found in the storage facility left as two unresolved pieces of evidence. Despite extensive investigation by a variety of detectives and FBI agents, authorities were also unable to identify the woman with the feathered hair posing in front of a jewelry store in the photo found in John's San Diego storage unit. Not a day goes by that Wayne County Sheriff's Detective Potts doesn't think about that woman, and wonder. Authorities did, however, solve the mystery of the woman in the other picture. The petite woman standing next to John in front of the airplane was located and identified around the time of John's trial. She had died, but not by violent means. Cancer took her long after she had parted ways with John Smith.

When the verdict in the Ohio case was reached, West Windsor police Detective Dansbury was not in the court-room. He was in upstate New York at the home he'd bought for his retirement, which he would take in April 2002 after twenty-seven years in the department. He couldn't help but see the irony in the fact that it was the New Jersey investigation that had jump-started the Ohio investigation and led to John's conviction, yet in the end, the New Jersey case never got any benefit. The investigation into Fran's 1991 disappearance technically remains an active case. If a tip comes in, the police will follow it up. Those who are convinced that John killed Fran don't think he'll take Judge Wiest's advice and "do the right thing."

If John is ever charged in the New Jersey case, he won't be looking at a fifteen-year-to-life term. It'll be death by lethal injection, unless prosecutors grant him immunity—something they haven't done. The location of Fran's body may forever remain a mystery.

"If I Die..."

A True Story of Obsessive Love, Uncontrollable Greed, and Murder

MICHAEL FLEEMAN

In January, 1995, skull and bone fragments of 64-year-old Las Vegas multimillionaire Ron Rudin were discovered in a remote and rocky ravine along Lake Mohave. He'd been shot at least four times in the head, decapitated, and set on fire. Who could have turned on the ambitious real-estate ace with such bloodthirsty fury? Even before the remains were found, circumstantial evidence was building against Rudin's tempestuous 52-year-old wife, Margaret, who stood to inherit a handsome share of her husband's fortune. Then a chilling caveat was discovered in Rudin's living trust: that should he die under violent circumstances, an investigation should be conducted. By the time authorities closed in on Margaret Rudin, she'd disappeared. It would take two and a half years to hunt the Black Widow down, and to discover the cold-blooded secrets at the heart of a poisonous marriage . . .

AVAILABLE WHEREVER BOOKS ARE SOLD
FROM ST. MARTIN'S PAPERBACKS